Winston Churchill

Eric Bolsmann, South African artist and author, is known for his meticulously researched books and magazine articles on subjects ranging from food and wine to art and history. His book on the young Winston Churchill is his first dealing with military history. Eric was inspired to research Churchill from a historical perspective set against the backdrop of the South African War. His research revealed much information about Winston Churchill that was generally unknown before. As an artist Eric has held numerous successful solo exhibitions. His paintings, in oil on canvas, are seen in the Pretoria Art Museum and in numerous corporate and private collections throughout the world.

Winston Churchill

The making of a hero in the Boer War

Eric Bolsmann

GALAGO

GALAGO BOOKS

Galago Books are published by Galago Publishing (1999) (Pty) Ltd
PO Box 404, Alberton, 1450, Republic of South Africa
web address: www.galago.co.za

Galago Books are distributed by Lemur Books (Pty) Ltd
PO Box 1645, Alberton, 1450, Republic of South Africa
Tel: (Int +2711— 011-907-2029. Fax 011-869-0890
Email: lemur@mweb.co.za

First published by Galago August 2008

Typeset in 11 point Times New Roman by Galago
Photographic reproduction by Galago
Printed and bound by CTP Book Printers, Cape

Front cover photograph: Winston Churchill in the uniform of the
South African Light Horse, 1900
Front cover design: Madelain Davies

This book is for the late Jimmy McLachlan who persistently nagged me into recording his search for the gold watches that Churchill had sent to his benefactors in Witbank after the war. If it wasn't for him the rewarding experience of getting to know young Winston would have eluded me.

Acknowledgements

Among the many who have helped me along on my journey with Winston Churchill, I would like to say a sincere thank you to Dr Christian Bolsmann of Aston University in Birmingham for his generous assistance in aiding me in my research in the UK. A heartfelt thank you is also due to Stephen Mafadi Bapela and Elize Retief of the South African National Library in Pretoria; to Caren Jansen, Frieda Green and Iona Gielen of the Pretoria City Library; to Marie Coetzee of the Archives of the University of South Africa (UNISA) in Pretoria; to the staff of the National Archives in Pretoria; to Ravina Wilkinson of the National Military Museum in Johannesburg; to Amanda Botha, manager of the *Witbank News* in Witbank, Mpumalanga, and Zita Goldswain journalist with the *Witbank News*; to Gail Loubscher, Kath Rapley, Jason Gates and Jill de Villiers of Pretoria; to Lisa

Contents

Chapter

In-text illustrations, maps and photographs

Foreword

One of the greatest talents that Winston Churchill was blessed with was his extraordinary command of the English language. He would go on to write a prodigious 65 books in his lifetime. He was rewarded for this in 1953 when he was awarded the Nobel Prize for Literature. Yet in Britain his abilities as a writer were already widely recognised by the end of the 19th century. Yet oddly enough he had not excelled academically at school and it was only on his third attempt that he passed the entrance examination to the Royal Military Academy at Sandhurst.

Before entering politics he went on to combine his military career with journalism and shortly after the outbreak of the South African War in 1899, he was contracted as a war correspondent for the *Morning Post*. He made his way to the Natal front where he was destined to become one of the highest-paid newspaper reporters in the world.

Much has been made of Churchill's heroism. The exceptional courage he displayed when defending the derailed armoured train at Chieveley in Natal made his reputation. Yet strictly speaking as a journalist he was a non-combatant, but on his capture, the Boers treated him as a combatant because of his actions at the armoured train.

This was not an isolated incident of bravery for on other occasions, in Cuba, India and in Africa, his sometimes almost reckless courage had drawn widespread comment. On three different occasions during the Malakand campaign in India, he rode his pony along the skirmish line while everyone else was ducking for cover. He admitted that his actions were foolish, but playing for high stakes was a calculated risk. 'Given an audience there is no act too daring or too noble', he wrote to his mother, and concluded his letter by saying: '... without the gallery things are different.'

Scaling the wall surrounding the prison yard in Pretoria and making his way through enemy territory to Portuguese East Africa was not considered a particularly great feat by the British military. Yet his escape — he was largely unknown to the British people until then — was hailed by many as one of the greatest military escapes ever.

His instant fame, to a large degree, came about because the war was going badly for the British Army at the time. A depressed British people needed a hero to bolster their sagging enthusiasm for the war, so Winston Churchill was their man.

He had the need to stay in the limelight to fuel his political ambitions and the best way to achieve that was by returning to the front as a journalist and part-time soldier after his escape where he continued to captivate the readers of the *Morning Post* with his dispatches, writing convincingly about his own and other's front-line experiences.

His stories of how he miraculously escaped the bullets that whistled around him in Natal and the Orange Free State and how he rode a bicycle through enemy-held Johannesburg, ending with his triumphant returned to Pretoria where he helped to liberate his former fellow POWs from captivity, earned his newspaper a fortune.

The fact that the adventures he described sometimes did not happen exactly the way he related them didn't seem to bother anyone. William Manchester wrote: 'Virtually every event he [Churchill] described in South Africa, as in Cuba, on the North-West Frontier, and at Omdurman, was witnessed by others with whom recollections were consistent. The difference, of course, lay in the interpretation.'

I set out to discover the real Churchill in those early years of his life. During this process I discovered many facets to this complex and controversial man. At times I felt like a certain painter described by Cervantes. This sage artist was asked, as he was starting on a new canvas, what his picture was to be. 'That', he replied, 'is as it may turn out.'

So this, my account of how the young and extraordinary Winston Churchill became a hero during the South African War, is how it turned out.

1

A troubled childhood

Blenheim Palace in Woodstock, about eight miles from Oxford, is a masterpiece of English baroque architecture conceived in 1705 by Sir John van Brugh. It was completed in 1722 and named after a town on the Danube in Bavaria where in 1704, John Churchill, the 1st Duke of Marlborough, routed the Sun King's armies. The gates are emblazoned with the Marlborough family crest, flanked on either side by dragon-like reptiles with raised wings, not dissimilar to the dragons marking the entrance to the City of London's financial district, or the Flying Reptile statue at Temple Bar.

The palace, described by Frank Brennan as a 'monstrous pile reared by an admiring nation for John Churchill, 1st Duke of Marlborough, the victor of Blenheim, Ramillies, Oudenaarde and Malplaquet; the man who had saved Austria and the Netherlands from the French armies, laid the foundation of British power in the Mediterranean; the ablest soldier and statesman of his day'.[1]

The palace is a vast building with 300 rooms surrounded by 2 100 acres of parkland and gardens unrivalled anywhere in Britain. In one of the smaller rooms just off Blenheim's great hall, a direct descendant of the 1st Duke of Marlborough, Winston Leonard Spencer Churchill, was born at 1:30am on Monday 30 November 1874.

The first Marlborough had no son and the dukedom passed to his grandson who was a Spencer. In 1817, by royal licence, the 5th Duke of Marlborough added the name Spencer to that of Churchill. Winston's father, the 25-year-old Randolph, was the second son of the 7th Duke. His wife Frances was a daughter of the 3rd Marquess of Londonderry.

Winston's mother, Jeanette — or Jennie as she was called — was the 20-year-old daughter of Leonard Jerome, a Wall Street millionaire of Anglo-Irish descent who lived in a mansion on Madison Square in New York. Leonard had a chequered but successful career. With the money he made on the stock market he founded the American Jockey Club, built a racetrack in the Bronx, was for a time co-owner of the *New York Times* and served 18 months as the American consul in Trieste, Italy.

His wife Clara was known as 'Sitting Bull' because of her strong, dark complexion and features she had inherited from her grandmother, an Indian maiden named Meribah who had been born in the very heartland of the Iroquois in the densely wooded hills south of Lake Ontario around Rochester, New York. Leonard loved Clara. He had four daughters with her, one of whom died. Jennie was the youngest. But there were other women in Leonard's life, and when the number of illegitimate children he fathered continued to increase, Clara went to live with her daughters in Paris in a large apartment on the Champs-Elysées.

When the Franco-Prussian war broke out in 1870, Clara and her three daughters left the French capital for fashionable Cowes on the Isle of Wight. Aged 19, Jennie was considered one of the most beautiful women about and with her musical talent, her charm and her wit, she quickly became a social celebrity. A society event or party without her was almost unthinkable.

It was not long before the Prince of Wales had noticed Clara and her daughters, and invited them to a reception and dance on board *H.M.S. Ariadne* at a Cowes regatta in honour of the visiting Czarevitch and his wife on 12 August 1873. It was there that Jennie met Lord Randolph Churchill.

Randolph was not concerned about the background of the Jerome family. He was smitten with Jennie and proposed to her within three days of their meeting. The Duke and Duchess of Marlborough, however, were totally opposed to their youngest son marrying Jennie. After all, Randolph was the son of an English aristocrat with a name that was among the proudest in the land; Jennie, on the other hand, was merely the daughter of a nouveau riche American stockbroker.

The Prince of Wales was an old family friend of the Churchills. He listened with empathy when Randolph came to plead for help. However, not convinced that royal intervention would be sufficient to secure the marriage, Randolph conceived a back-up plan. His brother George, Marquess of Blandford, had been a disappointment to his parents. He had been expelled from Eton and was, because of his obstinate and erratic temperament, not very popular. He was known to treat his wife badly. Randolph was thus expected to fulfil their parents' destiny.

Known as 'Randy' in London society, his bulging eyes — he suffered from exophthalmia — and walrus moustache were not his most attractive features, but then he was always impeccably dressed and could be witty and charming. He enjoyed the social whirl and being the son of a duke, was one of the most eligible bachelors of his time. About to be elected to take up his father's old seat in Parliament, Randolph was expected to marry a lady befitting his position in society.

The Duke and Duchess had, for many years, secured the loyal support of the voters of the small borough of Woodstock, of which Blenheim was a part, with cash gifts. Randolph was due to run for the constituency and maintain the old established traditions.

If his parents would not consent to his marrying Jennie, he would refuse to stand for Woodstock, or worse, withdraw at the last moment, leaving the Liberal candidate to take the seat.

Meanwhile Clara and her daughters had returned to France. Randolph visited Jennie frequently in February and March of 1874, and finally, on 15 April, they married in the chapel of the British embassy in Paris.

Although the intervention of the Prince of Wales had proved unsuccessful, Randolph had not withdrawn his candidacy for Woodstock. It is possible that he had decided to take another route to force the issue of marrying Jennie with his parents' consent. In the event, the Duke and Duchess had no choice but to give the two their blessing, but their disapproval of the match was demonstrated by their being conspicuously absent from the ceremony.

After the wedding, Randolph and Jennie moved into a house at 48 Charles Street, near Berkeley Square in Mayfair, London. They had planned for their baby to be born there, but fate would have it otherwise. After a very active social season in London they went to Blenheim to hunt. While walking with the shooters, Jennie stumbled and fell. She recovered well but a few days later a rough ride in a pony carriage brought on pains. She was confined to bed, but at the annual St Andrew's Ball held at the palace on 28 November, she made an unexpected appearance.

Later that evening, Jennie's labour pains began. She tried to make her way to the bedroom but did not get further than the great hall. There she fainted and was carried into the ladies' cloakroom to be attended by servants while the party carried on. The pains continued all day Sunday, and it was not until well after midnight that her first-born arrived. And so Winston came into the world.

Winston's parents had been married for only seven months, but there were no indications, other than the actual date of birth of the baby, that the boy was born prematurely as *The Times* reported.

The weight of the baby was not recorded, but both he and his mother were remarkably healthy. However, his father had a problem. Within a month of Winston's birth, Randolph took to visiting the family doctor. His ailment was not talked about, but it became known that he had contracted syphilis. The somewhat notorious author Frank Harris divulged the secret in his autobiography, *My Life and Loves*. Harris had heard the story from Louis Jenning, a close friend of Randolph. According to him it had come about during his student years at Oxford. Randolph woke up the morning after a drinking bout to find a seasoned prostitute in his bed.

All evidence suggests that Jennie became aware of Randolph's state of health very early in their marriage. Syphilis is highly contagious and if she had continued sleeping with her husband, she would surely have contracted the disease herself. It was not until World War-II many years later that a viable treatment was found.

Given their position in society and the mores of the time, a divorce was out of the question. So Jennie found other ways to amuse herself. Randolph had always detested dancing. Now Jennie was happy to attend parties alone, or with her sister Clara. Albert Edward — the eldest son of Queen Victoria — Prince of Wales and later King Edward VII, topped the list of men clamouring for her attention. He thought 'American women brought a little fresh air into society',[2] and it was not long before 'he granted her the rare privilege of using Buckingham Palace's private garden entrance'[3] when he requested her company.

The revelation of her husband's state of health less than a year after their wedding and only a month or two after their son was born not only brought about the severance of intimate relations with Randolph but resulted in Jennie distancing herself from her infant child too. But conversely, relations between Jennie and her mother-in-law improved radically.

Since Winston had arrived unexpectedly, no baby clothes or even a cradle were ready. The Duchess borrowed the essentials from the wife of a solicitor whose baby was expected only in January and she engaged a wet nurse. She also arranged for the baby to be baptised Winston Leonard Spencer Churchill. The ceremony was performed by the family chaplain in the chapel at Blenheim Palace on 27 December.

Elizabeth Everest, the nanny Jennie hired early in the new year was given total responsibility for Winston. She chose his food and fed him, cared for his health and cleaned up after him; she bought his clothes, washed his nappies, bathed him; held him when he learned to walk and hugged and comforted him when he was troubled. Winston needed to be shown love and affection by his mother, but Jennie had little time to spare for him. Even these short interludes were largely prearranged so as not to interfere with her busy social schedule.

Randolph's brother, the Marquess of Blandford, was in love with the wife of Lord Aylesford. Randolph felt obliged to meddle in his brother's affair. The Prince of Wales, who had taken Lord Aylesford with him on a tour of India in 1875, was involuntarily drawn into the quarrel. Randolph believed that his brother had been unjustly accused of running off with Edith while her husband was away.

With the help of a detective he found out that no less a person than the Prince of Wales himself had been involved with her before she surrendered to the charms of Lord Blandford. Love letters written by His Royal Highness to Lady Aylesford were produced in evidence. Randolph insisted that the Prince should use his influence to stop the impending divorce, if only to save his brother George from embarrassment. Failing this, the letters would be made public.

Queen Victoria, who was informed of the brewing scandal, did not take kindly to this blackmail. She consulted her Prime Minister, Benjamin Disraeli. 'Blandford I always thought was a scoundrel,' he remarked, 'but his brother beats him'.[4]

Ultimately Lord Aylesford decided not to pursue the matter, but he did divorce his unfaithful wife. Lord Blandford then married Edith and the two lived for a number of years in France. In 1888, after they too were divorced, he married the wealthy New Yorker, Lillian Warren Hammersley.

While Lord Blandford pursued his own happiness, his brother Randolph, who had in good faith tried to defend his honour, fell from grace. The Queen informed the Prince of Wales in no uncertain terms that she disapproved of particular members of society with whom he was involved. The Prince in turn let Blandford know that neither he nor the Princess would attend any social function at which the Churchills were present. The Churchills were, for all practical purposes, banned from London society. This was, of course, a scandal in itself, but Disraeli had a solution. He appointed the Lord Lieutenant of Ireland and suggested that his son Lord Randolph, act as his unofficial secretary.

In January 1877 the Churchills moved to Ireland. They lived in 'The Little Lodge' in Phoenix Park, Dublin. It was not a particularly happy time for young Winston. Because his father was away so much of the time sitting in Parliament in London while his mother spent endless days riding the countryside, he developed a constant fear of being abandoned. This lack of parental attention, in particular from his mother, turned him into — as he himself confessed in later years — 'a troublesome boy'.

Jennie's second son was born in Dublin on 4 February, 1880. Jennie had led an active social life in the Irish capital, passing much of her time with the dark-haired and handsome John Strange Jocelyn, a colonel in the Scots Fusiliers Guard who succeeded his nephew as the fifth Earl of Roden later that year. Jennie named her second son John Strange, after 'the delightful Strange' as she called the colonel, leaving little doubt in the family as to who the father was.

Jack, as the dark-haired boy became known, is said to have looked quite different to Randolph. His temperament, too, was unlike that of his quarrelsome father. Winston had inherited many of Lord Randolph's character traits. But Jack was calm and serene. Yet in spite of their differences, the two boys were close at various stages of their lives. This was particularly marked when Jack came to South Africa during the Anglo-Boer War early in 1900.

Winston was to write that his earliest memories were of Ireland. He was able to recall such events as his grandfather, the King's representative, unveiling a statue of Lord Gough, scarlet soldiers on horseback, his 'formidable grandpapa talking loudly to the crowd' and even using stirring phrases such as 'with a withering volley he shattered the enemy's line'.[5] He remembered being taken to Elmo Park where he was told that the tall white stone tower he admired had been blown up by Oliver Cromwell and later rebuilt. Young Winston thought of Cromwell as a very great man, for the tower was only one of many structures he was supposed to have blown up. Not surprisingly it was not a view shared by the British royalty. Many years later during World War II when he was prime minister of Britain, he asked permission from King George VI to name a newly launched warship the *Olive Cromwell*. Permission was refused.

Then there were the black-coated riflemen he saw in Phoenix Park, and the Fenians — the Irish rebels Mrs Everest had warned him about. One day when Winston was riding a donkey in the park, his nanny mistook the Rifle Brigade marching in the distance for Fenians. She let out a scream which frightened the donkey. She tried to control the kicking animal but to no avail. Winston was thrown off and suffered a mild concussion. 'This was my first introduction to Irish politics!'[6] he wrote in *My Early Life*.

In April 1880 the Disraeli government lost the election and the Duke lost his post as Lord Lieutenant of Ireland. Later that year Randolph and Jennie were back in London with the two boys and their nanny in tow. Randolph, with his party in opposition, worked hard to make his mark in Parliament. Jennie did her best to once again be accepted into London society.

Winston, as always, was looked after by Mrs Everest. He was often sent to Blenheim to stay with his grandparents, and it was from there that he wrote his first letter — to his mother — thanking her for the lead soldiers and flags and a castle he had been given as Christmas presents. He had already accumulated more than a thousand toy soldiers, and each year his collection grew. It is likely that Mrs Everest bought most of them with money from an allowance she could use at her own discretion, but relatives also knew of Winston's passion for playing war games and that a gift of tiny dragoons or lancers was always appreciated.

The Churchills settled at Connaught Place near Marble Arch. The house, the first one in Mayfair to have electricity, had a large nursery where Winston played with his toy soldiers and a steam engine. Jack was six years younger than Winston and there were no friends they could play with. Mrs Everest took the boys for walks in Hyde Park, and once to Ventnor on the Isle of Wight.

Her brother-in-law, John Balaam, was a senior warder at Parkhurst prison. Winston was enthralled by stories of riots in the jail and of how a warder had been attacked and injured by convicts. Then there were the tales he was told about the British fighting the 'black and naked'[7] Zulus in South Africa that made a lasting impression on him. He was angry with the Zulus for 'they killed a great many of our soldiers, but judging from the pictures, not nearly so many as our soldiers killed of them'.[8]

Winston enjoyed wearing fancy clothes and all his life he loved to show off his finery. In later years he owned more hats than most women in England, even the fashionable ones, and had a closet full of costumes and uniforms. He took every opportunity to parade his medals and decorations — in particular the Danish Order of the Elephant that was worn with a sash.

Mrs Everest photographed the seven-year-old Winston dressed in a sailor suit that was fashionable at that time. 'Freckled, red-haired, and pug-nosed, the likeness gives the impression of violent motion suddenly arrested, and in fact he was already hyperactive; from the time he had learned to talk his lips had been moving incessantly'.[9]

Winston was not the most handsome boy around. He had inherited marginally protruding eyes and a slight speech defect — from which he suffered all his life — from his father. He was prone to colds and had neither friends to play with nor loving parents who were there for him when he needed them. All this, coupled with the impetuous streak also bequeathed by Lord Randolph, led to him developing into a rebellious and self-centred individual obsessed with achievement and recognition.

There is no reference to Winston being particularly unhappy during his pre-school years, but his problematic childhood and the two years of abuse he was to endure at preparatory school brought on bouts of misery together with a tendency to be aggressive. Mrs Everest was the first to notice these depressive episodes that were a legacy of five of the seven dukes of Marlborough passed via Lord Randolph.

Winston's illness was fostered by parental neglect, and it was Mrs Everest who tried to help him to fight the 'Black Dog', as she called the melancholic spells he would suffer throughout his life. William Manchester wrote: 'We first encounter Churchill's awareness of his illness in a letter written when he was 20, complaining of mental stagnation and a slough of despond'.[10] He may not have understood his brooding moods in his younger years, but he realised that he had a recurring problem long before he wrote about the agonising stages of melancholia.

As is often the case with children who have inherited the genes of depressive ancestors, Winston was constantly on the go. He was quite a handful for Mrs Everest to manage. When he was not playing with his toy soldiers, he would either be far away in his thoughts, or rushing about, jumping on chairs, falling or banging into things and getting hurt in the process.

Shortly before his eighth birthday in November 1882, his mother took him away from his toy soldiers and the caring Mrs Everest. He was enrolled at St George's, a boarding school near Ascot 'that modelled itself on Eton and aimed at being preparatory for that Public School above all others'.[11]

Winston thought that it would be fun living with so many boys, and that he would make a lot of friends and enjoy adventures with them, but he was severely mistaken. The impression he gained of the school when the headmaster received him and his mother was anything but comforting. A sense of misery and a desire to be left alone overcame him, and the misery turned into fear.

The school was fashionable and expensive and had only ten boys to a class. There was electric light, a swimming pool, a soccer field, cricket grounds and a chapel. The teachers all had Masters degrees. The headmaster, however, believed that flogging his pupils with the birch was an essential part of the curriculum. 'But I am sure no Eton boy, and certainly no Harrow boy of my day, ever received such a cruel flogging as this headmaster was accustomed to inflict upon the little boys who were in his care and power'.

In fact the flogging ordered by the Rev H W Sneyd-Kynnersley 'exceeded in severity anything that would be tolerated in any Reformatories under the Home Office', Winston remembered. 'Two or three times a month the whole school was marshalled in the library, and one or more delinquents were dragged off to an adjoining apartment by the two head boys, and there flogged until they bled freely, while the rest sat quaking, listening to their screams'.[12]

Winston struggled with arithmetic and was unable to comprehend basic instructions in Latin and Greek. He failed a standard and had to repeat the course. But he received a good grounding in the English language which, as it turned out, compensated for all the other shortcomings. He was also fascinated by politics and his extraordinary interest in war poetry was remarkable for a child of his age.

'How I hated this school', he later recorded, 'and what a life of anxiety I lived for more than two years. I made very little progress at my lessons, and none at all at games. I counted the days and the hours to the end of every term, when I should return home from this hateful servitude and range my soldiers in line of battle on the nursery floor'.[13]

Even a brief period of indiscriminate punishment can be counter-productive in that the victim might respond by delivering quite the opposite of the desired result. He might, for instance, channel his energy into controlling his emotions instead of concentrating on the work at hand. Perhaps this was the case with Winston 'refusing' to learn Latin and Greek. The war games Winston so dearly loved possibly acted as a safety valve, helping him to control his aggression and to cope when the strains in his young life seemed almost unbearable.

The grandiosity that Winston displayed from a very early age can be seen as an attempt to mask his brooding moods and, to a lesser extent, a sense of worthlessness that would manifest in self-destructive thoughts. Many years later he confessed to Lord Moran, his physician, that he did not like standing near the edge of a platform when a train passed through. When he looked down into the water from the side of a ship, or from the balcony of a high-rise building, he had to fight a strange compulsion to throw himself over the edge. Even sleeping near a balcony was discomforting. 'A second's action would end everything', he said, and was adamant that he had 'no desire to quit this world, but thoughts, desperate thoughts, come into the head'.[14]

Jennie didn't visit her son at St George's and seldom replied to his letters pleading for her to take notice of him. But when the rebellious child finally fled the institution to seek solace in the arms of Mrs Everest, Jennie had to react. She didn't see the anguish in the boy's eyes, but the scars left by the birch on his back and bottom she couldn't ignore. The headmaster blamed Winston and insisted that the troublesome boy had no ambition and could not be trusted to behave himself.

At the end of the summer term of 1883, Winston was, on the recommendation of the family doctor, Robson Roose, removed from St. George's. In September of that year when he was not yet ten, he was transferred to a little school in Brighton run by two maiden sisters, Kate and Charlotte Thomson. Although at Brighton Winston 'found an element of kindness and of sympathy which I found conspicuously lacking in my first experiences',[15] he needed time to adjust to his new environment.

Within three months of joining the school, he was involved in a fight with another boy over a penknife. Winston was stabbed in the chest. The wound was superficial but the other boy was expelled. Jennie, though, was convinced it was Winston's fault. He had started the fight by pulling the other boy's ear. Lord Randolph, who was away in India during the second half of 1885 acting as the Secretary of State for seven months, was amused by Jennie's letter more than concerned. 'What adventures Winston does have', was his reply.

There were other incidents that would have prompted the headmaster at St. George's to take harsh measures — such as when Winston refusing to conform to the practice of turning to the east when the Apostles' Creed was recited in the Chapel Royal at Brighton. Winston expected to be severely reprimanded for his obstinate behaviour, but to his puzzlement, mixed with a measure of disappointment, his action was not commented on. He looked forward to the next similar occasion to make his point, but the two sisters had their own way of dealing with the rebellious youngster. At the following service the school was ushered into pews which faced east, thus obviating the need to turn in that direction. This clever tactic employed by the Thomson sisters made a strong impression on Winston.

At the end of the first term, Winston was ranked near the bottom of the class of 32. In his first report it was stated that 'frequent absence from the schoolroom made competition with other boys very difficult'. But progress was in the offing. He was allowed to study subjects that interested him, such as French and history, and he learned poetry by heart.

Realising that his physique was not his greatest asset, he resolved to learn to swim and rode three times a week. He played cricket until he made the first team as 12th man. After the third term the Thomson sisters again reported his progress. He was first in his class and received two prizes, one for English and the other for scripture.

Life, no doubt, would have taken another turn for Winston if his parents had shown a keener interest in their son. The psychological effect of the knowledge of Lord Randolph's illness on both his wife and himself must have been severe, and this surely contributed to their mutual need for escapism and the neglect of their two sons. Ever busy with their own affairs, this lack of parental responsibility was to have a profound and lasting effect on Winston's personality — and for all we know, on Jack's too. When Winston was seriously stricken with bronchitis with both lungs affected and Dr Roose was desperately trying to keep his temperature below 104° degrees, Randolph and Jennie did visit him, but separately.

In spite of Randolph's condition, Jennie still showed affection for her husband. She was an ambitious woman who took it for granted that his time as Prime Minister would come. She did her best to campaign for him, but other than that she led a life of her own. She had long since shed her American mannerisms and took on the lifestyle befitting a titled Englishwoman. The endless dinner parties offered by the beautiful and charming hostess demanded much of her time.

Jennie found it equally diverting to flirt with anyone who was anyone. Although she loved her sons in her own way, she did not allow parental obligations to interfere with her social calendar. Her intimate friendships with men — whether they were other women's husbands or eminent personalities such as Oscar Wilde or the famous attorney and MP Sir Edward Carson — took priority in her scheme of things.

Besides her 'delightful Strange', she was romantically linked to Sir Edgar Vincent, later Viscount D'Abernon while living in Ireland . 'My mother always seemed to me a fairy princess; a radiant being possessed of limitless riches and power',[16] Churchill wrote in *My Early Life*, and confessed that he appreciated the way Sir Edgar described her when he saw her for the first time at the vice regal lodge in Dublin.

> She stood on one side to the left of the entrance. The Viceroy was on a dais
> at the farther end of the room surrounded by a brilliant staff, but eyes were

not turned on him or on his consort, but on a dark, lithe figure, standing somewhat apart and appearing to be of another texture to those around her, radiant, translucent, intense.

A diamond star in her hair, her favourite ornament — its lustre dimmed by the flashing glory of her eyes. More of a panther than of the women in her look, but with a cultivated intelligence unknown to the jungle.[17]

William Manchester quoted the Irish novelist George Moore as saying that Jennie had bedded 200 men. 'That is absurd', Manchester insists, stating: 'Jennie was far too fastidious for that, and only she would have known the figure anyhow'.[18] A figure of 200 does seem rather excessive, but it is well documented that Jennie enjoyed the company of other men — with Albert Edward, the Prince of Wales, in prime position.

Lord Randolph had little choice but to accept his wife's escapades. There were those who — probably being unaware of his state of health — wondered why and speculated that he was homosexual. Once or twice he did raise his fist against a man whom he suspected of being more than friendly with his beautiful wife, and even ordered the Prince of Wales out of his Mayfair home. But by and large he showed admirable tolerance towards Jennie's needs. In the case of Count Kinsky, who was four years younger than Jennie and who won the Grand National on his own horse in 1883, Randolph didn't seem to object to their 'Austrian Alliance', as the liaison was referred to.

Winston, too, accepted his mother's 'desire to please, her delight in life, and the genuine wish that all should share her joyous faith in it', as Lord D'Abernon put it. But her neglecting him miserably, and 'his knowledge of her guilt undoubtedly contributed to his adolescent turmoil'.[19] Yet it seems strange that the young and impetuous Winston didn't rebel against her. He simply adored his mother. 'She shone for me like the evening star', he wrote. 'I loved her dearly — but at a distance'.[20] This explains the generous measure of patience, tolerance and understanding he had for the woman who gave little in return.

The adoration Winston had for his father was reciprocated by a distinct dislike for his son. Once, in Brighton, Winston wanted to come home during the Easter holidays. He wrote a letter, asking for someone to meet him at the station as he was too young to travel on his own, but no one turned up. Later he read in the local newspaper that Lord Randolph had made a speech in town, but he hadn't even bothered to call on his son. Although Winston could not comprehend why his father didn't come to see him, he resigned himself to the fact that he must have been just too busy.

Many years later when Winston was dining with his own son — called Randolph after his grandfather — the former remarked that he had talked more to him during the course of one evening than his father had talked to him in his entire life.

2

A school dunce for Sandhurst

Six generations of Churchills had attended Eton. Lord Randolph had been expelled from this prestigious institution and there was doubt that Winston would pass the entrance examinations, let alone manage to keep up with the classes there. Dr Roose had a ready answer. Eton lay among the foggy and misty meadows of the Thames Valley and he declared that it was therefore not a suitable place for a boy with a weak chest.

Harrow was situated on a hill and the local climate would therefore be more bracing and less injurious to his health. Winston was not concerned about his health when Harrow was mentioned. What concerned him was passing the entrance examination and he felt this would not be a problem. He was right. Although he did not answer one question on the Latin paper, the headmaster, the Rev Dr JEC Welldon, 'showed that he was a man capable of looking beneath the surface of things: a man not dependent upon paper manifestations'.[1] Winston passed the examination on 14 March 1888 and shortly after his 13th birthday he was admitted to Harrow and placed in the division of the fourth, or bottom, form.

That Winston was accepted at Harrow, however, was not due to the headmaster's ability to 'look beneath the surface of things'. Dr Welldon knew that Winston was a difficult child before he was enrolled, but the boy was the son of a lord who was a former cabinet minister.

On arriving at the school he was registered as Winston Leonard Spencer-Churchill. He was placed in a small house of 15 boys under the care of the assistant master, Henry Davidson. The boys were instructed to line up alphabetically according to their surnames. Spencer-Churchill was one of the last names called and Winston was so irritated by this that he dropped 'Spencer', a name the Churchills had been associated with since 1817.

In addition, Winston was constantly teased by his fellow pupils for his lisp — or stammer as some thought — which caused him difficulties with the sibilant 's'. He made an appointment with a distinguished throat specialist, Sir Felix Semon, who was one of the Prince of Wales' doctors.

He told Semon that he wanted to go to Sandhurst and then join a cavalry regiment in India, but he had no intention, he insisted, of being a soldier all his life. When he was finished with the cavalry he intended to enter politics and become as important a statesman as his father. He thought that he would only be successful if he were able to deliver speeches without worrying about his pronunciation of the letter 's'. Dr Semon was not perturbed. He assured Winston that it would not affect a career in the army, and that his father before him had the same speech impediment. With practice and perseverance he could cure himself of this minor disability.

Semon's advice led to a Miss Muriel Wilson, who tutored Winston to rehearse phrases such as 'She sells sea shells on the sea shore', and 'The Spanish ships I cannot see for they are not in sight', while walking up and down the drive of the mansion owned by her father. Miss Wilson did not cure Winston of his impediment, but he was nonetheless attracted to her because she had a very wealthy father. Money, he felt, was reason enough to marry her when he was old enough. As it turned out, the young lady did not share the sentiments of the noisy and pugnaciously shameless boy, nor did she — much to Winston's disappointment — have faith in his future.

At Harrow, Winston's phenomenal memory helped him to scrape through the grades. Although he did not excel academically, he could do anything — or almost anything — he turned his mind to.

In his first term he won a prize by repeating 1 200 lines of Macauley's *The Lays of Ancient Rome*. Yet, after three months at the school, his housemaster, Henry Davidson, felt compelled to write to his mother to complain about Winston's forgetfulness, his carelessness and lack of punctuality. He asked Jennie to have a serious talk with Winston about his irregular ways when he went home.

The housemaster lamented that Winston's behaviour had deteriorated as the term passed. 'Constantly late for school, or losing his books and papers, and various other things into which I need to enter — he is so regular in his irregularity that I really don't know what to do; and sometimes I think he cannot help it'. Davidson was adamant. 'If he cannot conquer his slovenliness, he will never make a success at a public school.'[2]

Winston, the school dunce, presented a disciplinary problem. In fact, at Harrow he was looked on as a hopeless case. He was constantly short of money and generally unpopular — characteristics that stayed with him for many years to come. As far as punctuality was concerned, he missed trains, ships, aeroplanes and appointments as long as he lived.

'I do think unpunctuality is a vile habit, and all my life I have tried to break myself of it', he wrote in *My Early Life* and agreed with his former headmaster, Dr Welldon, when he said: 'I have never been able to understand the point of view of persons who make a practice of being ten minutes late for each of a series of appointments throughout the day.'

The only solution to his habit of making people wait for him, he felt, 'is to cut one or two of the appointments altogether and catch up. But very few men have the strength of mind to do this'.[3] Churchill was not one of the few.

On being shown Davidson's letter, Lord Randolph realised that Winston would not be accepted into Oxford or Cambridge or be called to the Bar as he had hoped. As we have seen, he had thus far shown very little interest in his son. Winston later wrote: 'I would far rather have been apprenticed as a bricklayer's mate, or run errands as a messenger boy, or helped my father to dress the front windows of a grocer's shop. It would have been real; it would have been natural; it would have taught me more; and I should have done it much better. Also I should have got to know my father, which would have been a joy.'[4]

What his father was aware of, however, was Winston's love of playing war games with his toy soldiers and his fascination for things military. His collection had grown to almost 1 500 soldiers, all British, and he arranged them as an infantry division with a cavalry brigade. He placed Jack in charge of the hostile army, but according to the Treaty for the Limitation of Armaments, he insisted, his brother was only allowed to have men of colour in his ranks; and they were not permitted to employ artillery.

'Very important! I could muster myself only eighteen field guns — besides fortress pieces. But all the other services were complete — except one. It was what every army is always short of — transport. My father's old friend, Sir Henry Drummond Wolff, admiring my array, noticed this deficiency and provided a fund from which it was to some extent supplied',[5] Churchill wrote in *My Early Life*.

One day Lord Randolph looked at the display of Winston's lead soldiers, arranged in the correct formation to attack the enemy. After studying the set-up for some 20 minutes, there was no longer any uncertainty as to what career his son would follow. Being assured by Winston that the army was the place he wanted to be, all was settled. Winston was ecstatic. He had no doubt that his father had recognised in him the qualities required of someone destined to become an outstanding military leader. But to his dismay, he was to learn that he was not thought of as clever enough to be called to the Bar.

At Harrow the preliminary Army examination included the drawing of a map. Winston put the names of all the countries of the world into a hat and drew one out. The name was 'New Zealand'. He studied the outline of the two main islands of the country thoroughly and on the following day collected his exam paper. The instruction read: draw a map of New Zealand!

Having passed the preliminary examination, Winston spent the next three years at Harrow in the army class which Dr Welldon had introduced a year earlier as part of his far-reaching reforms in the curriculum of the school. Passing the examination to enter the Royal Military Academy at Sandhurst, however, was not as easy as drawing a map, learning its main characteristics by heart and copying down the information the following day.

While Winston struggled on at Harrow, his father, ever in need of finances, decided to sail to South Africa and travel to Mashonaland in search of riches he hoped to gain from the gold-prospecting syndicate he had formed. There was quite a stir at the news of his impending visit. Cecil John Rhodes had created a vast diamond and gold-mining operation in Kimberley and on the Witwatersrand, and he made sure that the arrangements made by his men were in line with the needs of the flamboyant guest.

Lord Randolph and his party, which included Captain Gwynydd Williams as his aide-de-camp, Dr Hugh Rayner, a surgeon in the Grenadier Guards and an American mining expert Henry Cleveland Perkins who was employed by Messrs Rothschild, arrived in Cape Town on 14 May 1891.

In South Africa Lord Randolph was treated like royalty. Percy Fitzpatrick, of *Jock of the Bushveld* fame, was asked by the Johannesburg mining magnate Alfred Beit to come to the Rand and take charge of the expedition. This was Fitzpatrick's chance to obtain a permanent position in Beit's financial empire — provided of course that all went well. The wealth that Randolph had hoped to accumulate from the newly discovered gold of the Witwatersrand reef, however, did not materialise.

One favourable outcome was that his health had improved remarkably during the dry and crisp winter on the South African Highveld. An invitation to a hunting expedition on the estate of wealthy industrialist Sammy Marks to the east of Pretoria was the highlight of his visit. But he couldn't hold his tongue on the subject of the Transvaal Boers even when it came to hunting. The Boers, he claimed, killed wild life to such an extent that there was nothing left for the sportsman besides feathered game. Things would be very different, he insisted, if 'God had only given a glimmer of intelligence to the Boer'.[6]

During the course of the morning he and his party were nevertheless able to shoot 'two springbok, four ducks, 50 partridge, four hares, 250 quail, eight koran, 11 snipe, one dikkop, one wild turkey and one blue crane'.[7] On leaving Pretoria his party stopped at a hotel in a hamlet called Nylstroom. The *Volksstem* reported on the visit, saying:

> In a flash the hotelkeeper was ready to offer the gentleman his fatted calf: fried chicken and ducks were waiting to tempt gentleman to the table. Imagine the host's surprise when the said gentleman carried several large cases into the dining room, lit a paraffin stove, requested the hotelkeeper to remove his 'little dinner' and to supply a leg of mutton, and then, like regular cooks, began to grill meat and prepare their own meal. After standing admiringly round the stove until the meal was cooked, they partook of a little here and there. Then they repacked their boxes, inspanned the coach, and departed, having rather grudgingly paid the hotelkeeper for the rooms they had booked as well as the dinner.[8]

On his way back from Mashonaland, it was said that Lord Randolph was told to take a different route instead of returning to Pretoria. According to rumours, angry burghers were ready to demonstrate their displeasure of the man by parading an effigy of him through the streets of the Transvaal capital for onlookers to throw rotten vegetables at.

Perhaps this added to Randolph's feelings about the Boers when, upon leaving Johannesburg, he predicted:

> The days of the Transvaal Boers as an independent and distinct nationality in South Africa are numbered; they will pass away unhonoured, unlamented, scarcely remembered either by the native or by the European settler. Having given to them great possessions and great opportunities, they will be written of only for their cruelty towards, and tyranny over, the native races, their fanaticism, their ignorance, and their selfishness; they will be handed down to posterity by tradition as having conferred no single benefit upon any single human being, not even upon themselves, and upon the pages of African history they will leave a shadow, but only a shadow, of a dark reputation and an evil name.[9]

Later, when his much-resented letters were published in the form of a book entitled *Men, Mines and Animals in South Africa*, Lord Randolph had these comments included. The book was an instant success and it was reprinted several times before he died, but the author did not care to change or delete his remarks about a people who had welcomed him and offered him and his companions their generous hospitality.

When he returned to England in January 1882, the rumbustious lord left a trail of rudeness and resentment behind that was to haunt Winston when he arrived on the scene some eight years later. As an amateur journalist, Randolph had been contracted to write for the *Daily Graphic*. He severely criticised the Transvaal Government, of which he knew little, and described the Boers themselves as being dirty, lazy and barbarous.

As a sort of poetic quid pro quo, the South African cartoonist William Howard Schröder drew some unforgettable pictures of an aristocrat of the more objectionable type. The character was immaculately dressed in frock-coat and striped trousers and was shown to be inconsiderate, supercilious and rude to whoever crossed his path. Randolph Churchill had made himself the laughing stock of the country. *The Natal Advertiser* opined: 'If he is not sorry he ever came here, the people of South Africa most certainly are.'

Loyal Jennie with Jack at her side was at the docks in Southampton to welcome him home. Winston was unable to go. He rather grudgingly left for Versailles to stay with one of Harrow's French masters, a Monsieur Minssen and his family, so that he could improve on his rather poor knowledge of the language. As it turned out, Minssen's mother was English, but Winston became acquainted with French customs through Baron Maurice de Hirsch, the Marquis Henri le Tonnelier de Breteuil and Monsieur Trafford.

These gentlemen were three of his mother's continental admirers to whom he had written to inform them of his stay in Paris. Being entertained by them in fine restaurants and introduced to the best Bordeaux wines was an unexpected but welcome pleasure.

Winston's masters at Harrow realised that he was no candidate for Woolwich, the military academy that prepared cadets for commissions in the artillery and engineers. At the military academy of Sandhurst he could possibly pass the examinations as a subaltern of infantry or cavalry if he applied himself. At the first attempt, he failed miserably, largely because his maths was hopeless. His second attempt was no more successful. He wrote to his mother that he was 'awfully depressed now that the examination is over'. In fact, Winston's 'Black Dog' had taken such a hold of him that he seriously considered forgetting about the Army and taking up the priesthood.

His father, desperate to find a solution to Winston's problems, had already written to Welldon asking for advice as to what to do with his son. Welldon suggested that the help of Captain WH James, the most successful 'crammer' for the Sandhurst examination, should be sought. Captain James was happy to oblige, but before Winston could report to him, early in February 1893 he met with an accident that nearly cost him his life.

While spending a holiday with his aunt, Lady Wimborne, at her Bournmouth estate, he was playing with Jack and a cousin in a forest. Winston was short of breath as the two boys chased him as he tried to cross a bridge over a deep cleft. The chine below was covered with young fir trees, the tops of which he could almost touch. In an instant he had jumped over the railing with his arms held out to embrace the tree nearest to him.

'It was three days before I regained consciousness and more than three months before I crawled from my bed', he wrote in *My Early Life*, but his son Randolph had it that Winston 'had somewhat exaggerated the length of his convalescence'.[10] The time Winston spent in bed was in fact less than two months, but a ruptured kidney delayed his lessons with Captain James for almost another month.

That Winston had also fractured his thigh was detected by neither Dr Robson Roose nor Harley Street specialist Dr John Rose. 'No bones were broken', reported *The Times* of 11 January 1893.

It was only in 1963 — 70 years after the fall — when the same thigh was X-rayed in Monte Carlo that the full extent of the damage became known.

Captain James had his share of problems with the headstrong boy who engaged him in a battle of wills. In a letter to Lord Randolph, James noted that he had to reprimand Winston about his casual manner. He felt that the boy showed a lack of attention and thought too much of his abilities. Another complaint James brought forward was that Winston tried to teach his instructors rather than making an effort to learn from them; this, he insisted, is not the frame of mind conducive to success.

But Captain James' patience and tolerance paid off. When Winston sat the Sandhurst entrance exam for the third time at the end of June, he was placed 95th out of 389. Fortified by what he regarded as a scholastic triumph, he wrote to his father — who was taking the cure with Jennie at Bad Kissingen — that he had qualified for a cavalry cadetship at Sandhurst.

Lord Randolph was aghast that his son was not eligible for the infantry. He had already made plans for Winston to enter the Duke of Connaught's regiment, the 60th Rifles, which was one of the finest regiments in the Army. This would have enabled him to serve for a couple of years in a Mediterranean fortress and then be transferred to India.

The additional levy of £200 a year required of a cavalry officer was even less to Randolph's liking. He made up his mind. He was not going to allow his son to remain in the cavalry and he told Winston accordingly by return of post. Winston was staying at the Hotel Couronnes in Brigue, Switzerland while on a walking tour with Jack and a young teacher from Eton. Lord Randolph must have been furious when he wrote:

> Never have I received a really good report of your conduct in your work from any master or tutor you had from time to time to do with. Always behind-hand, never advancing in your class, incessant complaints of total want of application, and this character which was constant in your reports has shown the natural results clearly in your last army examination.
>
> Do not think I am going to take the trouble of writing to you long letters after every failure you commit and undergo ... I no longer attach the lightest weight to anything you may say about your own acquirements & exploits. I shall leave you to depend on yourself giving you merely such assistance as may be necessary to permit of a respectable life. Because I am certain that if you cannot prevent yourself from leading the idle useless unprofitable life you have had during your schooldays and after months, you will become a mere social wastrel one of the hundreds of the public failures, and you will degenerate into a shabby unhappy & futile existence.[11]

Although Winston expressed regret that he had caused his father so much worry, he was nonetheless delighted he would have his own horse. This, he reasoned, gave him a distinct advantage over soldiers who had to fight battles on foot. An added bonus was wearing the cavalry uniform which was much more attractive than the one worn by the infantry, and that was important to him.

In a letter to the Duchess of Marlborough, Lord Randolph reiterated his deep disappointment with Winston. 'I shall try and get Brabazon who has a regiment of Hussars to take him and after two or three years shall exchange him with the infantry', he wrote, and asked her not to mention Winston's failure to get into the infantry to any of the family. 'After all, he has got into the army and that is the result which none of his cousins have been able to do, but still that is a very wretched and pitiable consolation'.[12]

Randolph's disillusionment with his and Winston's reputations and the annoyance over the extra expenses he would have to meet while his son served in the cavalry, were short-lived. As it turned out, a number of aspirants had failed to take up the cadetship and before the month was out, Winston was informed by telegram that he had the opportunity of serving in the infantry.

Although pleased with the turn of fortune, Lord Randolph was leaving nothing to chance. During Winston's third and final term at Sandhurst, he reminded the Duke of Connaught of his promise to accept his son into his regiment. Winston, however, had his own ideas about his future career as a soldier.

Colonel John Brabazon, who had been romantically involved with Jennie for a short time and remained a family friend, had taken command of the 4th Queen's Own Hussars at Aldershot, 32 miles from London. He invited Winston to stay with him during a weekend after Easter. It did not take much for Brabazon to convince Winston that joining the 4th Hussars would have great advantages over staying with the infantry. The regiment would be going to India soon, he told him, and the chances of rapid promotion, obtaining his own commission and a host of other benefits the infantry could not meet, left Winston in no doubt as to where his immediate future lay.

Lord Randolph's opinion about Winston joining the cavalry no longer mattered. The final stages of Randolph's disease had already set in. In June 1894 he and Jennie went on a world cruise on the *SS Majestic*. By the time they returned to London on Christmas Eve, Randolph's condition had developed into insanity.

Winston was well aware of his father's illness and had confronted Dr Roose on the situation when his parents were in Japan. On being shown the medical reports, he realised how grave the situation was. For a month Lord Randolph lingered in agony. Then on the morning of 24 January 1895, he passed away.

Within a week of Randolph's death, Jennie sent Colonel Brabazon a telegram. In his reply, Brabazon told Jennie that he had written to the private secretary of the Duke of Cambridge, Commander-in-Chief of the Army, and suggested that she follow up with her own letter to the Duke at once. He advised her to state that a vacancy had come up in the 4th Hussars, that Brabazon knew and liked her son and was very anxious that he should join the regiment.

He further instructed her to add: 'Winston passed very much higher than any of the candidates for cavalry and I hope that the Duke will allow him to be appointed to the 4th Hussars, and thus fulfil one of Randolph's last wishes.' Brabazon concluded his letter by assuring her that he was certain the Duke would make the necessary arrangements as far as Winston's posting was concerned.

The Duke shortly replied and promised Jennie that if the posting could be arranged, it would be. And so it was. Winston reported to the 4th Queens Own Hussars on 18 February and was officially commissioned as a second lieutenant on 20 February 1895.

Churchill wrote in *My Early Life*: 'My mother was always at hand to help and advise ... she soon became an ardent ally, furthering my plans and guarding my interests with all her influence and boundless energy ... we worked together on even terms, more like brother and sister than mother and son. At least so it seemed to me. And so it continued to the end.'

William Manchester is more direct when saying: 'His career would have been impossible without preferential treatment. His name, not academic competence, got him through Harrow and Sandhurst. Then his mother, finally taking an interest in his affairs, began pulling strings for him.'[14]

3

Platonic love and scandalous affairs

Life in the barracks at Aldershot where the 4th Queens Own Hussars were stationed, was pleasant. Churchill had his own room. At 7:45am the officers were served 'breakfast in bed', he wrote to Jack. A servant laid out his blue and gold uniform — for which his tailor had to wait more than six years to be paid. Churchill spent an hour each day in charge of a squad of 30 men, supervising the grooming of the horses and the cleanliness of both stables and the men's rooms. Attending the riding school for two hours and a drill in the afternoon was also on the programme. Dinner, a game of billiards and a hot bath ended the day. His pay was £120 per annum.

Churchill was quick to make friends and, unlike at Harrow, he was determined to be liked by his fellow officers. As a young boy he had lacked physical courage. Once, at Brighton, boys throwing cricket balls at him scared him. But he realised that hiding behind a tree was an act of cowardice and this made him determined never to back down. Being rather small and weak for his age, he decided that being good at sports would earn him respect. Learning to swim had been was one of his first priorities.

When he was about 14, he asked Mrs Everest to take him and Jack to Marylebone swimming baths. He must have been very frustrated for suddenly, without provocation, he pulled the foot racks from a changing cabin and threw them in the pool. The superintendent was called and demanded to know why Winston had done this. Not getting a reply, he threatened to call the police and have Winston locked up.

The boy was not impressed. His petulant lips were pouting. 'Oh, you are the superintendent, are you?' he said in a mocking voice and added: 'Well, I am the son of Lord Randolph Churchill. Please take off your hat when you speak to a gentleman.'

That this cocky behaviour would never earn him respect, the rebellious teenager still had to learn.

Besides riding and playing cricket, Winston took up boxing and excelled at fencing. Yet through all the years at school as well as at home, he suffered criticism and disapproval. Being accepted by his peers and assured that he belonged and was recognised as a worthy member of the inner circle of Sandhurst 'bloods' meant everything to him.

Still prone to accidents, he hurt himself badly while jumping a horse over a high bar without stirrups or saddle. This led him to promise his worried mother that he would take no further risks in steeple chasing. Notwithstanding, he did take part in the 4th Queens Own Hussars cavalry steeplechase Subalterns' Challenge Cup, coming third on Albert Savory's *Traveller*. Later a serious irregularity was discovered and the race was declared null and void. The horses that had taken part were disqualified from further racing under National Hunt Rules. All five subalterns involved were suspected of having substituted *Surefoot*, the outsider that tied for first place with another horse. Dishonourable conduct was a serious matter. It was cause for discharge from the Army — not to mention gossip in the public domain.

The War Office's explanation was that there was no dishonourable intention on the part of the riders as they were ignorant of the laws of racing. A year later the magazine *Truth* denounced the scandal. The editor, Henry du Preez Labouchere, who 'became a sort of combined Mark Twain and IF Stone, deflating pomposity and exposing fraud in the literary style no less humorous than it was lethal', had his day.

Churchill could not have ridden in the race without being told of the substitution, so he could not protest complete innocence. But as long as the War Office swept the shameful scandal under the carpet, he didn't care. Albert Savory, Allan Francis and Reginald Barnes, the senior officers who participated in the race, had accepted him and this is what counted as far as he was concerned.

Not being accepted by the inner circle was synonymous with being undesirable. Officers who did not have enough money to keep their own horses, or who showed poor horsemanship, were unwelcome. Cowardice and effeminacy were equally frowned upon. At the time of Churchill's arrival at Aldershot, one officer, named George Hodge, was considered by his peers to be unsuited to the cavalry. This prompted Barnes and Savory to mercilessly harass the subaltern.

They horse-troughed him at two in the morning and pushed him under the bars before forcing a salt and cayenne pepper mixture down the throat of the bruised and bleeding fellow. He handed in his resignation. This earned him the same stigmatisation as being expelled from the regiment, and Hodge had no choice but to leave for the colonies.

Second Lieutenant Alan Bruce was Hodge's replacement, joining the 4th Hussars in April 1895. Bruce was a good horseman and a good shot. Most of all, he was an excellent fencer having displayed his skill before the Duke of Cambridge. But the following January he was expelled from the regiment, an incident that was very much Churchill's doing. Churchill's disgraceful conduct in the affair, which led to questions in Parliament, 'must stand as the most shameful episode of his early life'.[2]

Before Bruce joined the regiment, Churchill invited him and five subalterns to dinner at the Nimrod Club in London. All went well but when dinner was over, Churchill — who had been merely two months at Aldershot and was acting as spokesman for the junior officers — told Bruce that he was not welcome at the regiment. Churchill had known Bruce at Harrow where they had been fierce rivals. Winston had beaten his fellow pupil into second place for the Harrow fencing cup at

England's public school competition which, as it happens, was held at Aldershot.

Winston was lauded in the school's newspaper, *Harrowian*, for his success 'due to his quick and dashing attack which quite took his opponents by surprise'. Yet he feared Bruce. He no longer lacked physical courage but he detested Bruce's manners; and most of all, he feared that his erstwhile rival would reveal the past. The easiest way to resolve a problem which he feared could tarnish his career at Sandhurst was to get rid of its source.

The reason given for rejecting Bruce was his annual allowance of £500. The fact that Churchill had only £300 at his disposal did not bother him at all. £500 would not be enough for Bruce to meet the expenses of keeping hunters and racehorses, he argued.

His friends chipped in, telling Bruce they would get rid of him just as they had done with Hodge. Bruce looked at them in disbelief; he tried to reason with them and pleaded to be given a chance. But for Churchill and his friends, the decision was final. Bruce went to see Brabazon, but as the Colonel was away, he reported the callous threat to the adjutant, Captain De Moleyns. There the matter rested for the moment.

Bruce was indeed a man to whom rough and ready behaviour came easily. He was known to swear at his subordinates and once, when he was under the impression that he had not been properly addressed by a sergeant of another regiment, he lost his temper. This placed Colonel Brabazon in the humiliating position of having to offer an apology to the other regiment. Brabazon was told that the officers did not want Bruce in their ranks. He silently agreed.

On Boxing Day Bruce was the orderly officer in the barracks. He heard that there was a veteran of Balaclava in the non-commissioned officers' mess. Wanting to meet a survivor of this famous battle of the Crimean war, he went across, knowing that the NCO's mess was off limits to officers. The set-up was perfect. A drink offered to him by the sergeant-major in the spirit of Christmas was readily accepted.

On the morning of 29 December he was placed under arrest. A week later Colonel Brabazon informed him of the charges. Bruce was guilty of misconduct by reason of 'improperly associating with non-commissioned officers'. The sergeant-major testified and Brabazon told him that either he or Bruce would have to leave the regiment. It was left to Lord Methuen, the major-general commanding the Home District, to tell Bruce that if he did not send in his papers, his services would be dispensed with. Bruce had no choice but to resign.

'Who', asked Labouchere in the House of Commons, 'were the ungentlemanly officers? Bruce or the men who had told him they would turn him out because he had only £500 a year?'[3] He added that he did not believe 'a more disreputable set of young men existed in the whole Army', and reported the incident in his magazine. Once again the War Office took no action, but the case was to have later repercussions.

Bruce's father, the respectable barrister Alan George Cameron Bruce-Pryce, was outraged over the treatment meted out to his son. Being rivals at Sandhurst in shooting, fencing and riding was only part of the problem, he believed. The reason for Churchill's dislike was 'that his son knew too much about Winston, particularly about the case of a Sandhurst cadet who had been flogged publicly by a subaltern for committing acts of gross immorality "of the Oscar Wide type" with Churchill'.[4]

Homosexual acts were a criminal offence in 1885. On hearing Bruce-Pryces' accusation, Lord and Lady Randolph consulted their friends and solicitors and sued Bruce-Pryce for criminal libel, demanding £20 000 in damages.

Colonel Brabazon approved the prompt action. Bruce-Pryce was unable to substantiate his claims and had no choice but to withdraw the charges. He was ordered to pay £500 damages, but in spite of the verdict, there were people who, for some time, looked at Churchill in a strange way. What was more troubling for him than curious glances, however, was that 'Labouchere, who was also a Member of Parliament for Northampton, demanded a full investigation by the Army and personally brought the matter up for debate in the House of Commons.[5] He further insisted that the race-fixing a year earlier had been instigated by the same subalterns, and that this too, should be carefully examined.

Labouchere was the defendant in many libel suits and was almost always the winner. 'In Parliament, he rapidly proved himself a gadfly whose radical sting raised many a Tory welt. He could thunder outraged indignation with Gladstonian eloquence; he could be incisive, demolishing an opponent with a relentless barrage of unassailable facts. He may have been at his best, however, when hitting below the belt with weapon of ridicule that often drew on distortion and outright misstatements'.[6]

Lady Randolph contacted her friends for help. Winston advised her: '.. what you must do from my point of view alone and not with reference to the regiment, which has no ideas beyond soldiering, and care nothing for the opinion of those who are not their friends'.[7] But everyone who was anyone in the army was Lady Randolph's friend. Colonel Brabazon discussed the affair with the hero of the Zulu War, General Sir Redvers Buller, VC — who was perfectly satisfied to put the incident to rest.

Later, Winston's son Randolph was to admit that 'neither the story of the Challenge Cup nor that of Buller's reception into the Regiment reads very pretty'.[8] He convinced himself that Winston was an innocent victim in both the race fixing and the Bruce affair. 'Churchill was a high-spirited youth and naturally any escapade in which he was involved was bound to attract attention. After a careful study of all the known facts and a prolonged meditation upon them the author can only conclude that although Churchill's conduct may have been injudicious it was in no way dishonourable'.[9]

That Churchill was anything but an innocent bystander in both scandals has been extensively written about. Winston himself, of course, was not satisfied with the outcome. Being stationed in faraway India when the scandal came to a head, he immediately wrote to his mother to have her pull her powerful strings. 'I leave matters in your hands — but in my absence my dearest Mamma — you must be the guardian of my young reputation',[10] he pleaded in his letter of 12 November 1896. A week later he took up the matter again. He branded Labouchere a scoundrel and said: 'One of these days I will make him smart for his impudence'. He was concerned about the damage Labouchere's attacks could do him and 'therefore do muzzle him if you can', he wrote.[11]

Lady Randolph had already seen Field Marshall Viscount Wolseley — who had taken over as Commander-in-Chief from the Duke of Cambridge the previous year — and the old family friend, Under Secretary of State for War, William St John Brodrick, who defended the Army position in the House of Commons. Lord Wolseley, in a report, stated that Bruce being drummed out of his regiment by Churchill and his brother officers without being able to defend himself was 'reprehensible'. To this it can only be added that the cover-up by the War Office and Wolseley was equally reprehensible.

But that still left the difficult Labouchere, who had been a friend of Lord Randolph, for Jennie to deal with. The Queen called the publisher of *Truth* 'that horrible, lying Labouchere'. But even his fiercest enemies found it hard to dislike Labby 'since he himself seemed incapable of personal malice'.[12] Jennie turned on her charm, reminded him of his friendship with her husband and told him of her formidable connections among the most powerful men in Britain. Labouchere knew when to draw the line.

Later he described the growing pressure to drop the case with the words: 'The public must bear in mind that the young officer who assumed the part of ringleader in the conspiracy to eject Mr Bruce from the 4th Hussars belongs to an influential family, and all the authority at his back has been used to prevent a reopening of the case, as I can testify from my own experience'.[13] And thus the scandal was finally put to rest.

Homosexuality was common in Victorian times but 'acts of gross immorality of the Oscar Wilde type' were kept discreetly quiet. At the time that the Bruce scandal was reported in *Truth*, Churchill apparently admitted to Max Aitken, the young Canadian millionaire who was to become Lord Beaverbrook, that he had in fact had a homosexual affair 'to see what it was like'.

William Manchester brushes this confession aside by saying: 'It was an absurd remark by Lord Beaverbrook. Nothing in Churchill's life offers the remotest ground for intimation of homosexuality'.[14]

According to Ted Morgan, Churchill 'seems to have avoided the homosexual attachment that boys at Harrow often formed, and the humiliation and inculcation of servility that derived from fagging, the practice by which younger boys were made to be the servants of older ones'.[15] Other authors of biographies on Winston Churchill are silent on the subject, but later reports of him having been engaged in homosexual activities — notably with the friend of his secretary, the actor and composer Ivor Novello — did appear.

At the time of the Bruce scandal, Jennie also seemed to be concerned about the rumours of her son being homosexual. She perhaps speculated that their family circumstances had been conducive to such an outcome. When she became aware of her husband's illness, she found satisfaction in the arms of other men. Lord Randolph — the always elegantly dressed 'Randy' — on the other hand, was never seen with a woman. He went away for lengthy periods with male friends, and there was gossip of his growing effeminacy. Lord Salisbury, who had succeeded Disraeli as the Tory leader, disliked Randolph. He told a friend that 'Randolph's temperament was essentially feminine', and added that 'he had never been able to get on with women'.[16]

The neglect with which Randolph treated both his sons was harsher than was common in upper-class English homes of the time. Ralph G Martin speculates that the absence of a father-son relationship in Victorian England 'was probably part of the reason that homosexuality and sadism were so rampant in public schools. All older public school boys were catered to by younger "fags", who were often brutalised if they failed to give quick and proper service', he wrote. At St. George's, where young Winston had spent more than two years, fagging and flogging occurred on a daily basis. At Harrow 'most seniors sought his company only when they wanted him to black their boots or make their beds; he had to fag for three years, performing menial tasks until he was nearly seventeen'.[17]

Winston's boundless devotion to his mother, overtly accepting her lovers as if they were members of the family, was a strange phenomenon.

As for his own relationships, Winston had shown an interest in only one girl before he met Pamela Plowden and formed a platonic relationship with her at the end of 1896. This girl was Muriel Wilson, the younger daughter of the wealthy shipping line owner, Arthur Wilson. While he was serving at Aldershot Winston invited her to the Queen's Birthday Parade. Privately he admitted that he was after her money.

When she rejected him — telling him that he had no future — he was relieved and vowed that he would never again think of marrying for money. Marriage was in any case not a subject that he brooded on. During the very month that Muriel turned him down, he joined the Bachelor's Club in London. He told his mother that he had many invitations and could go to a ball every night if he wished, but field days and drills made him 'more eager for bed than anything else'.

When Lord Randolph died, Jennie was devastated. She had looked after her husband with such devotion during the last agonising six months of his life that even *Harper's Weekly* reported on her love and loyalty with admiration. That Jennie was genuinely upset about the inevitable; there can be no doubt.

Her real grief, however, was not centred on losing her husband. She had hoped that Count Kinsky would be waiting for her, but two weeks before she and Randolph returned to England from their world cruise, he had married Countess Elizabeth Wolff-Metternich, a woman 20 years younger than Jennie. Winston, too, was drawn to Count Kinsky. Only two weeks after his father's death he wrote to his brother Jack, asking him to send a picture of Kinsky on Zoedone, the horse on which he won the Grand National — the first foreigner to do so.

Jennie never spoke with anyone about the nature of Randolph's illness, little realising that his condition had long since become an open secret. Only her two sons were spared. After Randolph's death an official from the Treasury called on Jennie, requesting that the robes her late husband had worn as Chancellor of the Exchequer be returned. Jennie would have none of it. 'I am saving them for my son', she replied with such conviction that no doubt was left in the messenger's mind that his visit was abortive.

Winston, too, had no doubt about his future parliamentary career. At the funeral he was overcome with emotions he described in *My Early Life* as dreams that had come to an end. These dreams were 'of comradeship with him, of entering Parliament at his side and in his support'.[18] His task as he saw it was to 'pursue his aims and vindicate his memory', of lifting again 'the flag I found lying on a stricken field'.[19]

Winston was aware of the obstacles that faced him in his ambitious attempt to follow in his father's footsteps. In order to enter politics and achieve his final goal — becoming Prime Minister of Great Britain — a university education was as much a prerequisite as money. He had neither, but he had ambition and had chosen a profession which his father said was 'the finest in the world if you work at it and the worst if you loaf at it'. As a soldier he would not earn enough to keep up the lifestyle expected of an officer, but he could become famous in battle. Money, which was a scarce commodity after Lord Randolph's debts had been settled, he could make by reporting on the wars he helped to fight, and by writing books.

That his young age was also against him did not worry him unduly, and he was anxious to pursue his career in parliament as soon as possible. Meanwhile he would have to obtain the attention of the voters. This, he believed, he could attain by showing extraordinary military heroism.

The 4th Queens Own Hussars anticipated moving to India the following year and would serve there for at least nine years. Winston made up his mind. Nine years in India, he convinced himself, would be an awful waste of his time and he dropped the idea of being a professional soldier. He wanted to see action immediately.

4

Adventures in Cuba

At the end of October 1895 the officers of the 4th Queens Own Hussars were given ten weeks leave prior to moving to India. This long break would provide them with the opportunity to enjoy steeple chasing, racing and riding with the hounds during the day and exploiting the social scene at night. Officers were gentlemen, or so it was held. After all they had been rigidly selected according to their bloodline and public school attended. Traditions were passed on through generations of military leaders jealously guarding their status — like the Duke of Wellington who maintained that officers from a lower social order would cause the Army to deteriorate; or Lord Roberts insisting that the family history of a candidate stood up to scrutiny.

The War Office took it for granted that the patrician families of the officers could support their sons in acceptable style, since their Army pay-packets were woefully inadequate. To go on leave for ten weeks was not a cheap exercise and a few of the Sandhurst men suffered some financial embarrassment. Churchill was one of them. He had spent his money on his two hunters and three polo ponies, and with Jennie being once again short of funds, he had to make a plan.

London's social life bored him to death. Women did not interest him and he had never bothered to learn how to dance. All that was on his mind was action of the military sort. He had simulated action with his toy soldiers for long enough. Now he was ready to experience what real war was about.

During Queen Victoria's reign not a year had passed without a war being fought in one or other part of the Empire. Now the British Empire was temporarily at peace. Only in Cuba was fighting taking place: some 200 000 Spanish troops were trying to quell a rebel insurrection. Here was the opportunity he was looking for. Travelling via New York would give him the excuse to see the place his mother had come from. Then he could make his way to Florida and from there sail on to Cuba.

He lost no time in activating his network of influential contacts in order to get a taste of the serious fighting he had dreamt about for so long. Sir Henry Drummond Wolff was an old friend of Lord Randolph and a great admirer of Jennie. He had suggested starting a politico-social organisation through which Conservatives of all classes could meet. Jennie was part of the original group of 12 who founded the Primrose League, as the highly successful organisation became known. Now Sir Henry was the British Ambassador to Spain. Churchill wrote to him. A favourable reply came by return mail. Her Majesty's Ambassador in Madrid met with the Duke of Tetuan, who was the Spanish Minister for Foreign Affairs. The Duke arranged clearance from the Spanish Minister of War and gave Churchill a letter of introduction to his friend, Marshal Arsernio Martinez de Campos, who had been the Prime Minister and was now Captain-General of the Spanish army.

With the formalities in Spain taken care of, Churchill now had to obtain permission from the military authorities at home. Colonel Brabazon had no hesitation in giving his consent but only the commander-in-chief, Viscount Wolseley, could grant final approval. The Field Marshall was another of Jennie's friends. He told her that it would have been better if Winston had gone without asking, but now, having received an official request, he had to act one way or the other.

Jennie had no difficulty in convincing him that her son's excursion was that of a private individual. Wolseley then instructed General Edward Chapman, the head of Military Intelligence, to supply Churchill with maps, and to request him, quite informally, to gather information and statistics on various matters — in particular, details on the latest bullets.

There were no restrictions on officers writing for the press, and the *Daily Graphic*, which had published his father's letters from South Africa, agreed to do the same with Winston's at five guineas each.

Thus Winston's expedition to Cuba was facilitated by his mother's former lover Colonel Brabazon, arranged by her friend Sir Henry Drummond Wolff and sanctioned by her admirer Lord Wolseley. On 2 November 1895 the 20-year-old subaltern set sail for New York on the Cunard Royal Steamship *Etruria* with his friend and fellow subaltern Reginald Barnes at his side.

In New York Jennie's intimate admirer, Bourke Cockran, met them and invited them to stay for a week in his spacious Fifth Avenue apartment. Winston was impressed with the beautifully furnished rooms and found Cockran to be one of the most charming hosts and interesting men he had met. On their first day, Cockran arranged a dinner at his home for 12 judges, including a Supreme Court justice.

The two young men were also treated to a meal at the Waldorf Hotel, taken around the harbour in a tugboat and toured the ironclad cruiser *New York*. They visited the West Point Military Academy, attended the annual horse show and accompanied the fire commissioner to five fires.

They were invited to the residence of tycoon Cornelius Vanderbilt — whose niece would be the next Duchess of Marlborough in an arrangement that brought her the title and him the money. Cockran introduced Churchill to his lifetime habit of smoking fine Cuban cigars — some fine examples of which are still named after him — during their long discussions held late at night after Barnes had gone to sleep.

On departing, Cockran arranged for Winston and Reginald to travel by rail in a private compartment through Philadelphia, Washington, Savannah, Tampa Bay and

Key West. From there the steamer *Olivette* took them to Cuba where they arrived on 20 November. They booked into the Grand Hotel Inglaterra, paid a visit to Alexander Gollan, the British Consul General, and again enjoyed Cuban cigars. The following morning they proceeded by train to the HQ of Marshal de Campos at Santa Clara.

During his sojourn in Cuba there were a number of occasions when Churchill came under fire. 'The 30th November was my 21st birthday, and on that day for the first time I heard shots fired in anger, and I heard bullets strike flesh or whistle through the air.'[1] He joined General Suarez Valdez's division on a march through the insurgent districts. As the men breakfasted on half a skinny chicken, a bullet passed within a foot of his head and mortally wounded a horse behind him.

The following day, while bathing at a beautiful spot in the warm and clear waters of a river, a volley of bullets whizzed over their heads. The men made their way back to the General's headquarters, to be greeted by rounds falling all over the camp. One of them ripped through the thatch of the hut in which Churchill was taking a siesta in a hammock, and another wounded an orderly close by.

'We knew nothing of the quality either of our friends or foes. We have nothing to do with their quarrels. Except in personal self-defence we can take no part in their combats', Churchill wrote.[2] But he and his friend Barnes were nonetheless awarded the *Rioja Crux* for gallantry during the Battle of La Reforma.

Ted Morgan writes: 'Although gallantry implied active participation in battle, he did not boast about what he had done to win it, for his position was delicate. As a guest of the Spanish Army, he was not supposed to take part in hostilities.'[3] Indeed, there is no evidence that Churchill was anything else but an observer travelling with the Spanish. When he told the American press on his return from Cuba that he had not even fired a revolver, and that the *Rioja Crux* was bestowed on him as a sign of courtesy, he must have spoken the truth.

Churchill's stint in Cuba drew considerable criticism from the press. 'American newspapers sympathetic to the rebel cause said he was a British agent sent to give military advice to the Spaniards',[4] whereas a British newspaper questioned his involvement in a dispute that was absolutely none of his business. 'Mr Churchill was supposed to have gone to the West Indies for a holiday ... spending a holiday fighting other people's battles is rather an extraordinary procedure even for a Churchill',[5] the *Newcastle Leader* complained.

The *Eastern Morning Post* was certain that difficulties would arise, and that Lord Wolseley would most likely order his immediate return and put him on the carpet. But Wolseley, of course, had given his consent, albeit hesitatingly, and Military Intelligence had requested Churchill to gather information on the war. Therefore, as was to be expected, Wolseley and the War Office did not choose to concern themselves further with their subaltern's adventures in Cuba. Churchill had his five *Letters from the Front* published under the head 'The Insurrection of Cuba' in the *Daily Graphic*.

On his return from Cuba, he held his first press conference in New York and his comments on the war made headlines throughout the United States. He denied newspaper reports claiming that he had fought on the side of the Spanish, but he was not shy of voicing his opinion of Marshal de Campos and freely gave his comment on the struggle. He praised de Campos' leadership, his judgement and great humanity and summed him up as one of the most distinguished men that Spain had ever produced. But he held the rebels in contempt. They might carry on with their war for a year or two, he said, but they are not good soldiers, 'but as runners would be hard to beat'.

The press, as a whole, did not take kindly to the observations of the young adventurer whose insight into the conflict was rudimentary. It was a reprise of their treatment of Lord Randolph after his insulting remarks about the Boers in South Africa. But Churchill had succeeded in imitating his father, and this is what mattered most to him.

As far as fighting in a war was concerned, he had, in his youthful mind, imagined it to be 'a thrilling and immense experience to hear the whistle of bullets all around and to play a hazard from moment to moment with death and wounds'.[6] Having chosen the temporary career as a soldier, he believed that it was his professional obligation to be engaged in battle — and be adequately rewarded for his courage with medals. Cuba was a kind of rehearsal for him — 'a secluded trial trip in order to make sure that the ordeal was one not unsuited to my temperament'.[7] There was no doubt that he was courageous, for he had invited death voluntarily 'near the firing line when, as a nonbelligerent, he might honourably have sought safety in the rear'.[8]

5

War clouds in the Transvaal

Early in 1896 the 4th Queens Own Hussars marched to Hounslow and Hampton Court in preparation for their transfer to India later that year. Churchill had passed out of the Royal Military Academy of Sandhurst with honours — 8th out of 150 when his course finished at Christmas in 1895. He was ready for active service, but dreaded the fact that India was waiting for him. There must be a way out, he reckoned.

He had followed the trouble escalating between Britain and the South African Republic. A brief but decisive armed conflict would enable Britain to take control of the country, he thought. In South Africa he could see action and demonstrate his courage when Great Britain annexed the Transvaal. Being part of the struggle of uniting South Africa under the British flag and incorporating the southern African continent as a vital part of the British Empire would greatly enhance his prospects of achieving his goals.

The British had taken possession of the Transvaal before, on 12 April 1877, when their special commissioner, Sir Theophilus Shepstone, rode into Pretoria, the capital of the South African Republic, with 12 mounted policemen to bring to an end 25 years of self-rule in the landlocked quasi-state. The *Vierkleur*, the four-colour flag of the Boers, was lowered and the novelist, Rider Haggard, hoisted the Union Jack next to the thatched *Volksraad*, the House of Assembly on Church Square in the heart of what was then only a dusty hamlet.

In December 1880 some 5 000 burghers headed by Paul Kruger, Piet Joubert and Marthinus Wessel Pretorius declared themselves and their country independent of Britain. Colonel Sir Owen Lanyon, who had taken over as Administrator of the Transvaal from Shepstone, called on Sir George Pomeroy Colley, Governor of Natal for help to fight the rebels. Of the 480 men sent in January 1881 to confront the Boers at Laing's Nek on the Natal border, 150 were killed by Boer sharpshooters.

Less than two weeks later the British lost another 150 men, and this caused panic in Whitehall. It was decided to grant the Boers self-government if they would agree to end hostilities. It fell to General Colley to inform the Boers of the decision. However, he considered the offer tantamount to capitulation and thus insisted that the time they had to react was limited to 24 hours. He knew this was an impossible request for the

Boer leaders who were spread throughout the country. But it allowed him time to scale Mount Majuba, 'the Hill of Doves', with 400 British troops on the night of 26 February. From the flat top, he surmised, his men could command the countryside and shoot the enemy at will.

The following morning, Sunday, the Boers spotted the Redcoats on the plateau. A group of 150 volunteers climbed the steep walls of the hill. Taking extraordinary care not to be spotted by the men above, it took them five hours to creep up the slope. Once they had reached the summit, there was no retreat for the British. The only way they could run was over the cliff. Many threw away their rifles and jumped to their death 50 feet below.

Colley, the last man to stand his ground, was hit by a bullet in the back of his head. Ninety British soldiers lost their lives, 130 were wounded and 57 taken prisoner. The Boers had one man killed and five wounded. It was one of the most humiliating defeats in the history of British arms.

Six months later the Transvaal was declared a self-governing state. Then in 1886 gold was discovered on the Witwatersrand and this brought an influx of foreigners, or *Uitlanders* as they were called in Dutch, to the emerging mining camp that was named Johannesburg. The investment that poured into the Republic was in the hands of a few mining companies whose proprietors were to play an increasing role in the economic and political future of the country.

For the *Uitlanders* to qualify for the vote they had to become burghers of the Republic. President Kruger ruled that they could only obtain citizenship after residence of 14 years. Further, to be allowed to vote for the State President and Commandant-General or actually stand as a candidate, a 'new burgher' had to be at least 40 years of age.

Kruger believed that if he gave the *Uitlanders*, many whom were English, the franchise immediately, he would have to give up his Republic. Most of the *Uitlanders* in any case cared little about the franchise and cared even less whether the *Vierkleur* — with its green vertical stripe nearest the staff and three horizontal stripes of red, white, and blue — or the red, white and blue Union Jack fluttered over Johannesburg.

The language issue was something that bothered the immigrants. The Boers spoke Afrikaans, a Germanic language that had evolved in the Cape mainly from Dutch and *Nederduits*, or lower German over a period of some 250 years. The official language and sole medium of instruction in schools was Dutch.

During his visit to South Africa Lord Randolph had expressed the hope that the *Uitlanders* would increase in such numbers that the Boers would have to yield to their demands. Ten years later there were 85 000 *Uitlanders* and 65 000 Boers living in the Transvaal. The foreigners owned nine-tenths of the assessable property and paid taxes accordingly. Their legitimate grievances had not been addressed, although the Transvaal National Union had been established to help them win their rights.

Dominating commerce and industry in Johannesburg at this time were men such as Julius Wernher and Alfred Beit, the so-called Randlords who owned the most profitable mines, including the enormously rich Crown Mine and Rand Mines. Cecil John Rhodes, the Prime Minister of the Cape Colony, had the controlling interest in the second largest company, Consolidated Gold Fields of South Africa. He had established a white settlement in Mashonaland (now part of Zimbabwe) and then tried, unsuccessfully, to seize the port of Beira in Portuguese East Africa from the Portuguese in an armed raid. 'In 1893 he authorised the illegitimate invasion and conquest of Matabeleland [now also part of Zimbabwe], on the pretext of a fabricated border incident'.[1] Now he was the head of the British South Africa Company, which ruled both the new country of Rhodesia and the De Beers Consolidated Mines at Kimberley.

The Johannesburg Consolidated Investment Company was run by the flamboyant Barney Bernato, the son of a London East End tailor. Most of the taxes came from the gold industry and those people who owned and worked the mines. During the second half of the 1890s the Randlords agreed that something had to be done about the government standing in the way of them making even bigger profits. They established the Witwatersrand Chamber of Mines to protect the industry against abuses by the Government.

Of the 65 000 Boers, only 25 000 were over the age of 16. Sir Henry Loch, the High Commissioner of the Cape, suggested to the Colonial Office that if the *Uitlanders* were supplied with arms, they could easily stage an uprising. Loch hinted to Lionel Phillips, a partner in Wernher, Beit and Company, at the possibility of a revolution. The Randlords began to work out details.

Dr Leander Starr Jameson, the administrator of Rhodesia, was nominated to lead a force of the Chartered Company's police and the Bechuanaland Border Police from Pitsani in Bechuanaland across border into the Transvaal. He would be equipped with extra rifles to help the people of Johannesburg seize the town, then march on to Pretoria to force President Kruger to grant them the vote. Both Colonial Secretary, Joseph Chamberlain, and the High Commissioner, Sir Hercules Robinson, were given inflated numbers of the *Uitlanders* in the Transvaal to emphasise the threat, but officially they were not informed of the conspiracy, nor was the board of the Chartered Company.

Getting rid of Kruger's government would free the Randlords from a corrupt regime that enjoyed a monopoly on the sources of supply. What irked them particularly was the dynamite concession, the control of which had been given to a group of German financiers. Dynamite was one of the most vital needs of the mining industry and the bosses wanted it in their hands.

Rhodes, the 'crude, racist and ruthless imperialist who rode roughshod over the rights of Africans as a political opportunist, callous exploiter and supreme egotist',[2] believed that God's finest product was the Englishman. The African map, from the Cape to Cairo, had to be painted red to accord with the natural order of things. Rhodes himself would be the master of Africa and a one-world government led by Britain would follow. It was his duty, he believed, to conquer the dark continent with its enormous wealth and savage inhabitants. The first step was to form a South African Federation. Only the Transvaal stood in the way of his dream and Dr Jameson would be his tool to fix that little problem.

Kruger's intelligence service was well aware of the planned attack on his beloved republic. It could only be described as a coup d'état. In April, 1895, Major the Honourable Bobby White was sent to the Transvaal to gather intelligence. He was shown around the artillery camp in Pretoria and noted with glee that the arsenal comprised some very old pieces of ordnance, such as a gun dating to the Second French Empire, a Maxim Nordenfeldt and a nine-pound muzzle-loader. What White failed to realise was that the Boers had shown him their artillery museum. The Honourable Major never discovered that the Boers had 12 field pieces, 10 000 rifles, and 12 million rounds of small-arms ammunition stored at Pretoria.

During the last days of December 1895 Jameson marched into the Transvaal with 400 well-armed troopers. He told the men that they were to invade Johannesburg in the name of the Queen. The men had no need to know that Queen Victoria was completely unaware of the raid. In his pocket Jameson carried a letter from the *Uitlander* Reform Committee asking him to come to their rescue.

A trooper cut the telegraph lines south of Mafeking instead of the lines to Pretoria with the result that Rhodes could not contact Jameson. On the other hand, the republican postmasters along the route were able to inform their government of the raiders' progress. At Doornkop near Krugersdorp the Boers surrounded the invading force. Jameson and his men tried to make a stand on Brink's farm. When they realised that there was no way out, they pulled a white apron off an old servant and hoisted it over the outhouse as a token of surrender.

Three weeks after their capture, the raiders led by Jameson were handed over to the British Government by Kruger. They were escorted to England where Jameson and his officers were eventually tried and convicted under the Foreign Enlistment Act. Jameson was sentenced to 15 months imprisonment and his officers to terms of imprisonment ranging from five to ten months imprisonment. They were released after serving shortened terms of imprisonment. The rank and file were discharged by a magistrate.

Sixty-four of the Reform Committee in Johannesburg were also arrested, charged and convicted of high treason before Judge Gregorowski in Pretoria. The leaders, including Cecil John Rhodes' brother Frank, were sentenced to death. These sentences were later commuted to 15 years imprisonment. The remaining reformers were sentenced to two years imprisonment, a fine of £2 000 and banishment from the Transvaal Republic. All those convicted were eventually released after the payment of hefty fines.

Rhodes resigned as Prime Minister of the Cape. The plans for a federation were ruined and relations between Britain and the South African Republic were severely damaged.

The ill-fated Jameson Raid stirred Winston Churchill's imagination. His father had treated everything and anything to do with the Boers with contempt and regarded Kruger's government as the main obstacle to a peaceful solution of the South African problem. Yet he did not condone an armed intervention in the Transvaal. In fact Winston was of the firm belief that if his father had lived he would have actively opposed a war between the two nations. Winston's aunt, Lady Sarah Wilson, was one of the original members of Randolph's syndicate and thus had a financial as well as a personal interest in South Africa. She had been informed of the uncertainties in the Transvaal and with her brother no longer available for help, she felt it necessary to get first-hand information on the situation.

Lady Sarah and her husband Gordon arrived in Durban on the P & O liner *Victoria*, a troopship that was to pick up Dr Jameson and the other raiders in Natal and transport them to England. From Durban the Wilsons made their way to Johannesburg to be entertained at Clewer House, the home of Abe Bailey. The mining magnate was a good friend of the Churchill family.

Unfortunately for the Wilsons, Bailey was a conspirator in the Jameson Raid and was by then incarcerated in the State jail in Pretoria. Sarah and Gordon decided to visit him there. There is no record of their meeting, but Sarah recorded that they took a good look at President Kruger '.. this remarkable personage, stout in figure, with a venerable white beard, in a somewhat worn frock coat and rusty old black silk hat'.[3] They left the *Raadsaal* and flanked by four burghers, climbed into his carriage to be taken home. To complete their visit to the Transvaal, the Wilsons travelled to Brink's farm to view the place where Jameson's mission had come to an ignominious end.

On their return to England, Sarah's comments on the Boers and their country were quite different from those of her late brother. She wrote: 'One could not forget that the Transvaal was their country, ceded to them by the English nation. They left the Cape Colony certain we should never have followed them into the Transvaal but for the sudden discovery of gold; it is equally true they had not the power or wish to develop this for themselves, and yet without it they were a bankrupt nation'.[4]

Churchill did not agree with this view. In a comprehensive memorandum on the problems in the Transvaal, the 22-year-old Winston wrote:

> Imperial aid must redress the wrongs of the Outlanders; Imperial troops must curb the insolence of the Boers. There must be no half measures. The forces employed must be strong enough to bear down all opposition from the Transvaal and the Orange Free State; and at the same time to overawe all sympathisers in the Cape Colony. There will not be wanting those who will call such a policy unscrupulous. If it be unscrupulous for the people of Great Britain to defend their most vital interests, to extend their protection to their fellow countrymen in distress and to maintain the integrity of their empire, 'unscrupulous' is a word we shall have to face.[5]

In conclusion he wrote: 'Sooner or later, in a righteous cause or a picked quarrel, with the approval of Europe, or in the teeth of Germany, for the sake of our Empire, for the sake of our honour, for the sake of the race, we must fight the Boers'.[6]

Unlike his father, Winston approved of an armed conflict in the Transvaal and he had little doubt that the simmering hostility would lead to war. He would have loved to be involved in a scrap with the Boers to avenge the battle of Majuba. This, he thought, would earn him the South African Medal which would possibly launch him to greater heights in politics.

Churchill's frantic attempt to obtain a commission elsewhere led to rumours that he was trying to dodge his regiment and Lord Lansdowne, the Secretary of State for War, warned his mother in a letter. Churchill was not perturbed by the reaction. He pestered his mother to make use of her many contacts to find him a posting where he could gain experience and advancement instead of stultifying in what he termed 'the tedious land of India'. Little did he realise that before the century was out, he was to fight in the Sudan and would sail for South Africa where he would gain the fame that opened the door to Parliament. But India couldn't be avoided.

6

In pursuit of glory

While waiting for his posting to India, Winston stayed with his mother in London. Two or three times a week he travelled by underground to Hounslow Barracks to play polo. 'I now passed a most agreeable six months; in fact they formed almost the only idle spell I ever had'.[1] He had five ponies and being considered promising as a rider, he was ready to take full advantage of what the London season had to offer.

English Society 'still in its old form' called the tune. 'England was governed by a few hundred great families and these', Winston observed, 'were related to an enormous extent by marriage. The leading figures of Society were in many cases the leading statesmen in Parliament, and the leading sportsmen on the Turf'.[2] Winston did not have to be reminded of the fact that the Churchills slotted comfortably into the top echelons of Society.

On 11 September 1896 the 4th Queens Own Hussars sailed from Southampton to Bombay, arriving there on 2 October. As Winston disembarked he put out his hand and, impatient as ever, grasped the iron ring set in the quay side. As he did so, the boat fell away steeply into a trough of the harbour swell. He dislocated his shoulder which resulted in his sporting endeavours being curtailed for the rest of his life. He could no longer play tennis and he was severely restricted while playing polo, swimming or fencing with the sabre.

In Bangalore, where the 4th Hussars were stationed, Winston shared 'a palatial bungalow, all pink and white, with a heavy tiled roof and deep verandahs sustained by white plaster columns, wreathed in purple bougainvillea'.[3] He and his friends Reginald Barnes and Hugo Baring each had a butler who managed the household, served them at table and supervised the stables. They also had a first dressing boy — or valet — who, in turn, had an assistant, and there was a groom for every horse and pony. Two gardeners, four washermen and a watchman completed the complement of retainers.

One of Churchill's spare-time activities — of which he had plenty — was to collect butterflies, which had been a hobby of his since his school days at Harrow. He asked his mother to send him collecting-boxes, setting boards, a net, a 'killing tin' and a box of pins. Before long he had more than 65 beautiful and rare insects stored in a cabinet.

When a hungry rat devoured all the specimens, he diverted his interest from colourful insects to the growing of 250 rose trees.

Playing polo was, in spite of his injury, another passion to which he devoted much of his time. While playing at Secunderabad he met and fell in love with the blonde and beautiful Pamela Plowden.

Life at Bangalore, of course, was not all butterflies and roses. At dawn the officers were woken up 'by a dusky figure with a clammy hand adroit at lifting one's chin and applying a gleaming razor to a lathered and defenceless throat'.[4] An hour and a half's ride and drill followed before they had their morning bath and breakfasted in the mess. Stables and orderly rooms were next on the list, but at 11.00am all activities ceased.

The late morning nap was interrupted by lunch, and then, while the sun was at its fiercest, sleep was resumed until five. This was the hour everyone looked forward to, the hour reserved for polo. Dinner was served at 8:30pm 'to the strains of the regimental band and the clinking of ice in well-filled glasses'.[5] After dinner the officers played games, such as the then popular whist, or simply sat on their verandahs talking and smoking until 10:30pm or 11.00pm when bedtime was signalled.

Winston could not stand being idle. Brooding about his future, he realised that his lack of university education could be a disadvantage in a political career. He thus resolved to exercise his 'empty, hungry mind'[6] by reading works on history, philosophy and economics when his fellow officers rested or played cards.

The 4th Hussars were stationed in India for almost nine years and individual officers remained there for a three-year tours of duty before returning to England. Winston stayed only 19 months and during this time he went to London twice for a few months, the first time after only eight months' service.

On his first voyage back to England he was introduced to Ian Hamilton, a colonel in charge of musketry training in India. Realising that the influential officer — who was 20 years his senior — could be of assistance to him, he befriended him, but his wife Jean did not enjoy Churchill's company. She later confessed that she could not bear him, 'which is rather a pity as Ian thinks such a lot of him and says he is bound to be commander-in-chief or Prime Minister — whichever line he cares to cultivate'.[7]

Winston had hoped that his mother would arrange for him to go to Crete, where the Greeks had revolted against their Turkish rulers. Britain supported the Turks and although he believed it to be 'a wicked thing' that the British were firing on the Cretan insurgents and preventing Greece from succouring them, he was ready to defend the Turkish Empire. When he reached Italy, however, he learnt that the Turks had defeated the Greeks.

He had no choice but to travel on to London where, at the Conservative central office, he asked the Party organisers to arrange some speaking engagements for him. On 26 June 1897 he delivered his first political address to the Primrose League at Claverton Manor, situated in a park near Bath. On the day that Winston delivered his maiden speech, news of a revolt by Pathan tribesmen on India's north-west frontier reached England.

A year earlier Winston had secured a promise from Sir Bindon Blood, whom he had met at Deepdene in Sussex, to include him on his staff whenever the General might take the field again. Winston immediately contacted Blood, who was in command of a field force of three brigades at Malakand, reminding him of the promise and saying he was keener than ever to see action. He took the next train to Brindisi in Italy, and from there returned to India on the *S.S. Rome*. In Bombay a telegram from Blood awaited him: 'Very difficult. No vacancy. Come as correspondent. Will try to fit you in', it read.

Winston proceeded to Bangalore where, with the help of his friend Barnes who had been appointed Regimental Adjutant, he was able to obtain a month's leave. He managed to secure a commission with the *Pioneer Mail*, a newspaper in Allahabad, and with the help of his mother, was also contracted to write 'picturesque forcible letters' for the *Daily Telegraph* in London.

Winston's dream had come true. In February 1897 he was promoted to Brigade Major, and he was now in command of British troops in a real war. 'I have faith in my star', he wrote to his mother, 'that is that I am intended to do something in the world'. Ted Morgan writes: 'This was his first explicit disclosure of a new fantasy that had been grafted on to the childhood vision of an ideal father'.[8]

Morgan believed that Churchill had developed 'an irrational conviction that he was on earth for a special purpose. This was why the hand of providence protected him in battle. Such grandiose thinking seemed like an aspect of infantile omnipotence; the child saw himself as the centre of the universe. But in Winston's case, instead of being an empty dream, the sense of destiny propelled him to act in order to make it valid. It was more than a need to compensate for childhood deprivation by gaining fame. It was a mystical certainty that he was marked for greatness, which nothing in his life thus far warranted it'.[9] Indeed, there are a number of references to Winston implicitly believing that he would do something extraordinary in the world.

Randolph Churchill, in his biography of his father, writes that when Winston first went to India, he met Captain Francis Bingham (later Sir Francis) of the Royal Artillery and Master of the Ootacamund Hounds. They struck up a conversation and Churchill made it clear that he had no intention of serving indefinitely in the army. He was going into Parliament and would eventually be Prime Minister. Bingham's son Humphrey confirmed this prediction.[10]

In 1963 Randolph received a letter from a Mr KM Clegg, whose grandfather, George Clegg, was station master at Estcourt during the South African War. Apparently he was also with Winston on the train ambushed by the Boers. Prior to this famous incident, Winston was allowed to pitch his tent in Clegg senior's back yard. Over drinks in the local bar Winston would tell his audience about his adventures in India and the Sudan. George and his friends would laugh at the tales, believing them to be grossly exaggerated, and accused Winston of trying to impress them with 'tall stories'. But Winston was serious. One day he said solemnly: 'Mark my words, I shall be Prime Minister of Britain before I am finished'.[11]

A third story of Churchill predicting that he would rise to the highest office in England comes from the Unites States. On 7 December 1900, shortly after he had been elected to Parliament, Churchill met his namesake, the American novelist Winston Churchill in Boston. As they were crossing a bridge over the Charles River and stopped in the middle and looked down at the water. The English Churchill asked the writer whether he had any plans of going into politics. He was himself going to be Prime Minister of Britain, he declared, and thought it would be wholly appropriate for his namesake to be President of the United States at the same time.

Randolph Churchill does not say whether the American Winston Churchill had a political career in mind all along or whether he was sent in that direction by his namesake's advice. What is known is that he was twice elected to the New Hampshire legislature, in 1903 and 1905. What a strange twist of fate it would have been if history had favoured him with elevation to the highest office in the land.

'If these records of Churchill expressing this audacious opinion to three people in three years, on three different continents, are correct', Randolph writes, 'it is legitimate to suppose that he must have expressed it to a score of others'.[12]

Churchill undertook the 2 028-mile, five-day train journey to the front in Malakand in the worst of the heat, at his own expense. Most of his fellow officers were anxious to gain battle experience and win medals; but few of them would have gone to the same lengths as Churchill in risking their lives to achieve fame.

For Churchill the Malakand Expedition was a rewarding experience. On 16 September he went reconnoitring with the 35th Sikhs in the villages along the Afghan border. Brigadier Patrick Jeffreys commanded Sir Bindon's 2nd Brigade. Churchill accompanied a troop of Bengal Lancers on their way to Jeffreys' camp. He could not understand their language but the words *maro*, meaning 'kill' and *chalo*, 'get on' — which he complemented with the English word 'Tallyho!' — were, he felt, all that was needed to converse with them.

Throughout the night bullets flew across their camp. Battles with local tribesmen raged until night fell. Out of 1 300 men, the British lost 150 killed and wounded — among them Lieutenant Victor Hughes. Churchill saw him fall. Four of his men picked him up, but when they were attacked by a number of Pathan swordsmen, they left him and fled. Churchill, from a distance of 30 yards, fired at the leader of the group who was slashing his sword at Hughes. The tribesmen ran and Churchill carried the officer back to the lines.

He was disappointed that no-one witnessed his gallantry, but later his mother wrote to him, telling him that he had been mentioned in dispatches by Sir Bindon Blood. 'If he gets a chance he will have the VC or a DSO — and here such chances are sometimes gone begging ..' General Blood wrote to Colonel Brabazon.

Brigadier Jeffreys, too, mentioned Churchill in dispatches, commenting: 'The courage and resolution of Lieutenant WLS Churchill, 4th Hussars, the correspondent of the *Pioneer* newspaper with the force who made himself useful at a critical moment'. Being mentioned in dispatches left him, as he put it in a letter to his mother, 'with feelings of hope and satisfaction'. In another letter to her two weeks later he said:

> To ride the grey pony along the skirmish line is not a common experience. But I had to play for high stakes and have been lucky to win. I did this three times, on the 18th, 23rd and 30th, but no one officially above me noticed it until the third time when poor Jeffrey — a nice man but a bad general — happened to see the white pony. Hence my good fortune. Bullets — to a philosopher my dear Mamma — are not worth considering. Besides I am so conceited I do not believe the gods would create so important a being as myself for so prosaic an ending.[13]

Churchill made no secret that his purpose in joining the Field Force was to exploit the glory earned in the cause of politics. 'I should like to come back and wear my medals at some big dinner or some other function', he said, but 'the awful thought crossed his mind that no medal might be struck for this expedition'.[14] And in the event, he did not get a medal for the bravery he had undoubtedly shown. Instead, his craving for recognition brought about difficulties which were not conducive to his reputation. However, he was not too concerned about generals disapproving of his overzealous behaviour at the front; or brother officers branding him a 'medal hunter', a bumptious 'self-advertiser' and querying him being granted so much leave.

Blood requested that he be made his orderly. The Adjutant-General in Simla refused. When Churchill requested his mother to clear this matter with Lord Roberts, the old friend of the family declined to intervene. The *Daily Telegraph* had appointed him permanent correspondent, but the authorities in Simla questioned the wearing of a uniform while in this position and were loath to allow him on the battlefield.

Churchill was fascinated by the excitement and drama of war and saw each skirmish as an opportunity to attract publicity for himself. The part he had played as a British officer fighting battles in and around the Swat Valley in northern India for the Queen, the Empire and his own glory, together with the 15 dispatches he had written for the *Daily Telegraph* and the telegrams for the *Pioneer*, did not, he felt, do sufficient justice to his own contribution. For his articles in the *Daily Telegraph* he had only been paid £5 a column as against the £15 or £20 he had expected. But worse, the by-line 'From a young officer' did not indicate the name of the author. To his way of thinking, it was an opportunity lost of bringing his name before the electorate and the country.

Jennie did her best to ensure that everyone who mattered was made aware of the fact that the columns were penned by her son, but ambitious Winston could not leave it at that. In far-away Bangalore he decided to expand the dispatches into a book. He knew that Lord Alexander Fincastle, *The Times* correspondent and winner of the VC, had the same idea. Realising that the market was rather small for two books on the same subject, he set out to work five hours a day, becoming one of the pioneers in the pasting up of frontier dispatches.

It took him seven weeks to complete his manuscript and Jennie saw to it that *The Story of the Malakand Field Force* was published by Longmans. Not letting the grass grow under his feet, her son — who had been granted ten days leave over the Christmas period — travelled to headquarters in Calcutta in an attempt to join the Tirah Field Force.

Again his mother was asked to pull her social strings. With the help of the Prince of Wales and Winston's new friend, Ian Hamilton — who suggested that he contact Aylmer Haldane, the influential aide-de-camp to Sir William Lockhart — he was appointed as an extra orderly on the staff of the commander-in-chief.

While Haldane knew of Churchill's reputation for being overbearing and conceited, the latter had his own ideas about this man whose contacts in the army were important to him. He thought the tall Scot arrogant, irritating and indiscreet, but he instinctively knew that he had to cultivate his friendship. As it turned out, Haldane would play a decisive role in his career at a different time and in a different part of the world.

It so happened that an orderly officer was leaving and Haldane, encouraged by Churchill's enthusiasm, went to see the commander-in-chief. It was only minutes before he returned, telling him to take up his duties at once.

'Red tabs sprouted on the lapels of my coat',[15] Churchill wrote in *My Early Life*. The Adjutant-General published his appointment in the *Gazette*. Horses and servants were dispatched by the regiment from far-off Bangalore, and Churchill became the close personal attendant of Captain Haldane. 'For the first fortnight I behaved and was treated as befitted my youth and subordinate station. I sat silent at meals or only rarely asked a tactful question',[16] he wrote with unusual modesty. It was a calculated exercise to gain the trust and confidence of his superiors, and indeed the commander-in-chief seemed pleased with him. But it was too late for his purpose.

The punitive expedition into the Tirah to quell the rising of Afridi and Orzkazai tribes that had upset Sir William was called off. The rebels had changed their minds and with peace having returned, Churchill had no choice but to return to Bangalore. 'Thus the beaver builds his dam, and thus when his fishing is about to begin, comes the flood and sweeps his work and luck and fish away altogether. So he has to begin again',[17] he observed as he contemplated his future.

7

With Kitchener in the Sudan

Churchill did not have to look around for long to find an area of conflict in the vast British Empire that he felt could be advantageous to his career. He had been in Cuba and fought in Asia; now he set his eyes on Africa.

In 1882, Arab tribes under the leadership of the Mahdi, an ascetic Moslem, wanted to separate the Sudan from Egypt and transform the country into an independent state ruled according to Islamic law. Britain sent General Charles Gordon from occupied Egypt down the Nile to conquer the Sudan and to keep the religious reformer at bay. The general had been besieged at Khartoum for ten months when Lord Salisbury's government gave Sir Herbert Kitchener orders to relieve him. But it was too late. Gordon was killed early in 1885, a mere two days before the arrival of the rescue column.

After his victory over the British, the Mahdi built a new capital, Omdurman, across the Nile from ruined Khartoum. Shortly afterwards he died of typhus and was buried in an ornate tomb. His successor, Abdullah Ibn Mohammed al Khalifa set out to continue the work of his predecessor. Before long he called on them to wage *jihad* — a holy war against foreign intervention. The British in Egypt were alarmed and King Leopold's mining syndicates in the Congo expressed concern.

Khalifa's action was seen by Britain as a threat to their expanding economy and therefore a danger to peace. Churchill fully approved of Britain's leaders wanting to push aside the hurdle that stood in their way. It would not only 'settle a long account', but the great waterway would be liberated and the establishment of an 'African India' could become a reality.

The main problem in the Sudan, however, was not Abdullah Ibn Mohammed. The real danger was France. The French had made plans to capture Fashoda on the upper Nile where they intended building a dam to control the flow of the river into Egypt. Whoever controlled the Nile had mastery over Egypt. At the close of the 19th century, Egypt was ruled by Britain and her leaders would not sit idly by while an arm of the Empire withered.

But there was more to British expansionism on the African continent than Egypt and the Nile. Churchill was well aware of this when he wrote of 'the foundation of an

African India'. By the 'settlement of a long account', he referred to General Gordon's defeat and death at the hands of the Mahdi. Revenge had to be exacted.

At the outbreak of the campaign to reconquer the Sudan, Churchill suggested that a statue of General Gordon should be erected on Trafalgar Square with 'the significant, the sinister, yet the somehow satisfactory word "Avenged" chiselled into [the pedestal]'.[1]

Sir Herbert Kitchener, with a British and Egyptian force of 20 000 men, was given orders to proceed to Fashoda (now Kodok) before the French could seize the town. The fact that Omdurman and the Khalifa's 60 000 Dervishes were in his way was merely a nuisance to Kitchener. To Churchill the inevitable battles were an opportunity to display his courage in order to win medals and gain fame. Unfortunately for him, the opposition had grown considerably.

'When I had first gone into the Army', he observes in *My Early Life*, 'and wanted to go on active service, nearly everyone had been friendly and encouraging'. As if genuinely surprised, he noted that as time passed, the people who had shown him their goodwill 'began to develop an adverse and even hostile attitude'.[2]

Churchill may have detected a measure of jealousy among fellow officers who questioned him being posted to campaigns of his choice, and writing for newspapers while simultaneously serving as a uniformed officer. They resented him for getting extra leave, and for his gall in openly criticising his superiors. He was conscious of the fact that officers of all ranks considered his quest for decorations and fame deplorable, but could not understand why.

'It is melancholy to be forced to record these less amiable aspects of human nature, which by a most curious and indeed unaccountable coincidence have always seemed to present themselves in the wake of my innocent footsteps, and even sometimes across the path on which I wish to proceed',[3] he recorded.

Criticism by his fellow officers in India was one thing, but being detested by Kitchener, the Sirdar or commander-in-chief of the army in Egypt — and now on his way to victory in Khartoum — was another. Churchill was entitled to three months' leave for having served in the Malakand campaign, and this he intended to spend between June and September in Kitchener's army. But the Sirdar — who had happily accepted Lord Fincastle, Churchill's rival officer-correspondent — refused to consider having Churchill in his army. Without Kitchener's approval he could forget about the Sudan.

Churchill's solution was to travel to London where he drummed up his mighty and influential contacts ranging from the Prime Minister and Lord Crome, the British agent in Egypt, to Sir Evelyn Wood, the Adjutant-General, and the less obvious Lady Jeune, wife of the President of the Probate and a friend of Jennie.

Kitchener knew all about Churchill. He disliked the 23-year-old lieutenant intensely for having dared to criticise his superiors in *The Story of the Malakand Field Force*. The Sirdar had approached his own career prospects with a similar attitude, but the way he had played off the Foreign Office against the War Office was not something he cared to remember. He had used official reports to advertise his own views and had employed every scheme imaginable, including forming a strong friendship with Lord Salisbury to get himself out of Cyprus and into the Egyptian Army.

'Churchill's career looked like being remarkably similar to Kitchener's own, with the possible difference that Churchill had begun from a much more favourable position, worked less strenuously, and was even less scrupulous'.[4]

Churchill had given his mother instructions to leave 'no wire un-pulled, no stone unturned, no cutlet uncooked'.[5] It must have been a busy time for Jennie for 'many were the pleasant luncheons and dinners attended by the powers-that-be of those days which occupied the two months of strenuous negotiations',[6] Churchill recalled in *My Early Life*. But success was not forthcoming. The indignant Jennie embarked for Egypt. There she would sort out what she thought was a misunderstanding. From the Continental Hotel in Cairo, where she took up a suite with her latest lover, Major Caryl John Ramsden, she wrote to the Sirdar. The reply was short: 'I have noted your son's name and I hope I may be able to employ him later in the Sudan'.

Jennie had met Kitchener before, but there is no evidence that she had offered her charms to him. Yet, not being used to having her wishes rejected by men she was acquainted with, she was infuriated. And more humiliation was on the way.

She had gone on a brief excursion to Port Said. On her return she found Ramsden in bed with Lady Robert Maxwell, the wife of another army officer. To rub salt into her wounds, the Prince of Wales sent her a note advising her: 'You had better have stuck to your old friends than gone on your Expedition to the Nile! Old Friends are the best!'[7]

For Churchill time was short. Then when all hope seemed to have run out, his lucky star appeared overhead. Unlike Kitchener, Lord Salisbury liked *The Story of the Malakand Field Force* and invited the author to discuss the book with him. The appointment was set for 12 July. 'The Great Man, Master of the British World, the unchallenged leader of the Conservative Party, a third time Prime Minister and Foreign Secretary at the height of his long career, received me at the appointed hour, and I entered for the first time that spacious room overlooking the Horse Guards Parade in which I was afterwards for many years from time to time see much grave business done in peace and war'.[8]

The Prime Minister praised the book. Churchill was told how much he reminded Lord Salisbury of his father, and on leaving was advised: 'If there is anything at any time that I can do which would be of assistance to you, pray do not fail to let me know'.[9]

There was of course something the Prime Minister could do for Churchill. On the strength of Lord Salisbury's backing, Churchill persuaded Sir Evelyn Wood, the Adjutant-General, to telegraph Kitchener. It so happened that a young officer in the 21st Lancers died in Cairo that day. It was left to Lord Cromer, the British Consul-General in Cairo, to suggest Churchill as a replacement. The next day the War Office informed Churchill that he had been attached as a supernumerary lieutenant to the 21st

Lancers for the Sudan Campaign. He was to leave for Egypt at once — at his own expense — and report to the regimental headquarters in Cairo.

Churchill borrowed £3 500. He also arranged with Oliver Borthwick — 'the son of the proprietor of the *Morning Post* and most influential in the conduct of the paper'[10] — whom he had befriended, to write a series of letters at £15 a column. The following day he travelled by train to Marseille and from there by boat to Egypt.

When Churchill reported at the Abbaiyeh Barracks in Cairo on 2 August 1898, he learnt that the 21st Lancers had already started up the Nile. He was informed that the troop in one of the leading squadrons reserved for his command had, due to the uncertainty of his arrival, been given to 2nd Lieutenant Robert Grenfell. The young officer had taken off in excitement and fear of being too late for the battle. He wrote to his family: 'Fancy how lucky I am. Here I have got the troop that would have been Winston's, and we are to be the first to start'.[11]

Fate, however, took a cruel twist. In the battle of 2 September Grenfell's troop was wiped out in the charge and the young officer who had praised his luck was killed.

Churchill set off in a paddle steamer, travelling for a fortnight on the Nile to Wadi Halfa. From there a military railroad took him to Atbara where he joined the 21st Lancers about 200 miles north of Khartoum. Duties on the east bank of the river kept him busy on the day that the Lancers marched on to Shabluka overlooking Omdurman.

He arrested a man who he thought was an Arab, but in fact was a British intelligence officer. The Reuter's correspondent wanted to do a story on the incident, but Churchill would have none of it. Evidence of his having made a mistake, no matter how insignificant, was not something he wanted to see in print. He persuaded the reporter not to write about it, saying that he detested publicity.

During the late afternoon he was ordered to ferry over the river and make for the Lancers' camp fires some 15 miles to the south. When darkness fell he realised that he was lost. He rode on trying to find his way by keeping the North Star at his back. When he stopped after riding in almost total darkness for an hour, clouds obscured his celestial guide.

He had no choice but to wait for the sky to clear. He settled down at a rocky place, but sleep he could not for 'a hot, restless, searing wind blew continuously with a mournful sound'. It was not until half-past three the following morning that the sky cleared and 'the glorious constellation of Orion came into view. Never did the giant look more splendid'. Riding towards his guiding star, he reached the Nile two hours later.

When he finally found the camp, the regiment had already left. He rode on until he came to a village. He was hungry. A crowd had gathered to stare at him. He addressed them in English, but there was no reaction. He pointed to his mouth and stomach, remembered the word *baksheesh*, and all obstacles faded away instantly. Three women brought him dates and milk and fed his pony with doura. A man tried to tell him that the troopers had moved on southwards. Omdurman was the word Churchill understood, and in the direction of Omdurman he rode until he caught up with the lancers that evening.

When Kitchener's men finally sighted the Dervish army on 1 September, it fell to Churchill to report this to the commander. 'It was the first time I had ever looked at that remarkable countenance, already well known, afterwards, and probably for generations to be familiar to the whole world', he wrote in *My Early Life*.

'He turned his grave face upon me. The heavy moustache, the queer rolling look of the eyes, the sunburnt and almost purple cheeks and jowl made a vivid manifestation upon the senses'.[1][2] "Sir", I said, "I have come from the 21st Lancers with a report."

Kitchener listened in absolute silence as the lieutenant explained that the Dervish army was advancing.

'How long do you think I have got?' asked the Sirdar.

'You have got at least an hour — probably an hour and a half, sir.'

'He tossed his head in a way that left me in doubt whether he accepted or rejected this estimate, and then with a slight bow signified that my mission was discharged'.[13]

Kitchener was clearly the master of the situation and it was clear that he did not rely solely on Churchill's report, he was far too experienced to acknowledge that.

Since Churchill did not mention his name when coming face-to-face with Kitchener, one wonders whether the commander recognised the messenger. He had feared that Kitchener would send him back before the battle began. Frank Rhodes, *The Times* correspondent, told Churchill that the Sirdar knew he had no intention of making the army his career. The sunburnt Sirdar with his purple cheeks knew, of course, that Churchill had joined his force, and if he did recognise the 'scheming upstart, who was also a detested journalist' who had brought the vital news 'at the most critical moment of the campaign, this must have been enough to turn anyone purple'.[15]

As it turned out, the battle commenced only the following morning, 2 September 1898, as the sun rose in the desert. It was a fierce scrap, with 60 000 foes cheering for their holy Khalifa as they stampeded towards the British line. Kitchener's 20 000 troops were ready to receive the massed charge. The big guns of the Anglo-Egyptian force killed 7 000 Dervishes at their first charge, and 20 000 at their second. The cavalry was sent in to clear the enemy from the ground to prevent them from regrouping in Omdurman.

The 21st Lancers were ordered to mount a frontal attack on a group of what appeared to be 150 or so Dervishes. As they came nearer, the force suddenly swelled to about 3 000 men bearing spears and rifles. The Dervishes had arisen from their concealment in the natural trench of a dry watercourse. They formed an enormous wave on the crest of which a multitude of gleaming swords reflected the rising sun like lightning. For seconds a deadly silence fell over the troops. Then, to the sound of a battle cry, all hell broke loose.

Churchill was almost instantly cut off from his troops. Aware that the shoulder he had injured in Bombay would not allow him to wield his sword effectively, he resolved to use his Mauser automatic pistol — the most advanced handgun then available — which he had purchased in London before coming to Egypt. He drew it from its wooden holster.

The whole plain of Omdurman with the vast mud city lay before Kitchener's men. The silhouette of minarets and domes formed the backdrop to the militant blue-black horde as the British cavalry wheeled into line and charged.

Churchill rode his Arab polo pony between two of the enemy who were perhaps a couple of yards apart. They both fired. A trooper immediately behind Churchill was killed instantly. Scattered Dervishes ran to and fro. One drew his curved sword back for a hamstringing cut. Churchill turned his pony out of the man's reach and fired two shots into him at about three yards. As he straightened himself in the saddle, another figure with uplifted sword was in front of him.

'So close were we', Churchill wrote 'that [my Mauser] itself actually struck him'.

Then an Arab horseman in a bright coloured tunic and steel helmet with chain mail hangings came at him. Churchill fired and pulled away. He slowed to a walk and looked around, noticing two or three riflemen crouching as they aimed their weapons.

It was then that the adrenaline that had pushed him deep into the midst of the enemy drained out of him. He told his mother in a letter that he never felt the slightest nervousness, but in *My Early Life* he confessed that, for the first time that morning, he felt a sudden sensation of fear. He was alone. His fate was in the balance and all he could think of was to clear out before he was hit and butchered to pieces. But a smiling providence again looked after him, for no bullet was marked with his name. He rejoined his men who were forming up a few hundred yards away, ready to return to camp.

Suddenly a prancing Dervish was among them, dancing and thrusting at the troopers with his spear. He was soon staggering from several lance wounds. Churchill ended his misery with a single shot fired at point-blank range. His magazine was empty. The battle was over.

'But now from the direction of the enemy there came a succession of grisly apparitions; horses spouting blood, struggling on three legs, men staggering on foot, men bleeding from terrible wounds, fish-hook spears stuck right through them, arms and faces cut to pieces, bowels protruding, men gasping, crying, collapsing, expiring'.[16] Churchill was luckier. He had killed 'several — three for certain — two doubtful', but he came through the fight 'without a hair of my horse or a stitch of my clothing being touched'.

The Dervishes fled, taking as many of their wounded with them as they could carry. The battle, from the time of formation to the retreat of the enemy had taken some 20 minutes. The actual fight — the last classic cavalry charge in the history of British warfare — took perhaps two or three minutes. Of the 310 men who faced the enemy, five officers and 65 men were killed or wounded during those chaotic moments.

Unfortunately for Churchill, no-one had witnessed him in close combat with the Dervishes, and even if someone had testified to his bravery, it would have made no difference. Three Victoria Crosses were awarded within the regiments but no medals for heroic deeds were won by the 21st Lancers.

Immediately after the battle, three Dervishe leaders knelt before Kitchener and presented the keys to the city and Omdurman was occupied that same afternoon.

Churchill scoured the battlefield for trophies among the thousands of fly-infested corpses swelling in the hot sun. Kitchener, too, was looking for a trophy. But his was of a different kind. He ordered the Mahdi's tomb to be destroyed and the corpse ripped from its shroud. The head was severed from the body and the bones thrown into the Nile.

Stories of the Sirdar using the Mahdi's skull as a drinking cup with which he toasted his victory could not be taken seriously. Nor could Churchill's suspicion that he had turned it into an inkwell. He later recorded: 'Being now free from military discipline, I was able to write what I thought about Lord Kitchener without fear, favour or affection and I certainly did so. I had been scandalised by his desecration of the Mahdi's tomb and the barbarous manner in which he had carried off the head in a kerosene can as a trophy.'[17] It was this report that led to gossip that Kitchener had the skull preserved in a kerosene can for submission to the Royal College of Surgeons in London where it would make an interesting exhibit next to the intestines of Napoleon.

There were people who gave credence to such stories, for Kitchener's reputation for brutality had become legendary. Queen Victoria was one of them. When she read about his exploits, she instructed her Prime Minister to inform Lord Cromer that the skull had to be retrieved and buried in a Moslem cemetery.

Whether her instructions were carried out has never been ascertained. Philip Warner has it that the skull was passed on as a personal trophy to Sir Reginald Wingate. 'He was said to have drunk champagne out of it for the rest of his life on each anniversary of the battle of Omdurman.'[18]

Using the skull of a defeated adversary as a drinking vessel harks back to the dark ages. If this ritual was still practised during Queen Victoria's reign, it was certainly not a national trait.

Whatever may have happened to the skull, Kitchener, the hero of the Sudan, certainly didn't care. The British victory had been absolute. Only the Lancers had failed him. He had lost fewer than 3% of his troops in the Omdurman campaign, but the casualties suffered by the 21st Lancers amounted to 22%. This was unacceptable to the commander.

Consequently, he barely mentioned them in his dispatches and, perhaps to remove the stink from under his nose, he sent them packing. Churchill had to stay behind for a week. The Sirdar placed him in charge of sick camels that he was supposed to take back to Cairo, but being merely attached to the 21st Lancers, the lieutenant tore up the order. He returned on the next steamer to Cairo without the camels. From there he made his way to England to join the Lancers parading triumphantly through London.

Churchill was horrified at Kitchener's distasteful behaviour and appalled by his sadistic streak. He wrote to his mother that the triumph had been disgraced by battle atrocities he blamed on the commander. More than 100 Dervishes had thrown down their arms during battle and pleaded for mercy. Mostly Egyptian and Sudanese soldiers fighting on the side of the British had butchered them out of hand. But Englishmen had also participated in the barbaric acts.

When Churchill arrived at the barracks in Cairo, he was told that the 21st Lancers had never seen action, and other regiments joked that its motto was 'Thou shalt not kill'. It took courage for him to acknowledge the brutality and war crimes he had witnessed, for such heinous deeds would become public knowledge and might rub off on him to his detriment.

There were many who had read *The Story of the Malakand Field Force* and they may have wondered whether Churchill didn't himself have an unhappy appetite for blood. His great admiration for war is evident in his description of gory battles and bloody scenes that feature throughout many of the 65 books he wrote during his long life — almost all of which dealt with war.

As far as the English were concerned, he considered them to be essentially a warlike people, though not necessarily a militaristic one — meaning that although they were always ready to fight, they were not always prepared to do so. That he himself was ready to fight he had already demonstrated; and that he had an abiding desire to conquer the enemy at all costs, he was not shy to hide.

Churchill's dispatches from the Sudan appeared in the *Morning Post*. Critics were at his heels. Even the Prince of Wales was upset. He did not approve of an officer writing for a newspaper, and said that he now realised why Kitchener was set against him joining his force.

Another person who was concerned about Winston's reputation was Pamela Plowden. She wrote to him from India, saying that he made unnecessary enemies. There was no doubt that Pamela cared deeply for Winston and would have married him if he had asked her. But he had other things on his mind. In his reply to her letter he quoted from General Gordon's journal: 'We may be quite certain that Jones cares more for where he is going to dine, or what he has got for dinner, than he does for what Smith has done, so we need not fret ourselves for what the world says'.[19]

The bad publicity that Kitchener received and the adverse comments levelled at Churchill were not detrimental to the future careers of either. Kitchener was a national hero. He won a peerage, the thanks of both houses of Parliament, and a grant of £30,000.

As for Churchill, he decided to quit the army and seek a career in politics. He toyed with the idea of studying at Oxford or Cambridge as this would pave his way into Parliament. However, when he learnt that he had to pass examinations in Latin and Greek before being admitted to university, he decided to follow another route to reach his goal. He remained in England for another two months, working tirelessly on his next book, *The River War*.

During this time he finished his first and only novel, *Savrola*, and addressed three Conservative meetings. Leading Tories encouraged his ambition to seek a seat in Parliament, but this was only attainable with a considerable amount of money. Churchill did not have money. He had earned 'about five times as much as the Queen had paid me for three years of assiduous and sometimes dangerous work'[20] from his newspaper articles and his book, but much more was needed to ensure him a political career. Another matter he had to deal with — one that for him was more pressing — was to take part in a polo match against the 2nd Dragoons in Meerut in India the following February.

He left England on 2 December for Bangalore, and from there the team, with its 30 ponies, went to Jodhpur to practise. The night before they were to leave for Meerut, Winston — their number one player — slipped down some stairs in Sir Bindon Blood's residence and sprained both his ankles and again dislocated his shoulder.

It was decided not to replace him with the substitute they had brought along, but to bind his elbow to his side and hope for the best. It proved to be a good decision for the 4th Queens Own Hussars, for Churchill hit the crucial goal that made the team victorious. It was the first time they had won the cup and this, Churchill wrote to his mother, was because he had hit three out of four goals in the winning match. He pointed out that his journey to India had therefore not been futile as far as the regiment was concerned.

In *My Early Life* Churchill gives a rather detailed account of the Inter-Regimental Tournament, but as with the number of Dervishes he claimed to have personally shot at the battle of Omdurman, there is some confusion about how many of the winning quartet of goals were his. Randolph Churchill, in his biography of his father, quotes the *Pioneer Mail's* account of the final match played on 24 February.

According to this report, the team's captain, Reginald Hoare who played number three, is credited with one goal, the team's number two, Albert Savory, with two goals, and Churchill with the fourth and final goal. Randolph believed it likely that the correspondent of the *Pioneer Mail* 'mistook the identity of the actual scorer of the Hussar's second and third goals than that Churchill should so soon after the match have assumed the role of hero when he could easily have been exposed as a braggart'.[21] Winston's detailed description of the game in *My Early Life* notwithstanding, eminent biographers such as Ted Morgan in *Churchill — The Rise to Failure 1874-1915* and William Manchester in *The Last Lion* do not credit the hero of the last Inter-Regimental Tournament of the 19th century with more than the fourth and final goal.

After the victorious tournament Churchill travelled to Calcutta to stay for a week with the newly installed Viceroy of India, Lord Curzon. He then returned to Bangalore to say farewell to the army. He sailed for Egypt from Bombay on 20 March. In Cairo, he spent ten days working on his book *The River War*. Kitchener had given instructions to Major James Watson, his aide-de-camp in the Sudan, not to hand over any documents to Churchill. But this proved no problem for the writer. He simply interviewed the major personally. Lord Cromer was of immense help and with the book nearing its completion, Winston returned to England to enter politics.

8

Defeat at Oldham

When Winston was still a boy and playing with his toy soldiers, he said that he would become a soldier first and go into Parliament later. In the early summer of 1899 he was given the opportunity to partner Robert Ascroft, a senior Conservative member for Oldham — a two-member working-class constituency in Lancashire — at the next election. The other Unionist member, James F Oswald, withdrew from the campaign due to ill-health and Churchill was accepted as a suitable substitute. He duly consulted a well-known palmist by the name of Mrs Robinson, who read a favourable outcome to his political endeavours in his hand. Whether this success as a Tory candidate would be immediate, he did not ask. He felt he was ready for politics. Pre-ordained destiny, however, had it that politics were not ready for him.

Ascroft, his sponsor, suddenly died and Oswald, Oldham's other MP, resigned his seat. This called for a double by-election. Churchill was advised to wait for the general election, but decided to go ahead with his campaign. The London papers had predicted his defeat, and indeed, the Tories were doomed from the start. On some days Churchill made as many as eight speeches, and due to his speech impediment and the stress he endured on the platform, he was in great discomfort. At times his words were almost unintelligible and at the end of a day's campaign he would be completely exhausted. His confidence grew as the campaign progressed, but still, there were moments when his diction was so hampered that members of the audience suspected that he had a cleft palate.

A few years later, when he had been elected to Parliament, he continued to battle with his tongue refusing 'to give the standard of eloquence he desired to the torrent of thoughts flooding from his brilliant mind'.[1] After he was married, his wife Clementine, ever ready to help him rehearse his speeches, realised that his difficulties were largely confined to the opening sentences. 'The painful effort of mastering his utterances would make his normally pale cheeks flush angrily. Directly he had managed to establish sympathy with his audience his speech became clear and the fiery patches in his cheeks disappeared'.[2]

During his first election campaign there was, of course, no Clementine to comfort him when he returned home. Pamela, though, was in London proof-reading his manuscript on the Sudan campaign. He asked her to come and campaign with him, but being actively engaged in politics was not something she wanted to do. Winston accepted her decision, telling her that it would be a mistake to have her involved, but that he was nonetheless sorry that she was not at his side.

Jennie, too, was not available. She was busy launching her own publication, the *Anglo-Saxon Review*. The fact that Winston had found difficulty in expressing the thoughts that had formed so clearly in his head and transferred to paper depressed him. But even if Pamela, his mother or Clementine had been at his side to guide him in the task of improving his then elementary oratory skills, his election campaign would still have been a failure. It was not how Churchill spoke that ensured the Liberals victory, but what he omitted to say and what he actually said.

His opening speech was on the issue of high church versus low. He started expressing his opinion with a diatribe on the 'lawlessness and disorder in the Church of England' caused by the introduction of 'ritualistic practice'. He was sure, he told his listeners, that this subject was uppermost in their minds.

He also fought on the well-known Tory platforms concerning 'unity of the Empire', the 'benefits of the existing system of society' and the 'virtues of Conservative rule'. As the election progressed, the Tithes Bill — which had been introduced to help the Church of England's poor clergy — was passed through the House of Commons. This Bill caused upset among a great many of the voters in Lancashire, and three days before the election, Churchill — knowing that many of his supporters rejected the Bill — promised not to vote for it if he was elected.

This daring statement caused uproar in the House of Commons. The Liberals jeered at the embarrassed Tories, and Churchill was beaten at the poll.

He was not unduly concerned when the votes had been counted, ascribing his downfall to a lack of experience. In *My Early Life* he noted sadly that no one came to see him when he returned to his mother's house in London 'with those feelings of deflation which a bottle of champagne or even soda water represents when it has been half emptied and left uncorked for a night'.[3]

Churchill apologised for his defeat in a letter to Arthur Balfour, Leader of the House under the Premier, Lord Salisbury. He was quick to point out, however, that the fault for losing the election did not lie with him. The registration and organisation he found wanting and the size of the constituency was too large for him to cover adequately.

Balfour was not disturbed. He replied in his own handwriting, assuring Churchill that the setback was only temporary. In the House he said that he thought Churchill was a young man of promise, but now, he told the members, it appears he is a man of promises. What neither of them foresaw was that before another year had passed, the younger man would become world famous for his heroism and adventures in South Africa, and that it would be his pen rather than his sword or his battlefield medals that would enable him to enter Parliament as the junior member for Oldham.

9

Problems with the Boers

At the close of the 19th century the British Empire was the most powerful the world had ever seen. But the rising industrial challenge of Germany and the United States posed serious threats to its hegemony. Yet notwithstanding its might, the gold reserves in the vaults of the Bank of England dwindled faster than its custodians liked to admit. Something had to be done to restore the situation.

Geologists had already established that the largest deposits of the precious mineral anywhere on earth were to be found below the windswept ridges that the Boers of South Africa called the Witwatersrand — the ridge of white waters. There were, however, a number of problems that stood in the way of the men in Whitehall in claiming the unheard of wealth for themselves and their mighty empire.

The small *Zuid Afrikaansche Republiek* (ZAR), otherwise known as the Transvaal, was founded towards the middle of the 19th century by a group of farmers — or Boers as they called themselves in Dutch — who had left the Cape Colony in rebellion against British rule in the 1820s and 1830s. The discovery of gold had brought undreamt of prosperity to their government. The British ambition was to form a federation of the ZAR and its sister republic, the Orange Free State, with the two British colonies, the Cape and Natal — all, of course, under the rule of the British Crown.

There was, however, an obstacle .. in the form of the Republic's President, Stephanus Johannes Paulus Kruger. The Transvaalers loved *Oom* Paul, as he was affectionately known, although he was seen by many as partisan and corrupt because he handed out concessions and monopolies at will.

However, the Jameson Raid had strengthened his position to such an extent that he was returned with a large majority to head his inefficient government for the fourth time in February 1898.

It was certain that Kruger would not agree to a federation of the Boer republics with the British colonies in South Africa. It was more likely that the rich South African Republic would unite with the Orange Free State with which it was already closely tied by treaties. The next step would be that the large population of Afrikaners, nominally British subjects living in the Cape and Natal, would insist on a confederation under the *vierkleur* flag of the ZAR. A united South Africa under the *vierkleur* would be a serious threat to Britain's naval base at Simon's Town. Control of the port was as important to Britain as controlling the gold mines in the Transvaal, for rival nations such as the USA, Germany and France were increasingly asserting themselves militarily and economically beyond their traditional spheres of influence.

A meeting between Sir Alfred Milner, the High Commissioner and Governor of the Cape Colony, and President Kruger was held in Bloemfontein at the end of May 1899. Milner had informed the Colonial Secretary, Joseph Chamberlain, that he would turn the *Uitlander* grievances into such an issue that Kruger would be compelled to end the proceedings on the basis that this was hardly a good enough reason for going to war. Predictably, the conference was unsuccessful. As far as Kruger was concerned, the *Uitlanders* would have to defend their rights on their own, rather than through British Government intervention. In frustration, Milner asked his government to assert British supremacy in a practical and visible fashion.

The British government arranged for another conference between Kruger and Milner, instructing the latter to advise the Boer president that he had to issue a formal statement of the precise reforms he proposed to implement with regard to the *Uitlander* franchise and other social and economic issues. If the declaration did not meet with the approval of the British government, Britain would have no choice but to make its own demands for a settlement of the *Uitlander* question. It would also dictate the nature of future relations between the two states.

The practical proclamation of British supremacy was the dispatching of 10 000 troops from India and the Mediterranean to South Africa. The first units from India reached Durban on 3 October 1899. An ultimatum had been drafted by Kruger's government a fortnight before, demanding that all British forces on Transvaal's borders be withdrawn; that all troops who had arrived in South Africa since 1 June be sent out of the country; and that reinforcements then on the high seas not be allowed to land at any South African port. At 5.00pm on 9 October 1899, the Boer ultimatum was handed to the British Agent in Pretoria, Sir Conyngham Greene. Britain chose to ignore the demands and after the expiry of 48 hours on 11 October, martial law was proclaimed in the Transvaal and by its alliance partner, the Orange Free State.

In his biography, *My Early Life,* Churchill wrote that he embarked on the RMS. *Dunnotar Castle* in Southampton, bound for Cape Town on 11 October. This was the day the Boer ultimatum expired, but records of the shipping company and dates on letters he wrote during the voyage, show that he was mistaken. In fact, the date that the 24-year-old war correspondent strode up the gangplank of the Castle liner was 14 October, two days after hostilities began at Kraaipan on the western border of the Transvaal.

There was a wildly cheering crowd at the English dockside singing 'For he's a jolly good fellow' and shouting: 'Bring back a piece of Kruger's whiskers.' The war in South Africa had stirred up the people, but the well wishers had not come to see the then largely unknown son of Lord Randolph Churchill. The excitement was reserved for 59-year-old General Sir Redvers Buller, a veteran of the Ashanti and the Zulu wars where he had won the Victoria Cross. The new commander-in-chief would, many of them believed, bring back the soldiers before Christmas. Standing on the bridge, the tall, imposing hero of the British people waved as the foghorn sounded. Lady Buller led the singing of 'God save the Queen'. As the ship steamed away from the wharf, the stirring notes of 'Rule Britannia' drifted over the water.

Churchill had no doubt that one day he would be the object of the same sort of pomp and ceremony. With his background, intelligence and determination, coupled with connections in the right places, it was only a matter of time. So far he had, 'with his prodigious appetite for "fixing things" and an extensive range of well-placed friends of the family to help him, albeit reluctantly at times, set out about the task of earning both his keep and, if possible, a reputation as well, with immense energy'.[1]

'I thought it very sporting of the Boers to take on the whole British Empire ..', Churchill wrote 30 years on. 'Let us learn our lesson. .. always remember, however sure you are that you can easily win, that there would not be a war if the other man did not think he also had a chance.'[2]

Two months before he left for South Africa, Alfred Harmsworth of the *Daily Mail* had contacted Churchill with a view to engaging him as a war correspondent for his newly established paper. Churchill, however, declined the offer because he had obligations to his friend Oliver Borthwick of London's *Morning Post*. Borthwick had published his *River War* dispatches and Churchill knew that he could strike a good deal with him. Being in a position to dictate terms, he demanded an initial payment of £250 per month for a period of four months plus the copyright on his articles. If the contract was extended after four months, he would require an additional £200 per month for his services. Further, all expenses incurred were to be borne by the paper. The terms, Winston noted, were 'higher, I think, than any previously paid to a British war correspondent, and certainly attractive to a young man of 24 with no responsibilities but to earn his own living'.[3]

He did not believe that war should be a needless hardship — at least not for himself — and to travel as comfortably as he possibly could, he brought with him an Indian soldier-valet, one Thomas Walden. Walden had already gained experience of conditions in southern Africa when he travelled with Winston's father to Mashonaland eight years earlier. Now one of his many tasks was to look after the liquor Winston had ordered from Randolph Payne and Sons of 61 St James St, SW, a distinguished firm of London wine merchants, a week before the *Dunnotar Castle* was to sail. His order comprised:

		Per dozen	£	s	d
6	x 1889 Vin d'Ay sec	110/-	2	15	0
8	x St. Emilion	24/-	1	16	0
6	x light Port	42/-	1	10	0
6	x French Vermouth	36/-		18	0

18 x Scotch Whisky (10 year old)	48/-	3	12	0
6 x Very old Eau de Vie landed 1866	160/-	4	0	0
6 x 1 dozen cases for sample, packing, marking etc			10	0

It was shipped to South Africa aboard the *R.M.S. Dunnotar Castle* [11]

Churchill carried a letter of introduction that the Lord Chamberlain had written to Sir Alfred Milner, recommending him as 'a very clever young fellow with many of his father's qualifications. He has the reputation of being bumptious, but I have not myself found him so .. and time will no doubt get rid of the effect if he had it. .. He is a good writer and full of energy. He hopes to be in Parliament but want of means stands in his way..'

Winston had always been a poor sailor, but during the first part of the voyage between Southampton and Madeira, exceptionally rough weather made life almost unbearable for him. The uncertainty of not knowing how the war was proceeding in South Africa was amplified by the frustration of being cut off from all the news concerning the armed conflict.

There was also his disappointment at not being present for the publication of his new book, *The River War,* during the first week of November and gauging its reception by the public. It was quite a feat to have turned six weeks of service in the Sudan campaign into a two-volume 1 000-page opus — although its author was severely criticised in the *Saturday Review* of 18 November as 'only this astonishing young man could have written these two ponderous and pretentious volumes ... the airs of infallibility he assumes are irritating ... he is perpetually finding faults ...' The book was nevertheless seen as an excellent piece of work. However, what concerned Winston most was that he might miss the action in South Africa. His mood was anything but jovial.

A fellow war correspondent aboard the *Dunnotar Castle*, John Black Atkins of the *Manchester Guardian,* seems to have taken a keen interest in Churchill. He described him as 'slim, slightly reddish-haired, pale, lively, frequently pluming along the deck with "neck thrust out", as Browning fancied Napoleon, folding and unfolding his hands as if trying to untie mental knots'. Atkins got to know Winston well, for he added: 'It was obvious that he was in love with words. He would hesitate sometimes before he chose one or would exchange one for a better ... when the prospects of a career like that of his father, Lord Randolph, excited him, then such a gleam shot from him that he was almost transfigured. I had not encountered this sort of ambition, unabashed, frankly egotistical, communicating its excitement, and extorting sympathy.

'He had small respect for authority until he had examined it; he had acquired no reverence for his seniors as such, and talked to them as though they were his own age, or younger ... he stood alone and confident, and his natural power to be himself had yielded to no man.'[5]

After four days at sea the *Dunnotar Castle* stopped briefly at Madeira. Although it was on this day that the first shot was fired at the British, there had been no news of the situation in South Africa, other than that the British troops were moving to meet the Boers on their way to Dundee in Natal and Kimberley in the Cape Colony.

As the vessel steamed on through calm waters on the second leg of the voyage, the mood of Sir Redvers and his headquarters staff was one of apprehension. Already rumours of terrible battles and great losses on the side of the British were making their rounds. Buller and his men feared that the war would be over before they reached Cape Town in another fortnight. While the passengers, civilian and military, passed the time playing deck games and attending fancy-dress balls, Churchill tried hard to gain Buller's attention, but the commander was unapproachable.

Churchill grew increasingly impatient as the captain of the liner, oblivious of his urgency to join the war, failed to increase her speed above the normal cruising rate of knots. The craving for action was by no means peculiar to Churchill, though he earned his unflattering reputation as a 'warmonger' early in his career and this defamatory accusation stuck to him for the rest of his life.

His friends regarded the appellation as a detestable slander. Some wondered whether the barb had its origin with Lloyd George, an outspoken critic of the South African War who, in the House of Commons, quoted an early Churchill dispatch to the effect that the only way to conquer the Boers was to grind them down — 'to kill them one by one, dozen by dozen, commando by commando'.

Churchill tried to justify his fascination with war by reminding readers of *My Early Life* that nearly 50 years had passed since Britain had been involved in a conflict with white people — during the Crimean War. 'The idea that time played any vital part in such a business seemed to be entirely absent from all her methods',[6] he lamented.

Churchill had no doubt that in the case of the amateur Boer force marching into Natal, General Penn Symons with his infantry brigade, a cavalry brigade and two batteries of artillery, would meet them with such force that they would never again dare to face disciplined and professional soldiers. Churchill found this thought heartening, and being convinced that Buller too, was as anxious as he was to get into the action, he no longer wondered why the commander-in-chief looked so glum.

If the British had mustered 50 000 men to fight the Boers, the war would have been over as quickly as Churchill predicted it would be. As it was, they had little more than half that number and of these one-third were volunteers from the Cape and Natal. The Boers had 20 000 burghers ready to invade the northern parts of Natal on two sides. Another 20 000 men were distributed along the southern and western borders of the Republic. It wouldn't be nearly as simple as that.

When a homeward-bound vessel from the rival company, the Union Line, passed them, the captain of the *Dunnotar Castle* refused to go near enough to read the flags. Two days before reaching Cape Town, however, they passed a tramp steamer, the *Australasian*, whose crew had painted in bold white letters: 'Boers defeated. Three battles. Penn Symons killed.' This news devastated the military personnel on board. The fact that a British general had been killed was serious, but of more concern was the obvious assumption that the Boers had exhausted their resources after a bitter fight. It appeared as if the war had ended before they even got there.

Only General Buller, having read the message through his field glasses without showing any emotion, was able to assess the situation in a dispassionate manner. 'I dare say there will be enough left to give us a fight outside Pretoria', he said when asked to comment on the situation. The promise of more bloody battles 'restored our morale'.[7] Buller's words ran through the ship like wildfire. They were repeated by everyone and 'every eye was brighter', Churchill noted with relief. 'The Staff Officers congratulated one another, and the aide-de-camp skipped for joy'.[8]

Carried away by the fresh optimism, Churchill raised his voice, complaining that it would only have taken ten minutes to stop the ship in order to get detailed news of the situation in the field. But his grumble was strongly rejected and put down to the impatience of youth. After all, the full story would be known to everyone soon enough. Besides, he was told, questioning the opinion of a superior officer was 'not done', even by a war correspondent — particularly one who had quite recently worn the uniform himself. Churchill was unconvinced that the criticism was justified.

The *Dunnotar Castle* docked in Cape Town at 10.00pm on 30 October to the news that a Boer offensive had been launched on three fronts. The main Republican force had crossed from the Transvaal and Orange Free State into the northern districts of Natal, compelling the detachments of the British garrison to retreat to Ladysmith where the main body of the Imperial force was stationed. On the western front the Boer commandos were besieging the garrisons in Kimberley and Mafeking.

Churchill knew that his Aunt Sarah was in Mafeking. She had returned to South Africa at the beginning of May 1899 with her husband, Captain Gordon Wilson and Dr Jameson. They then travelled to Bulawayo, Rhodesia, to stay with Major Heaney, an American mining pioneer who had been a member of Cecil Rhodes' original team. In July they were back in Cape Town. Rhodes, who had also returned from England, invited them to stay with him at his residence, Groote Schuur.

On 25 July Colonel Robert Baden-Powell arrived in Cape Town. In case of war breaking out — and the British War Office had no doubt that it would — he had been given instructions to raise two regiments of mounted infantry. He was rather unsuccessful in completing this mission, appointing only Gordon Wilson to his staff. At the end of September, when Boer commandos massed on the borders of the northern Cape, Wilson was ordered to Mafeking. Sarah decided to join him there for a week or two and then take a train back to Cape Town. From there she would sail to England.

Watching the town being prepared for a siege, Sarah decided to write a description of Mafeking and send it to the London *Daily Mail*. The paper that had been rejected by her nephew Winston already had a correspondent in Mafeking. Nevertheless, her contribution was accepted and it created a great sensation, being written from a woman's point of view. She was immediately engaged as a 'special war correspondent' and proudly introduced by the *Daily Mail* as 'the only woman acting as such for any paper in South Africa'.

When the Boer ultimatum was announced, Colonel Baden-Powell ordered Sarah to leave the town at dawn the following morning. A Cape cart and two mules were hurriedly organised so that a Zulu servant could take her to a small hotel run by a Scot at Setlagole some 46 miles from Mafeking on the road to Kimberley. There, a relieving column arriving from the Cape would take care of her.

Churchill was aware that events had caught up with his aunt in Mafeking. Because the two of them didn't get on, he had no intention of travelling to the western border to report on the besieged town.

First thing on the morning of 31 October, he called on Alfred Milner — to be told that the Boers had come out in far greater numbers than anticipated. The uprising 'contaminated' the two British colonies and the whole of the Cape was 'trembling on the verge of rebellion'. Buller's task was to relieve George White's army at Ladysmith on the railway line 150 miles north-west of Durban, and it was there that the fiercest fights were expected to take place.

Winston and John Atkins agreed to stick together. They had dinner at the Mount Nelson — Cape Town's newest and most luxurious hostelry at the foot of Table Mountain. It had been opened by the Castle Line only a few months previously. It is 'a most excellent and well-appointed establishment, which may be thoroughly appreciated after a sea voyage',[9] Churchill wrote.

There the correspondents were told that the quickest way to reach the front at Ladysmith was to travel by train to East London — halfway between Cape Town and Durban — ship from there to Durban and then take another train to Ladysmith. This routing would allow them to beat Buller — who was extending his voyage on the *Dunnotar Castle* to Durban — by four days.

They met up with another correspondent, Captain Campbell of the Laffans Agency, and the three duly took the next train to East London. There they embarked on the *Umzimvubo*, a 150-ton steamer that fought its way through a ghastly Antarctic gale to Natal's principal port. They reached Durban at midnight on 4 November, leaving Churchill enough time to visit the hospital ship *Sumatra* where he found a number of friends, including Reggie Barnes. Barnes told him that a third of his regiment had been killed or wounded in a single action in South Africa. But this did not diminish Churchill's impatience to reach the front. 'As far as you can and as quickly as you can' was his motto.

The three colleagues boarded a train carrying mail to Pietermaritzburg, but Natal's capital was still a long way from Ladysmith. To get there fast, the trio had to hire a special train. However, at Estcourt, a village of some 300 tin-roofed houses some 30 miles south of Ladysmith the train came to an abrupt halt. The Boers had cut the railway lines. The correspondents were shown to an empty bell tent in the shunting triangle of the railway station. For the moment they were stuck in the little town held by 2 000 British troops.

After a day or two at Estcourt, Churchill could hardly contain his impatience. If the British would not attack the Boers, he would try to make his way across their lines to find out what Ladysmith looked like from the inside. It seems it is not generally known that he offered to pay £200 to anyone who was willing to get him into the town. The details about this episode came to light in correspondence between Lieutenant Colonel W Park Gray and Dr R E Stevenson in 1963[10], and were related by HW Kinsey in an article in the *Military History Journal* of June 1987.

Gray, the 21-year-old son of a Natal farmer, at the time, was a trooper in the Estcourt Squadron of the Natal Carbineers. Two British cavalry regiments, plus the Border Mounted Rifles, the Umvoti Mounted Rifles and the Natal Mounted Rifles, were — with the exception of the Estcourt Squadron — besieged in Ladysmith. When the town was surrounded, the Estcourt Squadron, together with the Imperial Light Horse that had come from Johannesburg, comprised the only mounted troops available in Natal for scouting and reconnaissance work.

Soon the rumour that a war correspondent had offered £200 to smuggle him into Ladysmith came to Gray's ears. Keen to acquire this princely sum, while at the same time being free for a few days from the rigorous discipline in force, he came to see Churchill. He recalled the scene as the correspondent sat in his tent. Gray was surprised at the youthful looks of the man who, he said, created the impression that he was very lonely. 'He had a complexion that many a South African girl would envy and although four years older than I, looked to be about 17 or 18'.[2]

Churchill became very animated when Gray told him that he was willing to guide him into Ladysmith and readily agreed to pay the £200 for doing so. But the trooper had to obtain permission for three days leave before final arrangements could be made. This was refused. His commanding officer, Major Duncan McKenzie could not spare a single man and Gray was thus unable to collect the promised fee. Neither did the frustrated Churchill get the chance to cross the enemy lines and experience life within besieged Ladysmith.

But more excitement than Churchill had ever dared to dream of was awaiting him. The stage was set for him to report on what he believed would be a speedy and complete British victory.

10

Disaster at Chieveley

It is interesting to note that many of the men Churchill had met within days of arriving in South Africa, were old friends and acquaintances of his. Barnes was one, and Ian Hamilton was in command of troops nearby. He also knew Leo Amery, chief of *The Times'* war correspondent service. Soon after arriving at Harrow he had pushed Amery, a sixth-former who was small of stature, into the school's swimming pool. Young Winston was alarmed to see a furious face emerge from the water. Evidently possessing enormous strength the agitated boy made his way using fierce strokes to the edge of the pool.

Winston's friends feared for him. 'It's Amery', they said, 'he is head of his house; he is champion at gym; he has his football colours'. Churchill admits that he was not only shaking with terror, but with the guilt of sacrilege. The incident had long since been forgotten and now in Estcourt the two shared a tent with Atkins. Although they were never close there is no doubt that a good time was had by all.

Atkins later wrote: 'We found a very good cook and we had some good wine. We entertained friends every evening, to our pleasure and professional advantage and, we believed, to our satisfaction'.[1] Among the officers was Colonel GJ Long who had been in charge of the artillery at Omdurman and was now the commander at Estcourt. Another old acquaintance was Captain Aylmer Haldane, DSO, an officer of the 2nd Battalion the Gordon Highlanders, who had been on Sir William Lockhart's staff during the Tirah expedition in India.

To be surrounded by familiar faces in times of war in a strange country would have been welcomed by most men who found themselves facing an enemy who could deal them death at any moment.

Churchill was different. He was not interested in friends and acquaintances — unless, of course, they could be used to his advantage when he filed reports for his paper. He had come to report on the siege of Ladysmith and he intended to be there when the town was relieved.

On the night of 14 November, eight days after Churchill's arrival at Estcourt, his valet Walden poured him and his guest some of his precious St. Emilion. As they clinked their glasses, the sound of field guns being loaded into wagons could be heard.

Colonel Long said that the Estcourt position could not be held and they were pulling back to Pietermaritzburg. Churchill argued that Piet Joubert, the Boer commander, would not advance in force beyond the Tugela River. 'It would be a pity to show him the way to Maritzburg [Pietermaritzburg],' he added with an assurance his companions did not really appreciate. Later that evening they heard the guns being unloaded.

Churchill was wrong in his assessment of Joubert. Five hundred mounted raiders, led by the Boer general and his aide, Louis Botha, crossed the Tugela that very night. They placed dynamite under the bridge at Colenso before crossing the veld along the railway line to Durban. They stopped at Chieveley. Joubert, knowing that the British were out in strength at Estcourt some 20 miles north of Chieveley, had no intention of attacking them. He was merely assessing the enemy position.

On the same day Captain Haldane received orders to go on a reconnoitring mission in an armoured train the following morning. Having been wounded in the battle at Elandslaagte a month earlier, the convalescing Haldane was anxiously waiting to be reunited with the Gordon Highlanders at Ladysmith. Meanwhile he was attached to the Dublin Fusiliers and assigned to command routine excursions of an armoured train running between Estcourt and the outskirts of Colenso.

Haldane had taken Churchill and Atkins along on one of the forays a few days earlier. They travelled to the fringes of Colenso and there, from a hilltop, they could see the hot air balloon which the besieged British in Ladysmith had hoisted in order to observe the enemy's movements. Suddenly they were surrounded by British troops. Their passes were inspected and all was well. They even took a photograph of the sergeant-in-charge. Churchill and Atkins walked with an officer and a sergeant through the deserted British trenches on the outskirts of the town, and then into Colenso itself.

Five days after this, Haldane wrote in his official report that, on receiving his orders and leaving the military office, he noticed Churchill as well as some other correspondents hanging about endeavouring to pick up such crumbs of information for their newspapers as might be available. Remembering that Churchill had enjoyed the earlier outing in the train, he invited him to come along again the next morning. At first Churchill was not all that keen, but then he agreed to do so out of comradeship and because he thought it his duty to the paper. Churchill, in turn, asked Atkins to join the party. In *Incidents and Reflections,* Atkins remembers the conversation:

I said simply that I would not go; and a few moments later, as Winston lingered, I explained that my instructions were to follow the war on the British side, and that if after having put my paper to great expense, I got myself on the wrong side, I should be held very much to blame.

Winston listened and then said gravely: 'That is perfectly true. I can see no fault in your reasoning. But I have a feeling, a sort of intuition, that if you go something will come of it. It's illogical, I know.' He left and I did not see him again until he had escaped from his prison in Pretoria and presented the world with a famous story. Is this man accompanied by a demon who tells him things?[3]

The train's engine and tender pushed two trucks and pulled three. The front truck was equipped with an old muzzle-loading seven-pounder naval gun from *HMS Terrible*. Four sailors and a petty officer were responsible for manning and firing the deadly weapon when the need arose. The front truck was followed by roofless trucks reinforced with steel plating. The plating had crenels cut into it, through which the soldiers could observe the scene and fire their rifles at the enemy. Two more armoured trucks and a wagon, which contained breakdown equipment, completed what could be described as a moving fortress.

Haldane did not like the idea of transporting military personnel, let alone civilians, in the clumsy behemoth that could be seen bellowing smoke and heard huffing and puffing from miles away. He considered the monstrosity — which was called 'Wilson's death trap' after its designer, the local commander — an easy target. Why take the risk of being attacked when two or three horsemen could get the same information much more speedily? But orders had to be obeyed.

Churchill met Haldane at the station and the two climbed into the holding wagon. The train was already occupied by 120 troops of the Dublin Fusiliers and the Durban Light Infantry, as well as a small breakdown gang of civilian platelayers. It was half-past five on the wet morning of 15 December when the signal to depart was given. The train arrived at the next station, Frere, about an hour later. Eight men of the Natal Mounted Police there told Haldane that advance patrols were reconnoitring the area. No sign of the enemy had thus far been reported and the train proceeded to Chieveley crossing the iron bridge that spanned the Blaauwkrantz River.

On approaching Chieveley, Churchill saw a column of mounted Boers riding towards the railway line. Further on, rows of Boers lined the hills and, no doubt, were readying to attack the train. The telegraphist on board the train reported the enemy sighting to Estcourt. Colonel Long replied that the Boers had occupied the town the night before. Haldane was advised to go back to Frere station from where he could observe the situation and await further developments. If there was no cause for concern, he should make his way back to Estcourt after nightfall.

Haldane sensed that he was in trouble. More than ever he regretted his ill-advised mission. 'I do not wish to lay blame on anyone but myself', he later recorded, 'but had I been alone and not had my impetuous young friend Churchill with me, who in many things was prompted by Dante's motto, *de l'audace et encore de l'audace, et toujour de l'audace*, I might have thought twice before throwing myself into the lion's jaws by going almost to the Tugela. But I was carried away by his ardour and departed from an attitude of prudence'.[4]

In a dispatch for the *Morning Post* that Churchill wrote five days later from the State Model School in Pretoria, he confirmed that the patrol of the Natal Police at Frere had informed them that there was no enemy within the next few miles, and that all seemed quiet in the neighbourhood. But 'this patrol's report was fatally misleading', he fumed. It was usual practice for the commander in charge of the train to clear passage further north with the garrison commander. On the day in question Haldane sent a report to Colonel Long, but fired by Churchill's enthusiasm he did not wait for a reply. Haldane was an experienced officer with a Distinguished Service Order (DSO) already to his name, but he had clearly fallen under Churchill's persuasive spell. It would cost both him and his men dearly.

Haldane ordered the train's immediate return to Frere, but it was too late to make a safe retreat. The Boer General Louis Botha had come out in full force with some 500 men of the Krugersdorp and Wakkerstroom commandos to watch the clumsy contraption cross the iron bridge. They had not come to fight but, like the British, their intention was merely to reconnoitre the terrain. However, the opportunity that presented itself only a day after they had crossed the Tugela River was too good to be ignored.

Churchill, who had climbed onto a box to get a better view of his surroundings, saw the Boers riding on the crest of a hill, accompanied by wagons mounted with guns. At first no one was particularly worried. They didn't think a small group of patrolling Boers would dare to attack them. If they did their rifle bullets wouldn't penetrate the reinforced trucks. Besides, Haldane had the seven-pounder naval gun which would be enough to beat off the enemy.

They didn't have to wait long to find out how wrong they were. The Boers fired two artillery shots from a distance of 600 yards. Horrifying sounds of steel fragments hammering the armoured plates of the leading wagon echoed through the valley. Shrapnel, the first Churchill had seen in war, spattered all over the place. The engineer got the fright of his life. He opened up to full steam as more bullets hit the hissing train. Flying down a gradient, it rounded a curve at full speed — only to crash into large rocks that Botha's men had placed on the track.

The sound of crashing metal was deafening. Churchill and the soldiers in his truck were flung to the floor. Scrambling up onto his box, Churchill saw Boers coming down the hill and heard rifle bullets whistling about his head. They 'splattered on the steel plates like a hailstorm'.[5] However, no one in Churchill's truck was seriously hurt.

They put their heads together and discussed their predicament. It was agreed that Haldane would make his way to the rear and order his troops to pin down the Boer riflemen. Churchill would go to the front of the train to assess the situation and, if possible, ensure the naval gun was brought into action.

By this time the Boers had moved their guns. With shots being fired at the train from three sides, it seemed almost impossible to get out of the truck without being hit. But Churchill ran to the front, ducking and diving as bullets ricocheted on the metal around him.

The leading wagon loaded with the tools of the breakdown gang had been flung in the air and it lay upside down on the embankment. The two ironclad cars were jammed together, one derailed and thrown on its side, the other half on and half off the rail. Its occupants, the Durban Light Infantry, were scattered about on the ground.

As Churchill reached the engine, which was still on the rails, a shell burst overhead. Shrapnel flew in all directions prompting the driver to jump out of the cab and dive under the overturned truck. Churchill ran after him because he was the only one who could operate the locomotive needed to ram the obstructing trucks off the rails. Until that was done, no thought of escape could be entertained. To persuade the driver — who introduced himself as Charles Wagner — to return to his cab was no easy task. He was bleeding profusely from a wound in his head caused by a shell splinter. Dazed and angry, he complained bitterly about his treatment as a civilian. He was not paid to be killed, he said, and would not stay another minute.

Churchill remained calm. He pleaded with Wagner, saying that no man was hit twice on the same day. 'A wounded man who continued to do his duty was always rewarded for distinguished gallantry',[6] Churchill told him, and added that he might never have the chance again. It is unlikely that Wagner, in the circumstances, cared about a reward, but Churchill succeeded in persuading him to climb back into his cab. He wiped the blood off his face and 'thereafter obeyed every order which I gave him'.[7]

'I returned along the line to Haldane's truck', Churchill wrote in *My Early Life*, 'and told him through a loophole what was the position and what I proposed we should do. He agreed to all I said and undertook to keep the enemy hotly engaged meanwhile'.[8]

Churchill tried to muster volunteers from the breakdown gang to help him clear the tracks, but they were nowhere to be seen. Some had been killed or badly wounded when their truck overturned and the rest had fled. He needed 20 men, but eventually nine, led by Captain Wylie of the Durban Light Infantry, came forward. The first task was to uncouple the engine from the rear trucks. Churchill, ready to put his shoulder to the wheel, took off the belt holding his Mauser pistol and placed this, together with his field glasses in the cab. For a civilian to carry a pistol was against regulations, but in this dreadful situation no one cared whether he was armed or not.

With Churchill directing the engine driver, they began the precarious business of pulling and pushing the wreckage off the rails. Backwards and forwards the locomotive shunted, its wheels screeching violently and the boiler threatening to blow up under the strain. For more than an hour Churchill ran up and down the line while under heavy fire, shouting orders to the labouring men.

When the forward line was finally cleared, they made an unsuccessful attempt to couple the engine onto the rear trucks. A shell had smashed the coupling and part of the overturned truck blocked the locomotive from the undamaged trucks. Churchill ran back to Haldane and suggested the men push the trucks forward. 'Perhaps it was possible to again remove the wreckage and re-couple the trucks to the engine', Haldane wrote in his official report:

> … but as the cab of the latter was now crammed with wounded, who would have been scalded had a shell struck the boiler, as the pipe of the reserve water-tank was torn open and the water rushing out as the front of the engine

was in flames, and because I apprehended lest the enemy, seeing the entire engine free, should again tamper with the line, I resolved to allow the engine to retreat out of range towards Frere, and withdrawing the men from the truck, made a run for some houses, 800 yards distant, where I had some hope of making a further resistance.

Some 50 men, most of them wounded, clung onto the locomotive by whatever handholds they could find. Even the cow-catcher was covered with men trying to escape from the assault. The engine provided a solid shield behind which the remainder could walk to safety.

Churchill could hardly move in the cab as he gave directions to the driver. They moved on, slowly at first, while 'the shell-firing Maxim continued its work, and its little shells, discharged with an ugly thud, thud, thud, exploded with startling bangs on all sides', he reported in the *Morning Post*. 'One, I remember, struck the foot-plate of the engine scarcely a yard away from my head, lit up into a bright yellow flash, and left me wondering why I was still alive'. A private from the Dublin Fusiliers was not so lucky. Standing close by, Churchill witnessed a bullet strike his arm. 'The whole arm was smashed to a horrible pulp — bones, muscle, blood, and uniform all mixed together. At the bottom hung the hand, unhurt, but it swelled instantly to three times its ordinary size.'

As the pace of the engine increased, the walking soldiers could not keep up. Churchill ordered Wagner to stop. The Blaauwkrantz bridge was close by. Forcing his way out of the cab, he told Wagner to cross the bridge and wait on the far side. Meanwhile he would help Captain Haldane and his Dublin Fusiliers to reach safety. Why he asked the engine driver to wait on the other side of the bridge with his heavy load of wounded soldiers needing urgent attention, Churchill does not say.

The reunion with Haldane was not as he had expected. 'As the enemy had not relaxed his artillery and musketry fire, and there was absolutely no cover, the men became considerably scattered along the line, and a formation ill adapted to offer resistance', Haldane wrote in his report of 6 January, 1900. 'To my disgust', he continued, 'and in direct disobedience of my orders, I saw two men 200 yards in front of me holding up white handkerchiefs.'

Haldane shouted and ran towards them. But the Boers stopped shooting and rode up to the retreating soldiers. They obeyed the command to surrender and Haldane had no choice but to follow suit.

11

Churchill is taken prisoner

Churchill, unaware of the turn of events, had hardly started to walk when he saw two figures in plain clothes approaching from the opposite direction. 'My mind retains its impression of these tall figures, full of energy, clad in dark, flapping clothes, with slouch, storm-driven hats, posing on their levelled rifles hardly a hundred yards away.'[1]

In a letter he wrote shortly afterwards to the *Morning Post*, he recounted the anxious moments as he turned to run between the rails towards the engine. 'Two bullets passed, both within a foot, one on either side'. In his account in *My Early Life* he remembered that 'their bullets, sucking to right and left, seemed to miss only by inches'.[2] Looking over his shoulder, he saw one of the Boers kneeling to aim. Again he ran. Two bullets hissed over him as he threw himself against a bank in a cutting and, as he tried to scramble up, a bullet hit the ground next to him. Earth spurted up and something hit his hand. He managed to get up the bank and crawled through a wire fence before crunching himself into a tiny depression where he tried to get his breath back. There was a platelayer's cabin nearby, and about 200 yards further on was the rocky gorge of the Blaauwkrantz River. He decided to move towards the river. As he stood up he saw a 'tall, dark figure' galloping towards him. The rider's right hand held a rifle. Pulling up his horse 'almost in his own length and shaking the rifle at me he shouted a loud command'.[3]

LPH Behrens, a former public relations officer of the Pretoria City Council, in an article in *The Star* on Churchill's capture, wrote: 'There was no evidence at that time of a shot having been fired to stop him [Churchill].'

In *From London to Ladysmith via Pretoria* Churchill wrote that he knew nothing of white flags, and that the bullets had made him savage. It's him or me, he thought as he fumbled for his familiar Mauser pistol — only to realise that he had forgotten to recover it from the cab of the locomotive. 'It came safely home from the engine, I have it now!' he wrote, 'but at this moment I was quite unarmed.'

The thought of continuing his flight crossed his mind. There was a wire fence between him and the horseman which might have briefly held up the pursuit. But he soon realised that he couldn't possibly avoid being hit by another shot at such close range. 'Death stood before me, grim sullen Death without his light-hearted companion, Chance.' He grudgingly accepted his fate, shrugged and held up his hands in surrender'.[5]

Seeing that there was no resistance, the horseman lowered his rifle and ordered Churchill to step forward. He mentally defended his submission: 'The great Napoleon said that when one is alone and unarmed a surrender may be pardoned.'[6]

As the sullen prisoner plodded alongside the rider, making his way through high, wet grass to the Boers, he noticed that his hand was bleeding. The rain pelted down heavily. No words were exchanged.

Suddenly Churchill remembered that he had two clips of Mauser ammunition, each holding ten rounds, in the breast pockets of his khaki jacket. 'These cartridges were the same as I had used at Omdurman, and were the only kind supplied for the Mauser pistol',[7] he wrote. He had not given a thought to these soft-nosed bullets which disintegrated and mangled tissue as they ripped through a man's body. Dumdums had been outlawed at The Hague Conference the previous July and Churchill was fully aware of it.

Realising possessing them might prove dangerous, he furtively dropped a clip to the ground. He was about to do the same with the second one when his captor looked down sharply and asked him in English: 'What have you got there?'

Feigning innocence, Churchill responded: 'What is it? I just picked it up.'

The horseman took the magazine, glanced at it and threw it away.

The Boers also used dumdums, but it is likely that at the outbreak of the war they were unaware of the international banning. Otherwise Churchill's captor would no doubt have kept them as proof that his prisoner was not only armed, but was also engaged in unlawful warfare. But with or without such evidence the journalist knew that he was in serious trouble. At best he would be a failure as a war correspondent — while Amery was still free to send letters to *The Times*.

At worst he, a civilian, would be shot for having taken an active part in defending the ambushed train. 'It is sad to note that the following 9 March, Churchill indignantly informed his *Morning Post* readers that the Boers were using "expanding bullets" and commented that 'the character of these people reveals in stress a dark and spiteful underside. A man, I use the word in its fullest sense, does not wish to lacerate his foe, however earnestly he may desire his death',[8] William Manchester observed.

When the horseman and his prisoner reached Haldane and his men, they found them surrounded by 'hundreds of mounted Boers, many holding umbrellas over their heads to protect themselves from the pouring rain'. They had captured 52 soldiers and killed six in the encounter. Sixteen of the badly wounded casualties had escaped on the locomotive.

To be rounded up with other prisoners 'like cattle' was 'the greatest indignity of my life', Churchill later recounted to Atkins. His heroism notwithstanding, it was perhaps a small price to pay for the impetuous young man. It was his reckless zeal, fired by 'a sort of intuition, that if I go something will come of it' that contributed to Haldane throwing all caution to the wind. It is true, though, that as the captain in charge of the expedition he was to blame for not waiting at Frere station for clearance from headquarters before proceeding.

It can also be argued that if it were not for Churchill's gallant conduct, the wounded on the engine would not have escaped and many more soldiers might have been killed. Captain Haldane had given orders and defended the train to the best of his ability, but it was Churchill who showed extraordinary courage. Without his outstanding leadership and reckless bravery — everyone who had witnessed him in action agreed on that — all would have been lost.

Circumstances dictated the events and Churchill obviously told the story from his own perspective. Later, when Haldane mentioned the train disaster in his book *How we escaped from Pretoria*, he stated: 'I am not going to recount the events of that day, which already have been portrayed by an abler pen than mine'.[9] He did not in any way dispute Churchill's version.

In his official report of 3 January 1900 to Chief of Staff of the Natal Field Force, Haldane, while imprisoned in Pretoria, wrote: 'Mr Winston Churchill ... offered me his services and knowing him thoroughly I could rely on him, I gladly accepted them, and undertook to keep down the enemy's fire while he endeavoured to clear the line. Our gun came into action at 900 yards, but after four rounds, was struck by a shell and knocked over.'

When the order was given for the engine to leave, Haldane ordered his men from the railway trucks and told them to retreat to some houses in the vicinity. They scattered and ran as fast as they could, but the Boers on their horses were faster. At about ten to nine that morning white handkerchiefs announced the end of their war.

Captain Thomas Haldane, 2nd Lieutenant T Frankland, 2nd Royal Fusiliers, and 50 men were taken prisoner. Of Churchill, Haldane wrote: '... owing to the urgency of the circumstances, I formally placed him on duty.' He further pointed out that, 'while engaged in the work of saving the engine, for which he was mainly responsible, he was frequently exposed to the full fire of the enemy. I cannot speak too highly of his gallant conduct'.[10]

His son, Randolph S Churchill, writes: 'History depends wherever it can on first-hand accounts', and points out that it should be:

> ... one of the strictest precepts of the historian to subject everything that comes before him to a cold and sceptical scrutiny. This applies with special force to months of action, passion and excitement. The man who is hotly engaged in action has all his faculties fully absorbed in the current emergency. Unless he has special aptitudes or is a trained reporter it is unlikely that he will see things in their true perspective or even perceive what were salient or dominating events of the action. In retrospect, of course, many events may be reassessed and assigned in different proportions, many illusory fears dismissed, many fugitive hopes relegated to a proper limbo. But when

there are a number of witnesses, all of them equally prejudiced, all of them equally truthful, it may still be that some facts will be etched more sharply in one man's memory than in another's.[11]

Lord Randolph had once demonstrated how memory could play quirks. He had told Winston a story about Sir Walter Raleigh when he was writing *The History of the World* during his imprisonment in the Tower of London. One day, looking out of the window, he saw a man being killed by another. Six independent witnesses including Sir Walter were asked to give their accounts of the event. He noted that all the accounts differed in almost every detail. This led him to abandon his *History*.

Lord Randolph explained that he did not put these reflections forward with the purpose 'of inducing a similar mood of defeatism in other historians, but solely as a corrective to gullibility' and advises: 'The chronicler must assemble all the evidence he can, deploy it, weigh it judiciously, consider its plausibility and then tell his tale with his utmost candour'.[12]

As far as Churchill's surrender to the tall, dark horseman is concerned, 'there are two ambiguities', according to Roy Jenkins in his book *Churchill*.[13] The first relates to the identity of the Boer sharpshooter who had him so firmly in his sights. The second concerns the grounds on which Churchill claimed to be a non-combatant entitled to immediate release.

Churchill himself was adamant that his captor was no less a personality than General Louis Botha himself. After hostilities between Britain and Boer republics had ended in 1902, Botha travelled to London to seek assistance for his war-devastated country. While attending a private luncheon, he was introduced to Churchill. Their conversation turned to the war and the Briton spoke about his capture. 'Botha listened in silence', remembers Churchill, 'then he said: "Don't you recognise me? I was that man. It was I who took you prisoner. I, myself", and his bright eyes twinkled with pleasure.'[14] Churchill further told his readers:

> Botha in white shirt and frock-coat looked very different in all save size and darkness of complexion from the wild wartime figure I had seen that rough day in Natal. But about the extraordinary fact there can be no doubt. He had entered upon the invasion of Natal as a burgher; his own disapproval of the war had excluded him from any high command at the outset. This was his first action. But as a simple private burgher serving in the ranks he had galloped on ahead and in front of the whole Boer forces in the ardour of pursuit. Thus we met.[15]

Churchill and Botha met again in 1906. Botha, the newly-elected Prime Minister of the Transvaal, had come to London to attend the Imperial Conference. A great banquet was given to the Dominion prime ministers in Westminster Hall. Churchill, in his position as Under-Secretary of State for the Colonies, attended the function with his mother. As Botha passed by the two, he is supposed to have turned to Jennie, who was standing next to her son, with the words: 'He and I have been out in all weathers.'[16]

Few writers or indeed eminent historians who have dealt with Churchill's capture at Chieveley query his narrative of the events and the characters involved. It is true 'there was a pleasing symmetry in one great man being captured by another'.[17] Their meeting by chance had a touch of dramatic romanticism that appealed to Churchill. A trusting public has accepted it as the truth. But both his son Randolph and his granddaughter, Celia Sandys, have assembled the evidence, deployed it, weighed it judiciously, considered its plausibility, and cast serious doubt about the tale. Sandys asks: 'How can it be that Churchill could have got his facts so wrong?'[18]

One possible reason is that Churchill simply misunderstood what he heard. Botha's command of the English language is supposed to have been poor. Brian Roberts, in *Churchills in Africa,* thinks it likely Botha 'was referring to the fact that he was in command of the troops that captured Churchill and not that he was the lone horseman who brought Churchill in'. [19] But Churchill's statement on the matter is quite clear. Botha, Churchill insists, said: 'Don't you recognise me? I was that man. It was me who took you prisoner. *I myself'.'* Botha's words were unequivocal, leaving no room for misunderstanding. If he was referring to his troops as Roberts speculates, why would he have queried Churchill for not recognising him, and why would he have said that it was 'I myself' who took him prisoner?

Randolph Churchill studied all available reports on the matter and corresponded with South African historians. Not one accepted that Botha was the captor. 'The probability that it was not Botha who captured Churchill is fortified by the fact that it is not mentioned in the Boer documents', Randolph wrote that Danie Theron, the master scout of the Boers who had taken part in the ambush, sent a telegram to the Secretary of State in Pretoria on 28 November 1899. It is kept in the South African State Archives and in translation it reads:

> Churchill was involved in the fight with the armoured train at Frere Station. Churchill called for volunteers and led them at a time when the officers were in confusion. I humbly wish to state that in the *Natal Witness* and *Natal Mercury* of the 17th of this month full reports appeared of the active and prominent part taken by the newspaper reporter Winston Churchill.
>
> According to the *Volksstem* and *Standard and Digger News*, he now claims that he took no part in the battle. That is all lies. He also refused to stand still until Field Cornet Oosthuizen warned him to surrender and aimed his rifle at him. In my view Churchill is one of the most dangerous prisoners in our hands.
>
> The Natal papers are making a big hero of him ...[21]

Danie Theron was the first to identify Churchill's captor in writing. Botha had been appointed senior combat general under Piet Joubert and so it is highly unlikely that he would have left his command at that crucial stage to become the lone horseman who had captured Churchill. It is also unlikely that Botha would have known who had taken him prisoner. Even if he had been told the name, it probably would have meant little to him. In any event, he mentions neither the captor nor the prisoner in the letter he wrote to his wife Annie the day after the train disaster. In translation it reads:

16 Nov. Yesterday an armoured train from Estcourt came upon us. Our Commandos Wakkerstroom and Krugersdorp with their men and I immediately turned around and returned. Shortly the foremost truck was derailed where our burghers had placed rocks. Our canons were in order and quickly penetrated the armoured truck. The engine uncoupled and went back heavily damaged. The enemy lost four dead, 14 injured and 58 taken prisoner as well as a mountain canon that was captured by us. This took place at Blaauwkrantz. Later we encountered thick mist and rain en route from Ermelo to Brandwacht and two of our burgers died. The commando stormed into battle and pushed the enemy back. Their loss is unknown. Blood was everywhere. Much rain.

Many years after the war, when Churchill had become an internationally known personality, a considerable amount of prestige was attached to being associated with his capture in Natal. A number of Boers came forward with a claim to have taken him prisoner. 'Ultimately, more than 40 men were to assert that they had played some part in the event.'[23]

According to reports from the Boer side, Adolph de la Rey and his brother-in-law, François Changuion, chased Churchill before he was captured by Field Cornet Sarel François Oosthuizen of the Krugersdorp Commando. It has been said that the two riflemen accompanied Churchill as he plodded towards the Boer lines beside the mounted Oosthuizen. It seems logical that the two Boers whom Churchill described as 'tall figures, full of energy, clad in dark, flapping clothes, with slouch, storm-driven hats, posing on their levelled rifles hardly 100 yards away', had made their way back to their command after the capture. It seems reasonable too, that they would have accompanied the horseman and his prisoner.

Sarel Oosthuizen was a farmer from Krugersdorp with a distinguished military career. This included his involvement in combatting the Jameson Raid in 1895. When the Boers started preparing in earnest for the war that was looming on the horizon, he was in command of 970 men. The Krugersdorp Commando left Johannesburg by train for the battlefront and rendezvoused at Sandspruit on 28 September 1899. There the Commandant-General, Petrus Jacobus (Piet) Joubert, incorporated the Krugersdorp Commando under DEJ Erasmus.

When martial law was proclaimed on 11 October 1899, Joubert was ready to attack the British army in Natal. During the night of 19 October the Boers occupied two hills next to Dundee. Their first shots totally surprised the English and the frontal attack on the hills led by Major-General Penn Symons left him fatally wounded. During this first major battle in Natal, Field Cornet Oosthuizen was wounded in the hand, stomach and buttocks.

General Louis Botha later wrote that the biggest commando was the Krugersdorp led by the fearless and likeable Field Cornet Sarel Oosthuizen — the Red Bull of Krugersdorp. Oosthuizen fought with distinction in Natal and later, as a fighting general, in his own area, the Western Transvaal. Another man Botha singled out was Captain Danie Theron who, without a doubt, was the most efficient and devil-may-care scout of the war. Both Oosthuizen and Theron would meet with heroic deaths the next year.

The British forces attacked the Boer lines at Elandslaagte between Dundee and Ladysmith during a heavy rainstorm on 21 October, making use of the Lancers and Dragoon Guards to drive the enemy out. When the Boers occupied Dundee two days later, it had a favourable effect on the morale of the burghers.

General Sir George White by then was under siege in Ladysmith. But not all of White's forces were bogged down there. He had earlier dispatched 2 300 men to Colenso in an attempt to stop the Boer advance. This unit, under the command of General Wolfe-Murray, was posted to Estcourt. Being restricted in manpower, they could do little but send out scouts and make use of an armoured train to obtain information on the movement of the Boers.

A fast-moving Boer force of 3 000 men, which included the burghers from Krugersdorp, was established by Louis Botha on 13 and 14 November. Its purpose was to meet the advancing British troops south of Colenso. This task force slept under heavy clouds next to the railway line and then demolished bridge at Hermansspruit on 13 November. The next morning they crossed the river over the Bulwer Bridge and set up camp near Chieveley.

When Botha saw Colonel Long's armoured train puffing from Estcourt to Chieveley, he immediately recognised the opportunity to capture it. He left the burghers of Krugersdorp and Wakkerstroom next to a bend in the line near Frere, with instructions to block the rails with heavy rocks as soon as the train passed.

Churchill did not record the loud words of command the 'tall, dark figure' shouted at him as he pulled up his horse and shook his rifle at the fleeing enemy. What he did record was that, after his surrender, the Boer asked him: 'What have you got there?' referring to the Mauser clip in his hand. These five words were all he said, according to Churchill. None of the Boers knew that Churchill was among the soldiers on the train. Sarel Oosthuizen didn't care whom he had arrested, and even if he had heard the name, it would have meant as little to him as it did to Louis Botha.

Churchill's brief description of the horseman adds to the drama of the hero of the battle being captured. A photograph taken of Oosthuizen with his bride, Susanna Alberts, in 1882 shows he was not particularly tall. But it wouldn't be easy to estimate the height of a man in the saddle on a grey and rainy morning. To someone like Churchill, it wouldn't have been psychologically acceptable to admit submission to somebody other than a powerful and imposing figure.

Height notwithstanding, when Churchill walked towards him, the flaming red hair and matching full beard of the 'Red Bull of Krugersdorp', as Jan Smuts, the Boer general and later Prime Minister of South Africa, had called Oosthuizen, must have struck him. That Churchill failed to mention these peculiarities in the reports he wrote, seems odd indeed.

> ... one of the smartest and bravest men in the whole Boer army. Dashing and impetuous, he was not only brave to rashness but withal most genial, and in the hottest fight and amid the greatest hardship he would crack jokes with his men, while the contagion of his hearty laugh would send a thrill of good humour and spirits through his jaded commando.[24]

Nowhere in Churchill's report was Louis Botha mentioned, and Theron's telegram written three days after the event makes the identity of his captor quite clear. Celia Sandys admits that 'all evidence points to Field Cornet Sarel Oosthuizen'[25] and has ready explanations as to 'why Churchill's usually open mind remained closed for ever on the subject'. 'For one thing', she writes, 'he had no reason to doubt his understanding of Botha's description of events.'[26]

Before this account can be accepted we must ask ourselves what was Churchill's understanding of the events in question? There were no witnesses to Botha telling Churchill that he was the captor. And not once during his adventures in South Africa does Churchill, the reporter and main character in the drama at Chieveley, rely on anyone else's description of events.

'The man who is hotly engaged in action has all his faculties fully absorbed in the current emergencies', his son wrote.

Certainly Churchill would have had all his faculties fully absorbed when being chased by the Boers. His minutely detailed description of the action with himself at centre stage as the bullets 'sucked the air', plus the record of his emotions when being arrested, testifies to this.

From Haldane's account it is clear that white handkerchiefs had already been waved and that the firing had stopped when Churchill made his way back to the troops. There are no reports other than his own of him being fired at from close range. Nor are any details offered about the Boers who pursued him — including the tall horseman. The highly observant Churchill had ample time to scrutinise the man who had taken him prisoner as they plodded towards the group of British prisoners.

To be taken prisoner was a humbling experience for Churchill. 'A man tries his best to kill another, and finding that he cannot succeed asks his enemy for mercy. The laws of war demand that this should be accorded, but it is impossible not to feel a sense of humbling obligation to the captor from whose hand we take our lives'.[27] To ask his enemy for mercy would have been the greatest indignity imaginable, and that is probably why Churchill failed to acknowledge the Boer who forced his surrender.

Only by completely ignoring the individuality of the man in his report could he, in his thinking, combat the humiliation he felt. Contempt for his captor nonetheless gave his melancholic makeup a decisive blow as he lined up with the other prisoners.

The name Louis Botha came to his rescue two years later in London. The Boer who had taken him prisoner was no longer a mysterious 'tall, dark figure', but none other than the famous general himself. Botha had risen to become one of the most important men in South African politics and was destined to become the first prime minster when the country was unified in 1910.

In *My Early Life* Churchill turned his displeasure into a personal triumph by devoting more than three pages to his meeting with Botha. 'Few men that I have known have interested me more than Louis Botha', he wrote.

Words of praise for the 'wise and profound statesman, the farmer-warrior, the crafty hunter of the wilderness, the deep sure man of solitude', flowed from Churchill's pen like water down the throat of a man dying of thirst.[28] 'An acquaintance formed in strange circumstances and upon an almost unbelievable introduction ripened into a friendship which I greatly valued.'[29]

'This considerable digression will, I hope, be pardoned by the reader, and I make haste to return to the true path of chronology', Churchill promises as he ends his eulogy on Louis Botha.[30]

Churchill was delighted to have the world believe that he had found the man whose rank and status made him worthy to be his captor.

12

In the hands of the Boers

In the enemy camp the prisoners were disarmed and rounded up in a group — all 52 of them, including a few who were lightly wounded. The Boers crowded around, watching them eat the chocolate they carried in their pockets that was the substitute for the breakfasts they would have enjoyed at Estcourt. The prisoners were ordered to march away, leaving the seriously wounded behind to be attended to by burghers who remained. As they climbed a low hill from where, only a short while before, the Boers had emptied their rifles at the unfortunate soldiers, Churchill watched the engine moving out of reach of the enemy beyond Frere Station.

Rain drizzled on the subdued group while they were watched over by guards on horseback. 'You need not walk fast', one of them said and another, noticing that Churchill was the only man without a hat, felt sorry for him and gave him the forage cap of an Irish fusilier that he had picked up on some battlefield. Churchill expressed surprise at this act of kindness from a foe he had believed to be cruel and from whom he had expected only hardship and indignity. When the prisoners reached the Boer camp, they could scarcely believe that well over 3 000 men were there. 'It was plain to me now', recorded Haldane, 'that we were in the thick of a strong force which was on its way southward'.[1]

Churchill wasted no time in explaining that he was a correspondent and requested he be taken to General Joubert whom he believed was in the camp. This caused immediate attention. 'A crowd of rough-looking, and for the most part bearded, fellows soon gathered round us',[2] wrote Haldane. Churchill's request was refused, so he handed one of his captors a certificate identifying him as a correspondent and on which his name was clearly stated. However, the Boers had not forgotten Lord Randolph's crass behaviour when he visited South Africa and they held the name of Churchill in low esteem.

When Churchill's papers were eventually taken to the general, the news that the son of a real English lord was among the prisoners caused something of a stir. He was told to stand to one side and everyone wanted to take a good look at him. Fingers were pointed, his name was repeated and, while 'his case was under the consideration of the commandant-general, a running fire of questions on various matters connected with the struggle which had so recently begun was maintained'.[3] Churchill in his khaki jacket and fusilier's hat, didn't look like a civilian. What's more, he had been seen to be taking an active part in the battle. Being able to assess the size and the strength of the enemy commando, he decided his chances of being set free were slim indeed.

Contemplating his fate, he must have taken comfort in the thought that he did not have his Mauser on him and that his captor, unaware of the significance of the cartridges, had thrown the bullets away. His release would depend on General Joubert, 'from whom I had some hopes I should obtain assurances that my character as a press correspondent would be respected'.[4]

When examining the grounds on which Churchill claimed to be a non-combatant entitled to immediate release, it is evident the general was not particularly concerned about accepted principles pertaining to such a situation.

'I had enough military law to know that a civilian in a half uniform who had taken an active and prominent part in a fight, even if he has not fired a shot himself, is liable to be shot at once by drumhead court martial',[5] Churchill recorded. Standing anxiously in the pouring rain, he wondered 'what sort of appearance I could keep up if I were soon and suddenly told that my hour had come'.

Celia Sandys writes that General Joubert discussed the prisoner with 30-year-old Jan Smuts, then the Transvaal Attorney-General. The discussion did not centre on whether he was a civilian who had taken up arms, but simply on whether he was a civilian or a combatant. Smuts is supposed to have advised that Churchill's participation in the action cast him in the role of a combatant, so he should be held as a prisoner of war.

'In later years Smuts and Churchill would collaborate as world statesmen, but at their first meeting outside Joubert's tent, Smuts only saw a prisoner who was very young, unshaven, dirty-looking and very angry at my decision.'[6]

Smuts's greatest wish, during the first months of the war, was to take part in activities in the operational areas. He applied for permission to join General Erasmus in Natal, but this was turned down as the government believed that his administrative duties should take precedence. He visited the Natal front on occasions, but Churchill did not mention Smuts' presence in *My Early Life*, nor did Smuts mention discussing Churchill with Joubert in his book *Memoirs of the Boer War*.

The first time Jan Smuts and Churchill were known to have met was when the South African travelled on a private mission to London at the end of 1905 to present his *Memorandum of Points in Reference to the Transvaal Constitution*, setting out the case for self-government for the Transvaal to the Liberal Party. But he had to wait until the Liberal Party was elected to power in January 1906 before he met the new prime minister, Sir Henry Campbell-Bannerman, Lord Elgin, the Secretary of State; Winston Churchill, the Parliamentary Under-Secretary and David Lloyd George (a staunch supporter of the Boers) then president of the Board of Trade and later Prime Minister.

Churchill wrote in his dispatches to the *Morning Post* that, while he was waiting for a decision concerning his fate, unexpectedly 'a mounted man rode up and ordered the prisoners to march away to Colenso'. The escort was made up of 20 horsemen who closed around them. Churchill demanded from their leader that if he was not being taken to General Joubert, then his credentials should be given back to him. 'But the so-called field cornet [with them] was not to be seen. The only response was *Voorwaarts* [Forward]. As it seemed useless, undignified, and even dangerous to discuss the matter further with these people, I turned and marched off with the rest.'[7]

In *My Early Life* Churchill's version of the event had changed somewhat. As a result of the discussions in the tent, he was curtly told to rejoin the other prisoners. 'I felt quite joyful when a few minutes later the Boer field cornet came out of the tent and said, "We are not going to let you go, old chappie, although you are a correspondent. We don't catch the son of a lord every day."'[8]

Luck had again been on Churchill's side. His claim to be 'a non-combatant, immune from capture, or at any rate entitled to immediate release, if by ill-chance, his fate befell him, he pursued with considerable implausibility and great persistence'.[9]

Later when he was finally imprisoned in Pretoria, he submitted no less than three written requests for his release as a non-combatant to the Boer authorities, insisting that he had consistently adhered to his character as a press representative, and that, besides being unarmed, he had taken no part in the defence of the armoured train. When it seemed obvious that these letters would not secure his freedom and rumours came to his ears of an exchange of combatant prisoners, he changed his story. In a letter to the Assistant Adjutant-General at the War Office, he asked to be classified as a 'military officer'. This request he followed up — as will be seen later — with the promise that he would undertake 'any parole that may be required not to serve against the Republican forces or to give any information affecting the military situation'.

That Churchill fully appreciated the fact that his life had been spared by the Boers at Chieveley is evident from the following lines he wrote thirty years after he had been captured: 'The Boers were the most humane people where white men were concerned. Kaffirs were a different story, but to the Boer mind the destruction of a white man's life, even in war, was a lamentable and shocking event. They were the most good-hearted enemy I have ever fought against in the four continents in which it has been my fortune to see active service'.[10]

Churchill was elated when the prisoners' march continued. It is likely that the field cornet who brought him the news that he was not being released was the same Sarel Oosthuizen who had captured him earlier, but with Churchill being silent on the identity of the man we will never know for certain. What we do know is that he denied the Red Bull of Krugersdorp the glory of having caught the son of a lord. Churchill reserved this honour for a general who would become Prime Minister of a united South Africa.

In his autobiography *A Soldier's Saga*, Haldane noted the sudden change in his publicity-seeking companion when he wrote: 'Churchill must have been cheered by the thought, which he communicated to me, that what had taken place, though it had caused the temporary loss of his post as war correspondent, would help considerably in opening the door for him to enter the House of Commons. As we trudged wearily over the damp veld he remarked to me that in allotting him what I might call the "star turn" I had effaced myself, while his work of clearing the line had brought him into prominence'. The publicity-attracting hero had indeed been the 'star turn' of the armoured train disaster, but he was quick to promise that Haldane would get his fair share of praise.

Indeed, it was not long before Churchill's feeling of elation gave way to an immense sense of hopelessness. Walking alongside his fellow prisoners in the drenching rain to an unknown destination, the wretchedness of his misfortune hit him hard. There was no way he could suppress the brooding depths of melancholia as he thought of Atkins being free to send reports to the *Manchester Guardian* from the comfort of his tent at Estcourt, while his own future looked so gloomy.

By nightfall the weary band plodding along on the soaking veld had reached Colenso. Exhausted from the squelching six-hour march along muddy tracks, they were shepherded into a goods shed where at least they had some protection from the cold wind. The Boers lit two fires and invited the prisoners to come and dry themselves. The miserable group had not eaten since before they had left Estcourt that morning. They were given strips of meat cut from a newly slaughtered ox which they cooked over the fires. Some bales forage spread on the concrete floor provided them with bedding for the night.

Lying there buried in the short dry hay, too tired to sleep, Churchill listened to the Boers singing their evening psalms. 'A menacing note — more full of indignant war than love and mercy — struck a chill into my heart'.[11] He tried to justify the war and, being overcome with a severe bout of depression and mania, he wondered what kind of men the British were fighting. Fear that the Boers would gain the upper hand started to take hold of his tired mind.

The fires were probably insufficient to dry Churchill's clothes for he wrote in his despatch of 24 November: 'The night was cold and the wet clothes chilled and stiffened my limbs, provoking restless and unsatisfactory dreams'.[14] Rain fell heavily on the corrugated iron roof. Listening to the Boers chanting their psalms, the gloomy depression that had plagued him since his capture turned into a nightmare. His mind was telling him that the war was unjust. 'The Boers were better men than we, that heaven was against us, that Ladysmith, Mafeking and Kimberley would fall, that Estcourt garrison would perish, that foreign Powers would intervene, that we should lose South Africa, and that that would be the beginning of the end'.[15]

Haldane was not interested in philosophising about the causes of the war. He dismissed the 'pious God-fearing Boers' as hypocrites. 'Nightly, in every camp, the commandant assembles all his men who the call of duty does not take elsewhere, and before retiring to rest, a short time is devoted to prayer and praise',[12] he wrote in *How we escaped from Pretoria*. 'Honesty compels me to show the reverse of this picture. These very men, who are almost as full of apt texts as the great Cromwell's Ironsides, are far from acting up to the high religious sentiments that they profess. They are singularly untruthful, eminently boastful, lamentably immoral, and their ideas would do credit to a London pickpocket. My statement regarding their characteristics may seem sweeping; nevertheless it is true, and "Never trust a Dutchman" is a byword among the British in South Africa'.[12]

While his exhausted men made themselves as comfortable as was possible in the cold and damp shed, Haldane looked at the light filtering through the roof. Perhaps it might this very night provide the means of escaping from captivity, he thought. But finally, he was just too exhausted to put an escape plan into practice.

The following day the prisoners marched on until they reached a Boer camp at about midday. Haldane described it as 'resembling more a gypsy settlement than a military post'.[16] The commandant, Davel, invited them to share his tent. 'I have the most vivid and lasting recollection of the attention and kindness which this old Dutch farmer lavished upon us', Haldane noted in his report. 'Throughout the journey to the Boer metropolis we met with nothing but the greatest consideration; but this old commander not only gave us of the best he could — and at that time the Boer commissariat arrangements were in their infancy — but insisted on lending us some of his blankets, provided us with candles, and with his own hands brought us coffee on the following morning.'

He presented Churchill with a blanket, and we really felt quite sorry to leave his camp'.[17] The extraordinary hospitality shown by the commander towards the enemy who had invaded his country was perhaps what made Haldane empathise with a people he called rather unkindly 'rude tillers of the soil'.

On arriving at Elandslaagte station at 9:30am the rain started falling again. According to a Dr Keuzenkamp, who informed Randolph Churchill of the events in a letter dated 19 March 1963, the Boers rode to the small station of Modderspruit. It was still raining and the only dry place suitable to accommodate the prisoners was the baggage room. Churchill was singled out and shown to the ticket office. He noted that the copper grille under which tickets were sold made him think of a jail.

When the prisoners were ready to board the train, a young doctor named Thomas Visser, in charge of ambulances, attended to Churchill's hand. The wound had begun to fester, but after a new dressing was applied it seemed to heal rapidly.

On leaving Elandslaagte two Boers escorted the prisoners as far as Volksrust. One told Haldane that he had fired over a hundred rounds at the armoured train. To Haldane's amazement, for his successful feat he had been awarded 'a fortnight's leave to visit his wife, and not some costly war decoration.'[18] The other Boer, a bearded man who spoke little English, was indicated to the officers as the man who placed the rock on the line that derailed the train.

As for Churchill, there can no doubt that he would rather have had a medal for the part he played in getting the Chieveley wounded to safety than a spell of leave! 'In previous campaigns as a soldier he had sometimes been called a medal hunter', writes Celia Sandys, 'but in reality he had been seeking action, and having found it, he prized the medals which commemorate his participation'.[19]

At Volksrust, the first station inside the Transvaal border, Churchill, Haldane, and his second-in-command, Lieutenant Thomas Frankland of the Dublin Fusiliers, were joined by Sergeant-Major A Brockie of the Imperial Light Horse. Brockie had escorted Boer prisoners captured at Elandslaagte to Durban. While crossing the Klip River on his return to Estcourt, he was captured himself.

Brockie had removed and thrown away his regimental insignia and had told the Boers that he was a lieutenant in the Natal Carabineers. He knew that members of the Imperial Light Horse were despised by the Boers, for most of those serving in the corps — which had distinguished itself during the war — were residents of Johannesburg, and many had played roles in the Jameson Raid. Posing as an officer enabled him to join the officers in the first-class compartment of the train where he would be accorded courteous treatment. Also, in Pretoria he would not be locked up in a prisoner of war camp — or worse, in a jail — but would enjoy relative comfort amongst officers in a building reserved for them.

Brockie, a former miner from Johannesburg, was a talkative man. He had lived in Johannesburg for a number of years and knew the country well. Further, he could converse in Afrikaans, the language of the Boers, and he had some knowledge of Fanagalo, a kind of lingua franca that had evolved from numerous African languages. It was used by white miners to communicate with black miners on the Witwatersrand.

Finding a way to escape imprisonment is probably the first thing that comes to the mind of those unfortunate enough to find themselves in captivity. For Haldane it was an obsession from the outset. Brockie, with his knowledge of the country, the people and their language would be the ideal man to have at his side. Before long he was discussing the possibilities with the self-commissioned officer.

As for Churchill, everyone agreed that he would be released as a non-combatant on arrival in Pretoria, so the thought of including him in possible escape plans didn't enter their heads. They could not have foreseen, though, that newspaper reports concerning his heroic conduct during the attack on the armoured train would put paid to his chances of a speedy release.

As the train puffed along with its sullen captives, Haldane noticed the Boers following the 'strange and objectionable custom of firing at any game they may chance to see is within range'.[20] They passed a herd of buck at some distance, and although shooting animals from a moving train was prohibited by law, neither this nicety nor the fact that it was closed hunting season, mattered to them.

'Pop, pop, went the Mausers, the bullets knocking up the dust near the terrified animals. They galloped off apparently untouched, and I was glad to see that the vaunted marksmanship was at fault'.[21]

Sister Sophica Izedinova, the Russian nursing sister who came with the Russo-Dutch ambulance service to the Transvaal, described this behaviour as a characteristic pastime of the Boers. 'They are all crack shots and they regard it as the ultimate test of their skill to hit their target from a swift moving and jolting train, especially if the target is itself moving. Thus, when a distant buck is spotted running across the bare veld there is a salvo of shots and loud exclamations from the competing marksmen. At first we were alarmed by the sudden broadsides, which were strictly forbidden by the Government. Later we grew accustomed to them and either took no notice or ourselves followed with interest the result of the shooting'.[22]

Sister Izedinova relates an incident when a Russian volunteer on the side of the Boers shot a buck from a moving train and earned himself a great deal of respect. On the way to Bloemfontein EY Maximo — who was later appointed a general by the Boers — told inquisitive burghers that he was a correspondent. When a springbok was spotted on the veld, the Boers aimed their rifles at the animal but not a single bullet hit its mark. Maximov asked a burgher standing beside him to let him have a shot. The reply was that it was impossible to bring down the buck at that range, but he was welcome to try. Maximov adjusted the sights and fired. The bounding springbok fell. 'It was, of course, a lucky shot but reputations are made by shots like that in the Transvaal', Sister Izedinova recorded.[23]

Before the last light of day faded away, they passed a reminder that the Boers would not give up their country lightly. The prisoners stared at the distinctively shaped hill of solid rock called Majuba. It was there on 27 February 1881, during the first Anglo-Boer War, that 96 British soldiers were killed or wounded out of a force of 120. It was a British humiliation that Churchill intended to see revenged. That vengeance cannot bring true victory would had not have occurred to him at the time.

13

Captivity at the State Model School

The train took almost 24 hours to reach its destination, arriving at midday on 18 November in Pretoria. As soon as it came to a halt at the station, the doors of the carriages were unlocked. The officers were asked to step out and form a group, the other ranks another. It was a Sunday and many burghers had taken advantage of their day of rest to see the spectacle unfold in a town where diversions were limited. Churchill, always keen to be part of the attraction, was not exactly complimentary about the people who had come to stare.

'There was a considerable crowd of people to receive us, ugly women with bright parasols, loafers and ragamuffins, fat burghers too heavy to ride at the front, and a long line of untidy, white-helmeted policemen — Zarps — who looked like broken-down constabulary'. Thus did he unkindly record his first impressions in a dispatch to the *Morning Post*.[1] 'Zarps' was an acronym derived from the first letters of the official name of the Transvaal police, *Zuid Afrikaansche Republiek Polisie*.

As the prisoners disembarked from the train, the crowd parted to let them pass. 'About a dozen cameras were clicking, establishing an imperishable record of our shame', Churchill continued.[2] Reporters surrounded him and he became the only one mentioned by name in the Transvaal papers the following day. The fact that he was Randolph Churchill's son caused some excitement. One paper found his 'very youthful appearance' surprising, another stated that it was only necessary to get a glimpse of his 'mug' to see what a rogue he was.

The miserable looking officers stood around in the midday sun while the local populace gloated over them, Churchill could not suppress the dislike he felt for the enemy. 'The simple, valiant burghers at the front', he wrote, 'fighting bravely as they had been told for their farms, claimed respect, if not sympathy. But here in Pretoria all was petty and contemptible. Slimy, sleek officials of all nationalities — the red-faced, snub-nosed Hollander, the oily Portuguese half-caste — thrust or wormed their way through the crowd to look. Here were the creatures that had fattened on the spoils. There in the field were the heroes who won them.'[3]

The train ride had diverted Churchill's attention from the fact that imprisonment could not be avoided. He, the greatest hero of them all, had convinced himself that he was innocent of any wrongdoing. Now, he lamented, he was to be locked up like a common criminal. With the reality of the situation staring him in his face, he vented his misery by glaring at everyone in sight.

A hand on his shoulder interrupted his agony. 'A lanky, unshaven police sergeant' grasped his arm. "You are not an officer", he said; "you go this way with the common soldiers",'[4] and chivvied him over to the men forming columns of four. Haldane, anxious to keep Churchill with him, quickly pointed out to the 'burly, evil-looking police official'[5] that the prisoner was the son of a lord and he had come to South Africa not as a soldier but as a newspaper correspondent. As such he ranked as an officer and should be treated accordingly. But the sergeant pretended not to hear him.

More photographs were taken, one shows Churchill, wearing the Irish Fusilier's forage cap, standing clear of his fellow prisoners at the Pretoria station. The other ranks were to about be marched off to the racecourse camp in Pretoria West where temporary arrangements had been made to house captive non-combatant officers and men in tents behind barbed wire. Fortunately, Field Cornet Malan, a close relative of President Kruger, intervened and led him back to the line. Churchill described Malan as 'a superior official — superior in rank alone, for in other respects he looked a miserable creature'.[6]

British prisoners of war captured earlier had been marched from the station down Market Street, the main thoroughfare of the town (now known as Paul Kruger Street), to Church Square, and then on past the residence of President Kruger before reaching the prison. They were paraded as a kind of trophy for all of Pretoria to see. But since they were wearing khaki instead of the splendid red coats of the 1881 war, the burghers found it somewhat dull and boring and the novelty soon wore off and the parading discontinued.

The captured officers were taken to the State Model School at the corner of Andries and Skinner streets in central Pretoria, which had been converted into a prisoner of war camp. It is a handsome single-storeyed building of local sandstone and European red bricks typical of the late nineteenth century neo-Renaissance style. The South African Republic, anxious to establish a reputation as a prosperous and stable country, had commissioned the head of the Public Works Department, a Hollander by the name of Sytze Wopke Wierda, to design the school for the purpose of providing secondary education for boys and to serve as a teacher training institute. It was to be the 'model' for education in the young republic, hence its name, *Staatsmodelskool* or State Model School.

In a quadrangular 'playground', the Boers had erected a dozen tents for the police guards. Behind the school in a large open area were two tents for soldier batmen, a cookhouse and a shed where one could bathe. The latrines were at the south-eastern end of the property. An iron grill at the front of the building, facing Andries Street, extended along the northern boundary. Skinner Street at the southern side and a private property to the east were fenced off by a six-and-a-half feet-high corrugated iron fence.

There were 12 rooms in the main rectangle of the building. These were flanked at both ends by two large rooms, each of which were divided in the centre by a partition to form a total of 16 compartments. Seven or eight of these were used by the British officers as dormitories and one as a dining room. A lecture hall, which served as an improvised fives-court, and a well-fitted gymnasium were also provided. (The only dividing brick walls within the building were those in the rooms to the right and left of the main entrance, and through the large end-room abutting Skinner Street. The other dividers were made of solid wood. The partitions could be removed to provide larger classrooms when required.) Churchill, Haldane and his second-in-command, Lieutenant Frankland, were lodged in the centre of three rooms to the north of the main entrance, the windows of which faced Van der Walt Street.

Churchill, convinced that his incarceration was an act of gross injustice, lost no time in attempting to secure his release. His dispatch to the *Morning Post* could wait. What couldn't wait was a letter addressed to Louis de Souza, the Secretary of State for War of the South African Republic.

18 November 1899
Pretoria
Sir,

I was acting as special correspondent of the *Morning Post* newspaper with the detachment of British troops captured by the forces of the South African Republic on the 15th instant at Frere, Natal, and conveyed here with the other prisoners. I have the honour to request that I may be set at liberty and permitted to return to the British lines by such a route as may be considered expedient, and in support of this request I would respectfully draw the attention of the Secretary of State to the following facts:I presented my credentials as special correspondent immediately after the British forces surrendered and desired that they might be forwarded to the proper authority. This was promised, accordingly I was unarmed.

My identity has been clearly established. I desire to state that on my journey from the scene of the action to this town I have been treated with much consideration and kindness by the various officers and other burghers of the Republic with whom I have been brought into contact.

I am, Sir,
Your obedient servant
Winston Spencer Churchill
Special correspondent, *The Morning Post*, London[7]

Churchill wrote two more letters on the same theme to his mother and to Pamela. His

Name	Rank	Corps	Where captured	Date
Adye,W	Maj.	Staff	Nicholsonsnek	30.11.1899
Beasly, R. L.	Lt	I G. R.	Nicholsonsnek	30.11.1899
Blyth, E. W.	Insp.	C.M.P.	Barkley-West	15.11.1899
Breul, F. A.	Lt.	1 G.R.	Nicholsonsnek	30.10.1899
Brockie, A.	R.S.M.	1. L.H.	Bulwenskop	15.11.1899
Bryant, A.	Lt	1 G.R.	Nicholsonsnek	30.10;1899
Bryant, G. E.	Maj.	10 M.B.E.A.	Nicholsonsnek	30.10.1899
Burrow, A. R.	Col.	1 R.I.F.	Nicholsonsnek	30.10.1899
Cape-Vure, H.	Maj.	1 G.R.	Nicholsonsnek	30.10.1899
Carleton, F. R. C.	Lt. Col.	I. R.I.F.	Nicholsonsnek	30.10.1899
Churchill. W. S.	War Cor.	Morning Post	Blaauwkrans	15.11.1899
Conner, R.	Col.	I G.R.	Nicholsonsnek	30.10.1899
Crum, F. M.	Lt.	1 K.R.R.	Dundee	23.10.1899
Davy, R.M.M.	Lt.	1 G.R.	Nicholsonsnek	30.10.1899
Duncan, S.	Col.	1 G.R.	Nicholsonsnek	30.10.1899
Frankland, T.H.C.	2. Lt	2 R.D.F.	Blaauwkrans	15.11.1899
Gallway, W. J.	Lt.	N.C.	Bester-Station	19.10.1899
Garvice, C.	Lt.	2 R.D.F.	Dunde	20.10.1899
Ganillond, W. A.	Sub.Insp.	C.M.P.	Griekwastad	17.11.1899
Gray, R. J.	Lt/R.M.	1 G.R.	Nicholsonsnek	30.10.1899
Greyville, H. H.	Maj.	18 Hussars	Dundee	20.10.1899
Grimshaw. C. T. W.	Lt.	2 R.D.F.	Dundee	20.10.1899
Haldane, A. L.	Capt.	1 Gord. H.	Blaauwkrans	15.11.1899
Haserick, A. E.	Lt.	Rhod. Rgt.	Rhodesdrift	02.11.1899
Heard, A. E. S.	Lt.	1 R.I.F.	Nicholsonsnek	30.11.1899
Hill, W. J. B.	Lt.A.	I G.R.	Nicholsonsnek	30.11.1899
Hobbs, H.	Maj.	2 W.Y.R.	Willow Grange	23.10.1899
Hofmeyr, A. J. R.	Rev.		Lobatsi	15.10.1899
Holmes, H. B.	Lt.	1 G.R.	Nicholsonsnek	30.10.1899
Humphrey, S.	Maj.	1 G.R.	Nicholsonsnek	30.10.1899
Ingram, J.	Lt.	1 G.R.	Nicholsonsnek	30.10.1899
Jeudwine, R. W. R.	2/Lt.	1 R.I.F.	Nicholsonsnek	30.10.1899
Kelly, A. L.J. M.	Lt.	1 R.I.F.	Nicholsonsnek	30.10.1899
Kentish, R. J.	2/Lt.	1 R.I.F.	Nicholsonsnek	30.10.1899
Kinahaw, C. E.	2/Lt.	1 G.R.	Nicholsonsnek	30.10.1899
Knox, C. S.	Lt.	1 G.R.	Nicholsonsnek	30.10.1899
Le Mesurier, F. N.	Lt.	2 R.D.F.	Dundee	20.10.,1899
Lonsdale, M. P. E.	Col.	2 R.D.F.	Dundee	20.10.1899
Mcgregor, A.H.C.	Lt	1 R.I.F.	Nicholsonsnek	30.10.1899
Mackenzie, W. AS.	2/Lt.	1 G.R.	Nicholsonsnek	30.10.1899
Majandie, B. J.	Lt.	1 K.R.R.	Dundee	20.10.1899
Martin, G. H.	Lt.	1 K.R.R.	Dundee	23.10.1899
Moller, B.	Lt. Col.	18 Hussars	Dundee	20.10.1899
Moore, W. H.	Lt.	10 M.B.R.A.	Nicholsonsnek	30.10.1899
Munn, F. H.	Maj.	1 R.I.F.	Nicholsonsnek	30.10.1899
Nisbet, F. C.	Lt.	1 G.R.	Nicholsonsnek	30.10.1899
Nugent, G. H.	Lt.	10 M.B.R.A.	Nicholsonsnek	30.10.1899
Nugent, O.	Maj,	1 K.R.R.	Dundee	23.10.1899
Phipps, W. G. B.	Lt.	1 R.I.F.	Nicholsonsnek	30.10.1899
Pollock. W.P. M.	Col. A.	18 Hussars	Dundee	20.10.1899
Radice, A. H.	Lt.	1 G. R.	Nicholsonsnek	30.10.1899
Shore, F. H.	Lt.	1 G. R.	Dundee	30.10.1899
Shore, P. H.	Lt.	1 G.R.	Nicholsonsnek	30.10.1899
Smith, H. H.	2/Lt.	1 G.R.	Nicholsonsnek	30.10.1899
Southey, C. S.	Lt.	1 R. I.F.	Nicholsonsnek	30.10.1899
Temple, W. A. M.	Lt.	1 G.R.	Nicholsonsnek	30.10.1899
Wallace, W. W.	Maj.	1 G.R.	Nicholsonsnek	30.10.1899
Webb, G. T. W.	2/Lt.	R.A	Nicholsonsnek	30.10.1899
Wheeler, G. D.	Lt.	10 M.B.R.A.	Nicholsonsnek	30.10.1899

Roll of British officer POWs at the State Model School before Churchill's escape note to Jennie assured her that he had been unarmed when captured; was in possession of his full credentials as a press correspondent; and that he trusted her to do all in her power to procure his release. His letter to Pamela was confined to three short sentences. He noted that his current address was not a very satisfactory place to write from; stressed again that he had not been armed; had his full press credentials on his person; and how he often thought of her.

Stressing his status as an unarmed correspondent in both private letters was, no doubt, to divert attention from the active part he had taken during the ambush and, at the same time, to impress on the censors his non-combatant role.

In the dispatch he wrote later that afternoon on pages torn from an exercise book, he outlined the ambush and the actions he took in rescuing the wounded. He also mentioned the discussions he had with the Boers, calling them 'skilful pious soldiers' but deleting the word 'soldiers' and substituting it with 'burghers'.[8] His call for Boer prisoners to be shown all consideration was another tactic to arouse sympathy from the censors, but Commandant RWL Opperman was not impressed. He had been appointed chief officer at the State Model School a month before Churchill's arrival and was personally responsible for the safe custody of the prisoners. In his written objection to the letter, he pointed out 'persistent jingoistic attitudes which could encourage the enemy to send out more troops'.[9] Opperman's objection notwithstanding, a days later Churchill was given the privilege of writing whatever he wished.

While he kept himself busy with his correspondence, the *Natal Witness* compiled a report on the ambush of the train. In part, it said:

> Captain Wylie, who is doing well, describes Mr Winston Churchill's conduct in the most enthusiastic terms as that of a brave man as could be found. It was on Mr Churchill's initiative that Captain Wylie and a number of his men worked to get the trucks blocking the line out of the way. It was while he was co-operative with Mr Churchill in his work that Captain Wylie was shot through the hip. Before collapsing Captain Wylie succeeded in getting his head behind a large boulder, and there he lay on his face, helpless. While in that position, a shell struck the boulder and smashed it to pieces, without further injury to the wounded officer. When the engine came past again, he was placed on the tender. Previous to being shot down, Captain Wylie had seen that all his men were on the move in retreat.[10]

A letter by Inspector Campbell of the Natal Government Railways, addressed to the General Manager of the railways on behalf of the railway employees who escaped with the armoured train, was published along with the report. It read as follows:

> The railway men who accompanied the armoured train this morning ask me to convey to you their admiration of the coolness and pluck displayed by Mr

Winston Churchill, the war correspondent who accompanied the train, and to whose effort, backed up by those of the driver, Wagner, is due the fact that the armoured train and tender were brought successfully out, after being hampered by the derailed trucks in front, and that it became possible to bring the wounded in here. The whole of our men are loud in their praise of Mr Churchill, who, I regret to say, has been taken prisoner. I respectfully ask you to convey their admiration to a brave man.[11]

Randolph Churchill wrote: '... many of the reports on Churchill's part in the defence of the train suggested that he would be recommended for a Victoria Cross'.[12] He quotes a letter from Winston's servant Thomas Walden to Lady Randolph, informing her that Churchill was taken prisoner. The letter, published in the *Morning Post* of 12 December, gives details on what he had heard from Colonel Long about the fight on the armoured train .

There is no braver gentleman in the Army', the Colonel told him. The driver was one of the first wounded, and he said to Mr Winston 'I think I am finished.' So Mr Winston said to him: 'Buck up a bit, I will stick to you,' and he threw off his revolver and field-glasses and helped the driver pick 20 wounded up and put them on the tender of the engine. Every officer in Estcourt thinks Mr C and the engine-driver will get the VC.[13]

There was no doubt that the Boer authorities were fully informed of every detail concerning the conduct which led to his capture. They were also aware of the reports in the Natal newspapers and the letters and dispatches he had sent.

A day after Churchill's arrival in Pretoria, General Joubert addressed a telegram to FW Reitz, State Secretary of the Transvaal. The Dutch original can be found in the South African Government Archives in Pretoria. It translates as follows:

19 November 1899

I understand that the son of Lord Churchill maintains that he is only a newspaper reporter and therefore wants the privilege of being released. From a newspaper it appears entirely otherwise and it is for this reason that I urge you that he must be guarded and watched as dangerous for our war; otherwise he can still do us a lot of harm. In one word, he must not be released during the war. It is through his active part that one section of the armoured train got away.

A note on the telegram read:

The Government will act accordingly. Thereafter the Commandant-General's

Office will be instructed to act accordingly. F. W. R. (Reitz) 22. XI. 99.[16]

Joubert makes it clear that he had no intention of releasing the prisoner. But it was still early days. Churchill had only been in Pretoria for a day, and he had no doubt that he wouldn't remain a prisoner for long.

Meanwhile Sergeant-Major Brockie, who had been able to persuade his captors at the Pretoria West prison that he was indeed an officer, arrived at the school. He had been fortunate to find a Johannesburg acquaintance among the prisoners at the racecourse who suggested that he should keep his knowledge of Dutch to himself. He was thus able to follow the discussions of the officials and had sufficient time to prepare appropriate answers to questions of interrogation. Brockie was happy to be reunited with his friends and to share the dormitory with them. (Today the room is accessible from the inner passage and forms part of a larger one used as the Education Department's library. The marks of old partition walls are clearly visible on the flooring.)

Judging from Churchill's description of life as a prisoner, the inmate's lot was, under the circumstances, very tolerable. 'At the time of my coming into the prison, there was room enough for everyone',[14] he recorded. Every officer was given new clothes, bedding, and toiletries on arrival. In addition the storekeeper, a Mr Boshoff, 'was prepared to add to this wardrobe whatever might be required on payment either in money or by cheque on Messrs. Cox & Co., whose accommodation fame had spread even to this distant hostile town'.[15] The day started with a cup of coffee and a cigar or cigarette in bed. Breakfast was served at 9.00am. Churchill described it as a nasty and uncomfortable meal. 'The room was stuffy, and there are more enlivening spectacles than 70 British officers caught by Dutch farmers and penned together in confinement. Then came the long morning, to be killed somehow by reading, chess or cards — and perpetual cigarettes. Luncheon at one: the same as breakfast, only more so, and then a long afternoon to follow a long morning. Often some of the officers used to play rounders in the small yard which we had for exercise. But the rest walked moodily up and down, or lounged over the railings and returned the stares of the occasional passer-by'.[16]

The food consisted of 'a daily ration of bully beef and groceries. The prisoners were allowed to purchase from Mr Boshoff, practically everything they cared to order, except alcoholic liquors'.[17]

Among the prisoners was 'a very clever and energetic officer of the Dublin Fusiliers, Lieutenant Grimshaw, who undertook the task of managing the mess, and when he was assisted by another subaltern — Lieutenant Southey, of the Royal Irish Fusiliers — this became an exceedingly well-conducted concern'.[18]

Churchill mentioned that he usually sat next to Colonel Carleton at meals. The former spent a few days short of a month at the State Model School, yet Grimshaw, Southey and Carleton are the only officers he mentioned by name — besides, of course, Haldane, Frankland and the pseudo-officer Brockie.

The fact that alcoholic beverages were not allowed was contested by the officers. Representations were made to President Kruger himself, with the result that permission was granted for the buying of bottled beer. Meanwhile Louis de Souza, whom Churchill described as 'a kind-hearted Portuguese', would smuggle in a bottle of whisky 'hidden in his tail-coat or amid a basket of fruit'.[19] But there was the little 'fillip of excitement', Churchill wrote. 'One evening, as I was leaning over the railings, more than 40 yards from the nearest sentry, a short man with a red moustache walked quickly down the street, followed by two collie dogs. As he passed, but without altering his pace in the slightest, or even looking towards me, he said quite distinctly "Methuen beat the Boers to hell at Belmont."' [20]

Churchill had a sense of relief. The air felt cooler that night and the courtyard larger. He imagined the two Boer republics collapsing and the bayonets of the Queen's Guards in the streets of Pretoria. 'I had made a large map upon the wall and followed the course of the war as far as possible by making squares of red and green paper to represent the various columns', he claimed later.[21]

In spite of this assertion, it was Lieutenant Frankland — the artist among the prisoners — who drew the map of the Natal battlefields on a wall of the school. The officers who interpreted the various signals received from friendly Pretoria residents assisted him with the ongoing project and signed the cartographic mural. Frankland's signature can be clearly identified, but Churchill, who may have contributed to its early development by adding information he received from visitors, did not leave his name on the wall.

Next to the almost metre-high map, a drawing by Frankland of a large skeleton is a reminder of the senseless killings caused by the needless war. It can be seen to this day, along with the map itself, preserved behind glass in the historic State Model School building.

In order to explain the ingenious methods individuals employed to communicate developments in the war, a slight digression is necessary.

The person Churchill described as 'a small man sporting a red moustache' was unknown to the officers. He turned out to be a Mr Patterson who was the principal telegraphist in the Pretoria post office. Patterson passed the building rather frequently. It was not long before he attracted the attention of the men relaxing on the verandah facing Van der Walt Street by tapping out Morse code with his walking stick on the pavement.

The police became suspicious of the pedestrian, and realising this, he had to confine his messages to a few words, such as 'British victory', or 'Boers advanced'. The sentries also found his behaviour odd and it came as no surprise when he was asked to find another route for his daily walks. Undeterred, he devised another way of passing on information to the prisoners. A friend of his, a Mr Cullingworth, lived with his family in a house across the road from the school. Whenever Patterson visited the Cullingworths — and he did so often — he signalled his messages to the prison. His duties, however, did not allow him to pass by as regularly as he wished. Since he was by then well-known to the police and the sentries, there was also the danger that he could no longer hide his deception.

But Patterson was a resourceful man. He instructed two young ladies in the art of semaphore signalling. The police became suspicious of the attention the British officers paid to the house, but they never caught on that there was more to it than prisoners trying to sneak a glimpse of two young ladies. At a certain time the girls — believed to be Cullingworth's daughters — would appear well back from the open door. 'One would signal with a white flag, while the other, seated on the verandah, gave warning when a sentry or passer-by was approaching. By this means we now received, twice daily, the latest news, from the Boer point of view, of what went on at the front; and I believe that we were the recipients of the same telegrams which were laid before his Honour President Kruger'.[22]

Eventually, however, both Patterson and Cullingworth were conscripted as undesirable persons and sent to the front. The last message the officers received was that they intended to cross over to the British lines at the earliest opportunity. As it turned out, though, they were unsuccessful and were sent back to Pretoria as traitors. They were finally released by Lord Roberts' men when they entered the town.

'Lord Roberts showed his appreciation of what had been done for the officers by calling on the Cullingworths, and later on the officers, presented them and Mr Patterson mementoes bearing inscriptions indicative of the circumstances under which they came to be given.'[23]

The custody and regulating of the officer prisoners was entrusted to the board of management, four of whom visited them frequently and listened to complaints and requests. One of them, Louis de Souza — the 'kind-hearted Portuguese' — was the Secretary for War.

The second member was Dr WB Gunning, 'an amiable little Hollander, fat, rubicund and well-educated'. He had come to the Transvaal in 1896 and was the founder of the state museum and the zoological gardens in Pretoria. His enthusiasm for the zoo, however, led him into serious trouble. He had accepted the gift of a lion named Fanny from Cecil Rhodes. President Kruger is supposed to have reprimanded Dr Gunning personally, saying the presentation of this symbolic animal from the British imperialists was an insult to the Boers. Dr Gunning, so the story goes, confessed to Churchill that Kruger had spoken to him most harshly, and insisted that the 'objectionable' lion was returned forthwith.[24]

Also on the board was Commandant RWL Opperman, described by Churchill as 'a piece of miser'. In times of peace he was a *landdrost* or justice, but now he was too fat to go to the front. He would have gladly taken an active part in the fighting, but instead he had to be satisfied with being in charge of the prison.

A fellow prisoner was the Rev Adrian Hofmeyr. Celia Sandys describes him as 'a pastor of Dutch extraction, a colonial-born Afrikaner who had remained loyal to the Queen and who had urged both sides to compromise rather than go to war'.[25] Hofmeyr was pastor of Zeerust, a small town close to the present Botswana border. He had been suspended from his church for alleged immoral conduct. But that was not the reason for his captivity. Rather, it was because he had expressed an opinion about the conflict which did not coincide with the views of the Boers.

Hofmeyr readily agreed with Haldane when he characterised Opperman as 'not exactly the pattern of every virtue'. He called him 'a short, thickset man, generally very curt and uncourteous, and a terrible hater of the English'.[26] Opperman showed his lack of intelligence and common sense by telling the prisoners that if the country was conquered by the English, they would shoot him and reduce his wife to the rank of a servant; but before it came to that, he would shoot his wife and children himself and perish in the defence of the capital. However, he was convinced that the Boers would win the war.

The fourth member of the Board was Field Cornet Malan, the man who had rescued Churchill from being sent with the troopers to the racecourse. The two took an instant and intense dislike to one another. Not even the advantage of being Kruger's grandson 'could altogether protect him from taunts or cowardice, which were made even in the Executive Council, and somehow filtered down to us',[27] wrote Churchill. On one occasion, this 'foul and objectionable brute whose personal courage was 'better suited to insulting the prisoners in Pretoria than to fighting the enemy at the front, was reminded by Churchill that 'in war either side may win, and asked him whether he was wise to place himself in a separate category as regards behaviour to the prisoners',[28]

Churchill must have been pleased to learn that in August 1901, Malan was captured by the British and shipped off to a prisoner of war camp in Ceylon.

Churchill had only been at the State Model School a few days when fellow prisoners who had already explored all aspects of the building and observed the movements of the guards — began to formulate plans for an organised uprising that would include liberating the soldiers at the racecourse prison and end with Pretoria being occupied by the British. The seed for the plan had been sown by their erstwhile informant, Patterson, who offered to render any assistance he could.

Churchill had been busy with his correspondence. He had met most of the officers who had been taken prisoner in the early fighting, mainly at Nicholson's Nek. Although he agreed that their conditions of incarceration were very tolerable, he disliked nothing more than being locked up. 'I have certainly hated every minute of my captivity more than I have ever hated any other period in my whole life. You are in the power of your enemy. You owe your life to his humanity, and your daily bread to his compassion. You must obey his orders, go where he tells you, stay where you are bid, await his pleasure, possess your soul in patience.'[29]

The depressive Churchill had learnt that nothing would induce the recurring attacks of 'Black Dog' more readily than idleness and boredom. He had also discovered that action invariably remedied his suffering — when afflicted by a spirit of despair, throwing himself head over heels into action would lift his mood to extravagant heights. It was therefore not surprising that he was soon playing a leading role in the grandiose uprising the younger officers had been discussing.

The officers and their soldier servants were guarded by a total of about 40 Zarps. Ten of these were permanently positioned on the four sides of the enclosure in the centre of which the prison stood. Another ten were off duty and during the day they would be away from the school. The remaining 20 guards pursued their own interests in their tents in a corner of the yard, and at night the 30 Zarps not on duty slept the sleep of the just.

The whole compound was brightly lit by electric lights, fed by wires running through the officers' dormitories. An officer familiar with such matters had already demonstrated that it was easy to disconnect the wires and plunge the compound and its grounds into instant darkness. The guards in their tent could then be overpowered. Only the three sentries posted outside the spiked railing of the enclosure posed a problem. But Churchill was convinced that neutralising the men, who would be utterly bewildered, would not pose much difficulty.

Once the first phase of the break-out had been accomplished, the officers would have the rifles and pistols of their former captors. They would form 'an armed force superior in number and believed to be superior in discipline and intelligence to any organised body of Boers who could or would be brought against them for at least half an hour.[30]

Meanwhile the 2 000 hungry and dissatisfied prisoners at the racecourse had to be notified of the success of the operation at the school. They would be kept abreast of the plan by soldier-servants who, for one reason or another, were sent back in exchange for others. The soldiers would stage an immediate uprising and, assisted by the armed officers, would be able to break out and take control of Pretoria. Churchill had no doubt that 'President Kruger and his Government would be prisoners in our hands'.[31]

Some of the officers were so convinced that their scheme would succeed that they started stitching together a Union Jack to hoist on the day they occupied Pretoria and took the surrender of the Boers.

But the dream in reality bordered on the ridiculous and it never materialised. Churchill, who described the plan in great detail in *My Early Life*, wrote that it was vetoed by two or three senior officers, and he admitted that he could not fault their decision. One can sense Churchill's disappointment when he reminded his readers of the comic opera in which the villain impressively announces: 'Twelve thousand armed musketeers are ready to sack the town.' 'Why don't they do it?" he is asked. 'The police won't let them.'[32] With the great dream of occupying Pretoria and negotiating an honourable peace having come to naught, life at the State Model School dragged on.

The British officers were at liberty to exercise in the yard and borrow books from the government library. They could also divert their boredom by playing chess, whist and patience. They were allowed to receive visitors and read local newspapers, but the pro-Boer stance displayed by the Transvaal press was not exactly to their liking. The most widely read paper published in Dutch and English, *De Volksstem*, featured articles on Boer victories under bold headlines, and these reports Churchill found most depressing. It is true that not all was going well for the British forces, but Churchill dismissed the reports as lies disseminated for propaganda purposes.

It is understandable that the officers — professional soldiers who had come to South Africa to see action instead of idling around in a school building — were frustrated at their boredom. But no one was more irritated by their fate than Churchill. He needed to be out in the field achieving fame and glory. He was not a man who could sit around playing games and exercise in the yard which did not appeal to him. Neither newspapers nor visitors took his mind off the confined surroundings. He lodged a complaint about his captivity when Louis de Souza arrived in the company of a Reuter's agent, Mr Mackay, and a Mr Grobbelaar who was the Under Secretary of Foreign Affairs.

On 25 November Mr Macrum, the American Consul in Pretoria, visited him at the request of Jennie. Churchill expressed surprise at the lack of sympathy the Americans were showing for Britain, and he decided to tour the United States and lecture on the war as soon as he could.

It is possible that Macrum told him the Boers were considering an exchange of prisoners, for the following day he addressed a letter to Lord Milner. In it he reiterated his constant theme that he was unarmed at the time of his capture, and that his status as a press correspondent and non-combatant had not been taken into consideration by the Boers. He had no complaints about his treatment by the authorities and did not want to cause any problems, but if any exchange of prisoners was being arranged, Milner should do his best to have him included.

His numerous written and verbal requests to be set free had thus far been ignored by the Boer authorities. But Churchill was not a man to give up easily. Perhaps another letter to de Souza would change his attitude. He wrote:

26 November 1899

Sir,

In further support of my application for release on the grounds that I am a non-combatant and a Press correspondent forwarded to you on the 18th instant, I have the honour to urge the following facts:

1. I have consistently adhered to my character as a press representative, taking no part in the defence of the armoured train and being quite unarmed. Although in any case the onus probandi that I have departed from the non-combatant attitude would rest with the Government of the South African Republic, I append hereto a certificate from the officer who commanded the train. I have learned that it is alleged that I took an active part in the said

defence. This I deny, although being for an hour and a half exposed in the open to artillery of the Transvaal force, naturally did all I could to escape from so perilous a situation and to save my life. Indeed in this aspect my conduct was precisely that of the civilian platelayers and railway servants, who have since been released by your Government.

2. My case while under detention as a prisoner of war had doubtless attracted a great deal of attention abroad and my release would be welcomed as a graceful act of correct international behaviour by the world's press.

3. The kindness and consideration with which I have been treated by the burghers in the field and by various members of the Executive in Pretoria has left a pleasant impression in my mind and if I am released from my mistaken imprisonment, I am at least as likely as anyone else to chronicle the events of the war with truth and fairness.

4. My further detention as a prisoner will certainly be attributed in Europe and America to the fact that being well-known I am regarded as a kind of hostage; and this will excite criticism and even ridicule.

5. I am willing — though I desire to continue my journalistic work — to give any parole the Transvaal Government may require viz. either to continue to observe non-combatant character or to withdraw altogether from South Africa during the war.

6. The *Morning Post* newspaper will pay all expenses the Government of the South African Republic has been or may be put to on my account.

7. I have the honour to request that in the common courtesy of war I may be favoured with an answer to this and my previous application explaining the attitude whichthe Transvaal authorities propose to adopt respecting me, and the reason for it.[33]

I am, Sir, Your obedient servant
Winston Spencer Churchill
Sp correspondent, *The Morning Post*

Churchill's passionate plea again fell on deaf ears and his request to be treated with common courtesy was ignored. But he was not forgotten by the Boer authorities.

On 28 November, General Joubert sent the following telegram to Francis Reitz, Transvaal State Secretary:

I see a rumour in the newspapers that the son of Lord Randolph Churchill,

Lieutenant Churchill, reporter of the *Morning Post*, is to be released by the Government. I object most strongly against this. If this person is released then any prisoner of war whatever may as well be released for he played a very active part at the armoured train and led the soldiers in the attempt to let the train escape. He was thus made prisoner of war while seriously hampering our operation. He must therefore be treated like other prisoners of war, and, if necessary, be even more strictly guarded.[34]

Reitz was in full agreement with Joubert. When the former came to Pretoria for a few days, Churchill asked to meet him. 'We passed through the sentries into a large classroom where he was playing chess with fellow prisoners', his son Deneys, who accompanied him, wrote in *Commando*. 'He said he was a non-combatant but a war correspondent, and asked to be released on that account. My father, however, replied that he was carrying a Mauser pistol when taken and so must remain where he was. Winston Churchill said that all war correspondents in the Sudan had carried weapons for self-protection and the comparison annoyed my father, who told him that the Boers were not in the habit of killing non-combatants'.[35]

Reitz's reply to Joubert's letter was equally short:

Your telegram re Lieutenant Churchill. The Government does not intend to release Mr Churchill.

Early in December Churchill was notified of the government's decision not to release him, but this did not deter him from writing yet another letter to Louis de Souza:

8 December 1899

Sir,

1. I understand that the question of my release rests ultimately with the Commandant-General and I, therefore, request that my previous application may be forwarded to him so that he may have an opportunity of hearing my side of the case.
2. I would point out that I did not fight against the Boer forces, but only assisted in clearing the line from debris. This is precisely what the civilian platelayers and railway staff did. They have since been released.
3. I have now been kept a close prisoner for 24 days.
4. If I am released I will give any parole that may be required not to serve against the Republican forces or to give any information affecting the military situation.

I am, Sir, Your obedient servant
Winston Spencer Churchill
Sp correspondent, *The Morning Post* [36]

After reading the letter General Joubert decided to look more favourably at Churchill's case. On 12 December he wrote the following letter to FW Reitz:

Referring to your request by Lieutenant Churchill which was forwarded to me, I desire to state that he is entirely unknown to me; and I would not in the least have noticed him if the British newspapers had not mentioned him as being Lieutenant Churchill, with an account of all the highly appreciated services rendered by him in the British Army for years and on different occasions. These culminated in the attacks on the armoured train, when, owing to his actions, the engine or a section of the train escaped being captured. It is even mentioned in an exaggerated way that but for his presence on the train, not a single Englishman or soldier would have escaped. After the train was forced to a standstill, the officers and men would definitely have fallen into enemy hands had he not directed proceedings in such a clever and thorough way, whilst walking alongside the engine, that the train together with its load escaped capture. This became known throughout the world, and I suppose the British Empire, through the newspapers. All this however is denied by Mr Churchill, and I have to accept his word in preference to all the journalists and reporters. If I accept his word, then my objections to his release cease. Seeing that a parole was promised him and that he suggested leaving Africa to return to Europe where he would report and speak only the truth of his experiences — and if the Government accepts this and he does — then I have no further objections to his being set free, without our accepting somebody else in exchange.

PJ Joubert, Commandant

PS Will he tell the truth? Or will he also be a chip off the old block? [37]

Joubert's postscript leaves no doubt that he did not fully trust Churchill. 'Will he tell the truth, or will he also be a chip off the old block' is a reference to Randolph Churchill's cavalier treatment of the Boers when he visited South Africa in 1891.

Churchill claimed that he 'wrote two letters, one to the Secretary of State for War and one to General Joubert; but needless to say, I did not indulge in much hope of the result, for I was firmly convinced that the Boer authorities regarded me as a kind of hostage, who would make a pleasing addition to the collection of prisoners they were forming against a change of fortune. I therefore continued to search for a path of escape'.[38] The fact that Churchill wrote three letters to the Boer authorities during his

24 days of imprisonment; that he requested Lord Milner to have him exchanged for a Boer prisoner; and that he persuaded Captain Haldane to vouch for him being unarmed at Chieveley; points to him believing that it was only a matter of time before he was set free.

The following day De Souza told Haldane that he had received a telegram from General Joubert authorising Churchill's unconditional release from imprisonment. But ironically, Churchill had already escaped. Even if he had known that he would be allowed to walk out of the State Model School, it is difficult to imagine him following the conventional route, rather than testing his proverbial luck.

14

The escape

Churchill, of course, was unaware of Joubert's letter. He might have believed that it was his divine right to be set free, and that it was only a matter of time before the Boers came to the same realisation. Nevertheless, when the opportunity to escape presented itself, he was not prepared to wait for fate to deliver his freedom.

Apart from the fantasy of overpowering the guards, freeing the prisoners held at the racecourse and occupying Pretoria, there is no evidence that Churchill had devised any independent plans to escape. Why risk being caught and thrown in jail — or even killed — when there was an easier way out?

In a despatch of 12 December, 1899 he wrote: 'Before I had been an hour in captivity I resolved to escape. Many plans suggested themselves, they were examined, and rejected. For a month I thought of nothing else. But the peril and difficulty restrained action. I think it was the report of the British defeat at Stormberg that clinched the matter'.[1]

In *My Early Life* he wrote that as soon as he learned of General Joubert's decision to have him treated as a prisoner of war, 'in the first week of December, I resolved to escape'.[2] Churchill had heard that Lieutenant-General Gatacre had been defeated at Stormberg in the Cape on 10 December and that 696 of his men were missing or captured. Whether General Joubert's decision to keep him as a prisoner of war decided him on escape, or the upsetting news of Gatacre's defeat was the turning point, does not matter. His despatch as well as his report in *My Early Life* leaves little doubt that by the second week of December he was serious about escaping.

As we have seen, Captain Haldane was also obsessed with escaping. He did not, however, believe in an uprising and was one of the officers who had turned down the ambitious plan the younger men had hatched. But Haldane had his own plan. On arriving at the school, he carefully noted that the guards comprised 27 men and three corporals; nine sentries at a time worked in relief shifts of four hours. Five sentries were posted outside the enclosure and four guarded the grounds within. Equipped with Lee-Metford rifles and revolvers, they wore bandoliers of cartridges and had whistles dangling around their necks with which to sound the alarm. These ragged men must have looked scary, but their rifles were not loaded and their discipline showed a distinct lack of training. They didn't seem to be any great obstacle for a prisoner who was determined to escape.

Haldane soon suggested to Brockie, whom he considered an essential ally because of his linguistic skills and knowledge of the country, that they could escape by jumping the fence behind a circular latrine at the eastern border of the property. The area was not fully lit and the sentry had a habit of moving away to chat with a fellow guard while dinner was being served to the prisoners. If they hid in the latrine they could climb onto its roof at sunset and jump into the garden on the far side of the fence. Once clear of the school, they would have to find the railroad, hide on a coal train and travel to safety in Portuguese East Africa (now Mozambique).

The guards who patrolled the streets of Pretoria came on duty at sunset — round 6.30pm to 7.00pm. Armed with revolvers, and in some instances accompanied by dogs, they were primarily concerned with protecting property; pedestrians walking around the area were not bothered unless they looked suspicious although at night they could demand to see passes. The guards patrolling the streets near the school seemed to be kept busy, for whistle blasts were frequently heard. Haldane was not overly concerned about them. What worried him were the mounted patrols on the outskirts of town because they kept a close watch on the main exit routes and checked the passports of people leaving by train.

On 1 December Haldane and Brockie decided that the time had come to take action. The first set of clothes offered to Haldane's party were bright mustard in colour which would certainly have turned the heads of passersby. Fortunately they were found to be too small so they were exchanged for less conspicuous ones. Suitable headgear, too, posed no problem. Almost anything — besides guns of course — was for sale from Mr Boshoff. A railwayman had already given Haldane a slouch hat at the time of his capture and Churchill borrowed one from Rev Hofmeyr shortly before his escape.

In addition to clothing and luxury items Boshoff gathered in snippets of information concerning the outside world while the attention of Commandant Opperman, who supervised all transactions, was distracted. Haldane found that even a forged passport could be obtained at a price.

Haldane resolved that his only method of successfully escaping and getting back to the front would be by hitching a ride on a train leaving Pretoria. Timetables were published in the local newspapers and he tore out a small map from a book in the library. A compass and food rounded off the emergency supplies that he and Brockie required. The easiest way to get out of the State Model School, they agreed, was to offer a bribe to the guard nearest to the latrine.

According to the timetable a train left the station daily at 11.10pm. They would find a steep gradient where it was forced to slow down and jump aboard If this proved impossible they would trek 13 miles through the bush to Eerste Fabrieken Station and somehow get aboard a train when it stopped there. The trains travelled to the terminus at Middelburg via Balmoral and Witbank. The fugitives planned to get off in the vicinity of Balmoral station where there were coal mines and transfer to a coal truck in a siding and, hopefully, this would take them across the Portuguese East African border and on to Lourenço Marques.

Haldane and Brockie made ready to put their plan into action, but on 7 December, two soldier servants, David Bridge, a trooper of B Squadron of the 19th Hussars, who was billeted in a tent in the yard, had managed to scale the fence, together with a man called Joe Cahill, a 'Cape boy sent in to help us cook' of the 18th Hussars, had escaped by climbing over the six-foot corrugated iron wall at precisely the same spot that Haldane had chosen for his and Brockie's escape route.

Some officers there had assisted in their escape. Captain Pollok had lent Bridge £3.7.6 and Major HF Greyville had given them a tin of biscuits. Both officers wished the men good luck and for days talked with delight about the two getting away successfully. Some of the guards knew about the incident, but obviously felt it was in their interests not to notify the prison authorities. They would no doubt have disciplined the sentries for their laxity and tightened up security. Since no roll call was ever taken, the powers-that-be remained none the wiser.

Haldane mentioned his and Brockie's plan to Churchill. The two had not considered including him because they knew he was expecting an early release because of his status as a non-combatant.

On 9 December Churchill told Haldane that his hopes of an early release had faded and he asked to join in their escape plan. Haldane, however, was apprehensive about agreeing to this. 'Besides, he felt that Churchill was attracting too much attention to himself by engaging in animated discussions as to who was to blame for the war. Added to this, he was temperamental and unaccountable.'[4] Another point that bothered him was Churchill's impatience and intolerance towards others. He had noticed that when men were whistling, Churchill made no effort to hide his irritation. So Haldane told him that he had received too much publicity and he would easily be recognised which would pose a danger to them all. The risk of him joining them was simply too great.

Churchill had indeed become a public figure. He had been visited by Louis de Souza, Secretary of State for War, FW Reitz, the Transvaal State Secretary, the American Consul, and a number of journalists. People walked along Van der Walt Street in the hope of spotting this son of an English lord among the officers on the verandah. Some had even tried to photograph him. On Sunday afternoons the young folk of Pretoria promenaded up and down the street in groups opposite the school.

The number of ladies amongst those curious onlookers was surprisingly high and could perhaps be ascribed to the fact that many men had signed up for commando duties. One such lady was said to have shown such an inappropriate interest in trying to attract Churchill's attention that a policeman could not help but notice her.

Later, after Churchill's escape, anyone English in Pretoria was immediately suspected of complicity. There was no evidence that the young lady concerned could in any way be linked to the breakout, but she was nevertheless arrested by the observant policeman and fined £25.

Churchill had made up his mind. He refused to accept Haldane's decision and continued badgering him to be taken along. He even tried to entice the captain by pointing out that if they were successful, he would ensure his name was emblazoned triumphantly across the press. Haldane was taken aback. He knew that as an officer it was his duty to try to escape, but seeking publicity for escaping was not something he was prepared to indulge in. He nonetheless told Churchill that he would discuss the matter with Brockie and inform him of their decision. Brockie was as much against taking Churchill along as Haldane was. But Churchill would have none of it.

Churchill cornered Haldane. 'I could have escaped aboard the armoured train at Chieveley', he argued, but had chosen to stay. When Haldane proved adamant, Churchill reminded him of the gratitude he had expressed for his, Churchill's, conduct on the day of their capture.

Haldane again discussed the question with Brockie. Although both believed that a third person would be a hindrance, they finally succumbed to Churchill's emotional pressure. 'We consented', Haldane later wrote, 'though the certainty that he would be missed within a few hours lessened the chances of success. As for Brockie and me, we knew that our absence would hardly be noticed since at this time no rollcalls were held and no apparent record of the number of prisoners at the State Model School were kept'.[5]

Churchill was well aware of the difficult situation in which he had placed his comrades, but emphasised that he didn't think it would be fair to blame him if the escape was unsuccessful. Haldane accepted this, but insisted that as the leader of the group his orders should be obeyed.

The date for the escape was set for 11 December. Churchill was 'in a great state of excitement, telling everyone he was escaping, even though Haldane had asked him to keep quiet'.[6] Aghast at Churchill's enthusiasm, he had renewed doubts about whether it was wise to take the impulsive and loquacious fellow along.

Another problem of concern was Churchill's state of fitness. Haldane had noticed that he stood aloof while the other prisoners played fives and rounders and tried to keep themselves fit by skipping. Furthermore, Churchill had been complaining that the shoulder he had dislocated when disembarking in Bombay three years earlier was still causing him considerable discomfort. Haldane was concerned that Churchill might not be able to reach the top of the latrine without a 'leg up', and this would considerably hamper their escape bid. But Churchill could not be held back.

Shortly before the bell rang at 7.00pm to announce dinner, Haldane, Churchill and Brockie, accompanied by a few officers who had been told of the plan, walked to the lavatory. The officers would return to the main building separately at short intervals giving the impression that everyone had done so. They thought it doubtful that the sentry would pay much attention to this and in any case he would soon resume his routine patrolling.

It was intended that Haldane would give Churchill a leg up to avoid him kicking the metal side of the structure and attracting the sentry's attention. Haldane would follow immediately afterwards. Brockie would follow after checking that the two had got safely over the fence.

Luck, however, was not on their side. The sentry remained in position and after waiting for some time, Haldane and Churchill had no option but to postpone their breakout for another evening. To Churchill this meant the following evening. 'I was determined that nothing should stop me taking the plunge the next day',[7] he wrote in *My Early Life*. It was clear that his mind was set on escaping,, regardless of what his compatriots did.

Over the years there have been various interpretations of what happened on the following day. In his own account Churchill claims to have been compelled to obfuscate in order to protect his fellow prisoners as well as helpers on the outside. According to an account that he wrote in 1912 in connection with a court case concerning libellous interpretations of the escape, he was 'a party to all the discussions about plans for escape from the very first day of our captivity, and the only reason why I did not decide to go with them until about a week before the time, was that I expected to be released by the Transvaal Government as a civilian'.[8] With regard to who should go first, he wrote 'there was no more agreement, or bargain, or stipulation, or how we should go, than there is among a dozen people in the hunting field who are waiting to take their turn at an awkward gap'.[9]

The next day Churchill's depression had reached its zenith. Haldane looked on with concern as he paced up and down the yard, his head lowered and his hands clasped tightly behind his back. When Haldane spoke to him he insisted he would be going that night. Haldane was alarmed. He tried to calm his agitation, saying that if circumstances were favourable, they would certainly try again. But Churchill must remember, he added, that there were three of them involved.

'As the 12th wore away, my fears crystallised more and more into desperation',[10] Churchill recalled in *My Early Life*. Haldane must have felt the tension when the two went back to the roundhouse to await their second attempt to scale the fence. Once again a group of officers accompanied them and then returned to the main building singly as a diversion. Haldane and Churchill, conscious that the sentry was watching them, dawdled around for some time. After much hesitation they decided it was too dangerous and returned back into the camp

Brockie wanted to know why they had not made the breakout. He brushed Haldane's explanation aside and accused them of being afraid. 'I could get away any night', he grumbled, but Haldane cut him short, telling him to go and see for himself. Brockie accordingly walked across the yard to the latrine.

Before he returned Churchill's impatience overcame him. According to the account he wrote in 1912, he felt strongly that they would waste the whole night in hesitation unless someone acted. He told Haldane that he was going over the fence and asked not to be followed immediately. He met up with Brockie as he was leaving the roundhouse. Brockie whispered something but Churchill didn't catch what he had said and being within earshot of the sentry they dared not hold a conversation.

Churchill watched the sentries through a hole in the metal wall of the latrine. The moon was full and his anxiety peaked as he waited for the guards to move on. He was simmering over Brockie's remark of being afraid and this added to his agitation. Finally, after half an hour, one of the guards walked over to his colleague for a chat and their backs were turned.

The moment had come. In 1912 Churchill described it thus: 'As the sentry turned to light his pipe, I jumped to the ledge of the fence, and in a few seconds had dropped into the garden safely on the other side'.[11]

In *My Early Life,* published in 1930, Churchill's escape via the roundhouse was not quite as simple as he had portrayed it in 1912:

> Through an aperture in the metal casing of which it was built, I watched the sentries. For some time they remained stolid and obstructive. Then all of a sudden one turned and walked up to his comrade, and they began to talk. Their backs were turned.
>
> Now or never! I stood on a ledge, seized the top of the wall (sic) with my hands, and drew myself up. Twice I let myself down again in sickly hesitation, and then with a third resolve scrambled up and over. My waistcoat got entangled with the ornamental metal-work on the top. I had to pause for an appreciable moment to extricate myself. In this posture I had one parting glimpse of the sentries still talking with their backs turned fifteen yards away. One of them was lighting a cigarette, and I remember the glow on the inside of his hand as a distinct impression which my mind recorded. Then I lowered myself lightly down into the adjoining garden and crouched among the shrubs. I was free![12]

The seconds Churchill needed to scale the fence — as recorded in his 1912 memorandum — had by the 1930 version of the events, become a daring escape. What he had described as a straightforward jump over a fence had, some 18 years later, turned into three desperate attempts to reach the top of a wall. Once he had mounted the barrier, he needed an 'appreciable moment' to disentangle his waistcoat; while doing so he had enough time to get a 'distinct impression' of the glow of a cigarette — as opposed to a pipe — in the sentry's hand. These contradictory statements admittedly concern minor details, but they come from a man who ruthlessly attacked others for their interpretation of this event. What is surprising is that Churchill, who did not lack imagination when it came to embellishing his adventures, never mentioned his injured shoulder.

In *My Early Life* Churchill claims to have waited for an hour 'in great impatience and anxiety'[13] for his friends to come. Covered by the dark shadows of the bushes protecting him from the light of the full moon, he observed General Meyer's house, in whose garden he had landed. The lights were burning and many people could be seen passing the windows. A man came out of the house and walked towards him. He stopped within a few yards of the fugitive and stared into the dark. Then another man joined him and lit a cigar. The moment they started to move on, a cat being chased by a dog screeched out as it collided with Churchill. The two men turned their heads, but seeing the cat and the dog running away, they walked on towards the gate in Skinner Street.

Having caught his breath Churchill heard men talking on the other side of the fence. He could not make out what they were saying, but then he caught his own name. They were officers sent by Haldane to contact him. He crawled close to the wall and coughed to make his presence known. While one of the officers jabbered noisily to cover the speech of the other, Churchill heard: 'They cannot get out. The sentry suspects. It's all up. Can you get back again?' [14]

General Meyer, the owner of the house bustling with activity, had been wounded during the Battle of Ladysmith and sent home. A gathering of some sort was taking place at his house at the time of Churchill's escape. It is unlikely that Churchill was aware that the garden in which he was hiding belonged to a Boer general who was a prominent veteran of the First Anglo-Boer War (1880-81), for he would no doubt have mentioned this in *My Early Life*.

Churchill's claim in *My Early Life* that he had waited for an hour for his friends to join him, extended to more than an hour and a half in a lengthy report he prepared in connection with the lawsuit he instigated against William Blackwood in 1912. Haldane knew that the moon would rise at about 7.45pm 'and illuminate the dark spot where we meant to break out'.[15] The opportunity was a fleeting one. 'There is many a slip, as the proverb has it, and Brockie and I were doomed to disappointment',[16] he wrote later in *How we escaped from Pretoria*. 'Churchill saw his chance and took it, but when I tried to follow, the sentry, who now obstinately stuck to his post, saw me and escape was impossible. I will not dwell longer on this unsuccessful attempt, for on the principle that things without remedy should be without regard: what's done is done'.[17]

Churchill must have wondered if Haldane and Brockie had managed to get away. When he heard an officer in the latrine, he tapped the iron fence to attract his attention. He asked him to let Haldane know that he was out of the compound and waiting for him. In a while Haldane arrived. He and Brockie had gone to the dining-room to have a quick dinner. They then went to the dormitory to see if Churchill was there. When an officer told them that he was on the other side of the fence, they thought of following immediately. But the sentry was back at his post and they had to wait until he moved again.

By the time Haldane returned to the latrine, he was getting desperate. He pulled himself up the barrier, but he had not chosen his moment carefully enough. The sentry saw his head and shoulders rising from the darkness into the light of the full moon. He pointed his rifle and ordered him to turn back.

As he dropped to the ground Haldane heard Churchill asking for Brockie who, with

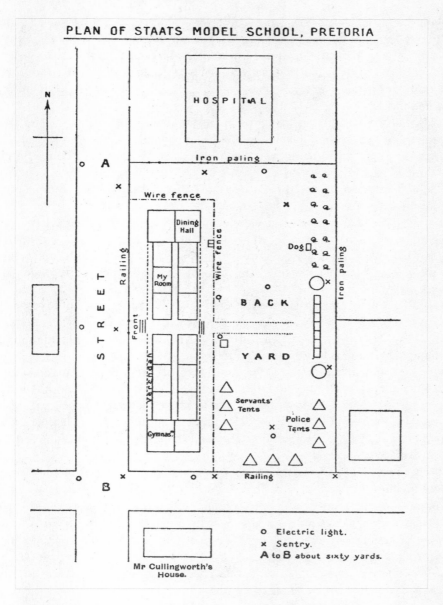

Plan showing Winston Churchill's escape from the State Model School.
Taken from Capt Haldane's *How we Escaped from Pretoria*.

his knowledge of the local language, could help him find food. Haldane was disgusted at the thought that Churchill was concerned only with his own well-being and he replied that neither of them could make it.

Churchill was in a dilemma. He could not climb back into the yard for there was no ledge on the garden side of the fence. As the excitement of getting away subsided, it occurred to him that he was somewhat lost without Brockie. Since he did not speak Afrikaans or any African language, how could he buy food without being detected? Without a compass or even a map, he would have to hide during the day and walk by night through hostile country he knew nothing about. This was more than he had bargained for.

But Haldane, designated as leader of the group, had surely discussed the railway timetables and how to find a train that could take them to the border of Portuguese East Africa. Yet Churchill painted his situation as so hopeless that he would gladly have climbed back over the fence.

As he contemplated his predicament, Haldane urged him to move on. Suddenly Churchill realised that he was on his own.

It is not difficult to imagine that Haldane and Brockie were furious. The escape had been planned by them; Churchill had begged to come along yet he had left them high and dry. They felt betrayed. Their fellow prisoners agreed, complaining that Churchill was not even a legitimate officer, but his actions had spoiled everybody else's chances.

Churchill's own version of his escape was first published by way of his dispatches in *The Morning Post*. The articles were reprinted in his book *From London to Ladysmith via Pretoria*. Thirty years after the event, an embellished and dramatised account appeared in his biography *My Early Life*.

Before we follow the footsteps of Churchill further, it is imperative to remember the two soldier-servants who had escaped only five days earlier.[18] Churchill made no mention of the two men in his writings. That he knew about them is beyond question.

Perhaps Churchill felt that any publicity given to Bridge, a private soldier, and his companion, a 'Cape boy', might have lessened the impact of public opinion on his own dramatised escape.

Churchill made a brief reference to others who escaped from the school. 'Curiously enough three out of our four at different times and in different circumstances made their escape from the State Model School; and with one exception we were the only prisoners who ever succeeded in getting away from them',[19] he wrote in *My Early Life*. The escapees mentioned included himself, Captain Haldane, Lieutenant Frederick Neil Le Mesurier and Sergeant Brockie.

The 'Cape boy' was neither seen nor heard of again. But this was of little or no interest to the officers, least of all Churchill.

Trooper David Bridge described in a diary the details of his and Joe Cahill's escape and his subsequent recapture and imprisonment at Waterval prison outside Pretoria. This was later published in the *Kettering Guardian* in Britain under the title 'Prison Life with the Boers'. The story was many years later reprinted in Johannesburg as Diary of David Bridge in the March 1979 issue of *Africana Notes and News*.

Bridge had landed in Durban on 29 October 1898. His regiment was garrisoned in Ladysmith before being ordered to march to Dundee. When war was declared, the

Hussars were engaged in patrolling the Natal border.

Early on Friday 20 October, 900 Boers with three guns under the command of Generals Lucas Meyer and Louis Botha, took possession of Talana — a hill rising about 600 feet to the east of Dundee. They began shelling the British camp, but a counter-attack ended with the Boers being driven off. Later that day another fight broke out and the British made a stand in a farmhouse. The Boers brought a gun into play and with no artillery to fight back with the Hussars decided to surrender.

The prisoners were taken to the Navigation Mines where they spent the night in the workmen's houses before being marched off to Dannhauser station about 12 miles away. From there they travelled by train to Pretoria. A large crowd gathered to watch them paraded through the town. On reaching the race course the prisoners were put into the pavilion enclosure. They were each issued with a blanket, a plate, a mug and a spoon, as well as a communal cooking pot. The daily food consisted of a small loaf of bread, a half pound of tinned meat, a few potatoes, a little rice, tea and occasionally sugar. Two weeks after this a further 1 200 more prisoners arrived from Modderspruit. With this large influx, the food ration was halved.

On 4 November the officers were moved to the State Model School. Trooper Bridge was detailed to help with the cooking there. He and the other soldier servants were accommodated in two tents in the yard. Their day started at 5:30am and they worked throughout the day until dinner was over at 8.30pm in the evening. They were paid ten shillings per month and had to put up with continual complaints about the quality of the cooking. Bridge recorded in his diary that he soon had enough of this and he began to think of a way of escape. He persuaded Joe Cahill to buy him a map, compass, civilian clothes and hats for both of them. Once out of prison he would make his way to the border. According to the map, the distance between Pretoria and Portuguese East Africa was 296 miles. He would somehow get to Lourenço Marques and from there travel by sea to Durban.

On the night of 7 December Bridge thought the sentries looked sleepy and so at 7:30pm while the officers were having their dinner, the two of them, boots in their hands so as to make as little noise as possible, crept towards the fence. Cahill said that he would take the food and get out first and wait for Bridge down the road. When the sentries turned to walk away from the proposed crossing point, Cahill scaled the fence, but instead of following him immediately, Bridge waited for about ten minutes to give his companion a good start. The guards were only eight yards away from him.

Eventually Bridge jumped up and without being detected by the guards, lowered himself down into General Meyer's garden. He caught his breath, put his boots on and walked to the street, passing within a few yards of another sentry. Three policemen conversing with each other gave him no more than a cursory glance. Then a man carrying a rifle stopped him and asked a question in Afrikaans which he didn't understand. He merely replied 'yes' and continued walking.

At the end of the road he crossed a small wooden bridge, on the other side of which he expected Cahill to be waiting for him, but he was nowhere to be seen. Bridge called out his name as he continued walking but no one answered. He began to realise that Cahill hadn't waited for him. He passed another three police guards but they took no notice of him. When he finally reached the open veld, he accepted that he was alone.

The two escapees had discussed their route in detail, so finding his way didn't pose an immediate problem. But Cahill had taken off with six tins of meat and the tin of biscuits so he had no food. Then it started to rain. With no food and the night wearing on, he had no choice but to press forward.

He came to a barbed wire fence, but as he climbed through he startled some ponies that made a great deal of noise as they galloped off. A man appeared from a nearby house with a lantern. He shouted something in Afrikaans but Bridge ignored him and walked on. More people appeared from the house and were obviously discussing him in loud voices. He took off and ran as fast as he could to get away from the potential danger zone. He ran into more barbed wire fences that were invisible in the dark. His clothes were torn and he was bleeding when he reached a railway line. He crossed the rails and continued walking only to encounter the line again a few miles further. While resting he heard a train approaching from between two hills and soon two big lights mounted on the engine appeared. He hid behind a large termite heap until the train had passed, knowing that every train, bridge and culvert was probably guarded. He climbed a rocky outcrop from the top of which he could see the lights of Pretoria.

He walked throughout the night. At dawn he found a spot among bushes on a river bank and decided to sleep in the wet grass. He woke up later in the morning and pressed on. He met an African boy herding cattle and offered him two shillings for food, but the only reply he got was '*niks*,' which meant he had nothing.

Bridge climbed another hill from the summit of which he saw five farmhouses and two African huts beyond them. Driven by hunger he began circling the farmhouses to get to the huts when a horseman carrying a rifle galloped towards him. The rider stopped and asked him where he was going.

'To Middelburg', he replied and asked if he was on the correct road.

'This might be the road but as you have no pass, you have to come with me to see the field cornet', the horseman said and loaded his rifle.

Bridge tried to ignore him, but he saw about 20 more horsemen approaching from the farm. Two men galloped up to them.

The field cornet listened to Bridge's cover story. He said he had been left behind at Dundee, because he was out scouting when the troops left. The Boers were between him and Ladysmith so he couldn't rejoin his regiment. He had been given civilian clothes by an Indian trader and he had made his way to Johannesburg where he had stayed for a month. His name, he claimed, was George Beattie of the 18th Hussars.

The Boers were unimpressed and told Bridge that he would have to be taken to Pretoria and placed in the prisoner-of-war camp at Waterval. 'If you try to escape, we will have to shoot you', they warned.

The next day was a Sunday and his captor and his daughters entertained him and discussed the war. The next day he was handed over to nine men with two wagons who would escort him to Pretoria. They arrived at Bronkhorstspruit on the Tuesday from where they were to take a train. Several old men were taking a particular interest in the prisoner. A young lad from the station was acting as an interpreter because the men escorting him had a scant knowledge of English. Noticing that the men were talking about him Bridge asked the boy what they were talking about.

'The old men are not going to the front and have to stay here to guard the railway', he told Bridge. They were lamenting 'that it a pity that we will not have a chance to shoot a *rooinek*. But we have one here, [so] let us shoot him!'[20]

Noticing that Bridge had turned pale, the lad was quick to add that he shouldn't be too concerned as the field cornet, being responsible for the prisoner wouldn't allow this to happen.

Before the train left the following morning, a telegraph was sent to Pretoria, informing the authorities that an Englishman had been caught. The immediate reply was that it had to be Winston Churchill. Bridge laughed at the Boers mistaking him for Churchill, but deduced that Churchill had escaped after he had gone on the run.

In Pretoria no fuss was made about Bridge and he was merely given a ticket which said he was a *Krygs Gevangenen* (prisoner-of-war), and locked up at Waterval.

He and 4 000 other prisoners were set free on 6 May 1900, the day after the British Army marched into Pretoria.

While Churchill was hiding among the bushes in General Meyer's garden, the fate of the two troopers who had jumped the fence before him might have crossed his mind, but it was none of his concern. He had to move on and he donned the old felt hat given to him by Rev Hofmeyr, and walked straight towards the house. He passed the lit-up windows not caring whether he was seen and headed for the gate that was manned by two sentries. Most sentries knew Churchill by sight, but he didn't even look at them. Whether they looked at him or not he couldn't say. Most likely the darkness, his hat being pulled down over his face and his brisk, self-assured walk gave the sentries the impression that he was just another visitor to Meyer's house who was on his way home.

Churchill's heart was pounding. He tempted to run and it was only with great difficulty that he restrained himself. After passing the sentries his anxiety subsided. 'I walked on leisurely through the night, humming a tune and choosing the middle of the road. The streets were full of burghers, but they paid no attention to me. Gradually I reached the suburbs, and on a little bridge I sat down to reflect and consider',[21] he wrote in *My Early Life*. The 'little bridge' spanned the Apies River, the natural boundary that separated the then fashionable suburb of Sunnyside from the centre of the town.

Reflecting on conditions in Pretoria at the close of the 19th century and considering the prevailing circumstances a couple of months into the war, it seems that Churchill, however audacious he may have been, must have used some literary licence when describing his stroll among the burghers down Skinner Street.

Before the outbreak of hostilities, the white population in the district of Pretoria had reached about 40 000. It was estimated that some 17 000 of them lived within the town limits. The number of Africans, Coloureds and Asians was just over 38 000, and many of these people lived in Marabastad, a black location to the west of Church Square, and in other areas outside the town.

As early as May 1899, when the voices of war between the Boers and the British were becoming louder, many people started to regards their future in the Transvaal with concern. During July and August an increasing number of *Uitlanders* — and there were many of them, mostly from Britain, but also Jews from Lithuania and Poland as well as other European immigrants — moved to the safety of the British colonies of Cape and Natal.

By mid-September the crush of women at the station taking their children to the coast was so great that special trains had to be organised by the government to cater for them. In a letter to his mother in Holland dated 26 October 1899, Johan van den Veer writes of the chaos as many British subjects fled from Pretoria, 'often packed into open coal trucks like a ton of herrings'.[22] Consequently many houses were empty and the town had taken on a deserted appearance.

On 28 September men were called up to register for commando service, and on 2 October the prohibition of the sale of intoxicating liquor was announced and all bars were closed. When Churchill strolled down Skinner Street, the number of people living in Pretoria had dropped to about 10 000.

The distance from the State Model School to the bridge is less than a half a mile. If we accept that Churchill scaled the fence at 7.15pm and that he spent an hour and a half behind the shrubs in General Meyer's garden, it must have been close to 11.00pm when he crossed the bridge to freedom. On this eastern side of town, away from the centre, the moonlit street was flanked by simple corrugated iron-roofed houses separated from the narrow thoroughfare by little rose-hedged gardens. With the bars closed and the town offering its residents few diversions at that time of the evening, it is unlikely that many burghers would have had reason to venture beyond their stoeps.

Whether Churchill strolled along the unpaved sides of the road, or walked briskly down the middle, it is unlikely he would have been observed — unless, of course, his behaviour attracted the attention of a guard on duty. That he was in a hurry to get away from his former place of captivity is understandable. So to reach the wooden bridge over the Apies River should have taken him no more than 15 minutes.

This far Churchill's escape attempt had been easy. It was certainly audacious, but in the annals of great escapes, it doesn't rate that highly. His bid for freedom required neither careful planning nor vast ingenuity. All it took was a modicum of courage and much determination.

Today few people in Pretoria are aware of the details of the escape, but during the 1950s when the episode was given much publicity in local newspapers and written about in books issued by the city council as part of celebrating the town's centenary, it was widely discussed. He was supposed to have claimed that he had swum across the 'mighty Apies River'. Some say he had told this story during his lecture tour in the United States, but Professor Paul Botes wrotes in *The History of Witbank* that Churchill had said that he 'swam through a deep water hole', and that this remark kindled the 'mighty Apies River' legend.

Indeed, Paul H Butterfield also wrote: 'Churchill made his escape from detention on 12 December 1899 and swimming the flooded Apies River, he travelled roughly in the direction of Delagoa Bay'.[23] Legend has it that a member of the House of Commons in England was supposed to have asked the Secretary of War why the British fleet did not sail up the river and shell Pretoria!

But nothing about swimming the river ever appeared in Churchill's writings.

With the little bridge sited conveniently at the eastern end of Skinner Street there was, of course, no need for Churchill to swim the river, no matter how fast or broad its flow. Today one might chuckle at the idea of anyone swimming across the Apies — which for most of the year is an insignificant trickle flowing down a concrete canal. But during the rainy season before it was tamed, like many African rivers, the gently flowing waters could transform within minutes into a torrent. The angry flood frequently caused damage to the homes and gardens of those living along its banks, and on more than one occasion caused the loss of livestock and people too. However, during Churchill's stay at the State Model School as a guest of the Boer government, no floods were recorded.

Sitting at the bridge while catching his breath, Churchill felt relieved at leaving behind him the days of captivity he had described as the most monotonous and most miserable of his life. Yet a sense of loneliness overcame him as he realised there was no turning back. He took stock of his situation and realised he had four slabs of chocolate and £75 in his pocket. He knew from maps he had seen in the State Model School's library and from discussions with Haldane, that the railway line to Portuguese East Africa ran from Pretoria station in a south-easterly direction.

Once again, 'Orion shone brightly. Scarcely a year before he had guided me when lost in the desert to the banks of the Nile. He had given me water. Now he should lead to freedom. I could not endure the want of either'.[24]

The story of Orion does have a ring of romance to it, but in this instance using the star as a guide served little purpose. Having crossed the Apies River, Churchill knew he had to turn right and head south to find the railway less than a mileaway. In the event, he followed the route already decided on at the State Model School. He recorded in *My Early Life* that he walked for half a mile before he found the railway. 'The night was delicious', he remembered. A cool breeze fanned his face, spurring a sensation of adventure while 'a wild feeling of exhilaration'[25] took hold of him. He followed the line of rail, taking little care to avoid guarded bridges.

Lieutenant Frankland was to term the escape project a 'primitive' one, but Churchill instinctively knew that his escape would be met with success. He later claimed it was because he took scarcely any precautions that the venture succeeded.

On seeing the signal lights of a station, he left the track and hid in a ditch on an uphill gradient not far from the small complex. He told himself that sooner or later the train he was waiting for would arrive. An hour passed before he heard the whistle and saw the bright lights of the engine pulling into the station. It stopped briefly as if to catch its breath, and then, accompanied by much steam and noise, resumed its journey. Churchill — concealed by an outward curve from the engineer and the guard — readied himself to jump board before it gathered speed.

'Then I hurled myself on the trucks, clutched at something, missed, clutched again, missed again, grasped some sort of handhold, was swung off my feet — my toes bumping on the line, and with a struggle scaled myself on the couplings of the fifth truck from the front of the train'.[26] The truck was laden with coal sacks filled with empty coal sacks that were being returned to the Witbank coalfields. He buried himself under these warm and comfortable coal dust impregnated bags and resolved to sleep to the 'clatter of the train that carries an escaping prisoner at 20 miles an hour away from the enemy's capital'.[27]

John Howard, the mine manager of the Transvaal and Delagoa Bay Colliery in Witbank, remembered in an interview published in *The Star* of Johannesburg in 1923 that Churchill boarded the train near where Pretoria College now stands at the foot of Rissik Station in Sunnyside. In a 1955 article in the *Natal Mercury,* Charles Burnham, another of Churchill's benefactors, mentioned Muckleneuk, the hilly Pretoria suburb next to the railway station where 'he jumped on a moving goods train'. Clearly, Churchill himself told the men in Witbank how he had clambered over the wall (or fence) of the State Model School and made his way to the railway line. Burnham agrees with Aylmer Haldane who wrote in 1901: 'Next to the railway line at Muckleneuk in Pretoria he lay waiting for the eastward bound train which would take him to Lourenço Marques'.[28]

These statements directly contradict Churchill's claim in *My Early Life* that he had walked for two hours along the railway line until he saw the signal lights of a station. It is certainly true that more than three hours had passed since he had scaled the wall. He had spent an hour in Meyer's garden; close to an hour making his way to the Apies River and then on to the vicinity of the station; and another hour hiding in the long grass before jumping aboard the slow moving train.

Churchill was unfit, so clambering aboard the moving train might not have been easy for him. But all went well. While trying to sleep amongst the bags of empty coal bags, his mind again focussed on the difficulties that lay ahead. He decided it would be wise to leave the train before the sun-up and find a hiding place for the day.

It was probably around 5.00am when he awoke. He saw that he was in a wide valley surrounded by low hills. The train reduced speed at a gently rising slope somewhere close to Brugspruit. Realising that it was probably about to stop, possibly at a colliery siding in the Witbank district, he decided it was time to jump off.

He was very thirsty but fortunately he soon found a pool of clear water. He drank deeply and quenched his thirst, feeling that would last for the rest of the day. He headed for the nearby hills and searched for a hiding place. The sun was fully up when he found a clump of shady trees alongside a deep ravine. He was soon well hidden but he had a panoramic view of the valley below. The setting was idyllic. There was a village of tin-roofed houses in the distance. Farmsteads surrounded by huge trees dotted the verdant landscape. At the foot of his hill he could see the round huts of a native kraal that added an exotic touch to the picturesque scene. The kraal dwellers could be seen working in the patches of cultivated land, while small herds of goats and cattle grazed peacefully on a carpet of green grass for it was the height of the rainy season.

To complete the picture that Churchill painted he observed two or three trains travelling in both directions along the railway. Although vultures had never been recorded in that part of the Transvaal Highveld, he claimed that above him an unusually large bird of this species eyed him with curiosity as it hurled hideous gurglings from time to time.[29] Whether the vulture had its mind set on an early English breakfast, he did not say. For his own breakfast he had a slab of chocolate which had to suffice for the whole day.

The long and hot summer's day did not pass without incident. Churchill became very thirsty, probably from eating the chocolate. The pool from where he had drank earlier was a mile or two away, but he did not dare leave his hide for he could see white men riding and walking around in the valley. While he nervously contemplated his future, a Boer rode up close to his hiding place. The horseman fired two shots at birds but Churchill, who 'dreaded and detested more than words can express the prospects of being caught and dragged back to Pretoria',[30] kept his head.

Lack of sleep, hunger and thirst increased his intense depression. 'I realised with awful force that no exercise of my own feeble wit and strength could save me from my enemies, and that without the assistance of that High Power which interferes more often than we are always prone to admit in the eternal sequence of causes and effects I could never succeed', he wrote later.

In India he had not hesitated to ask for divine protection when about to come under fire. It was no different in Africa. 'I prayed long and earnestly for help and guidance. My prayer, as it seems to me, was swiftly and wonderfully answered'.[31] In the report he sent to the *Morning Post* from Delagoa Bay on 28 December he added: 'I cannot now relate the strange circumstances which followed and which changed my nearly hopeless position into one of superior advantage. But after the war is over I shall hope to somewhat lengthen this account, and so remarkable will the addition be that I cannot believe the reader will complain'.[32]

The somewhat lengthened account that Churchill had promised to write about the adventures he encountered on his way to neutral Portuguese East Africa proved to be remarkably entertaining, and as he had predicted, few people complained about the narrative. That the descriptions of his experiences sometimes varied from the accounts of those who had helped him to escape — not without great risks themselves — is a matter for conjecture.

15

Great day at the State Model School

While Churchill was hiding in the shady grove with the peaceful valley at his feet, all hell broke loose at the State Model School in Pretoria. In spite of Haldane and Brockie feeling that they had been let down by their compatriot, they did their utmost to conceal his absence. They arranged a dummy in his bed that looked so lifelike that a batman bringing the morning coffee on Wednesday 13 December, didn't realise it was a mock-up. At 8.00am when the prison barber — a little Hollander named Henri Adelaar who came to the school on certain days of the week to ply his trade, failed to find his client at the appointed time and at once became suspicious. No one is better able to tell the tale of the frantic search that followed than the Rev Adrian Hofmeyr who witnessed the unfolding spectacle:

> He knocked at the door of the empty cage, in vain of course. Sorely afraid of losing his sixpenny fee the little man ran up and down the building, interrogating everyone he met. Some gave him no answer, just looked at him up and down, the little there was of him; others referred him to the most unlikely corners; a third said: 'In the bath'. And so outside the bathroom, barber and a bobby took up a strong position, holding it against all comers for fully half an hour. Then it struck the little man that perhaps they had been guarding an empty bath, so he knocked gently and apologetically. No answer. A louder, rather self-assertive knock then, and still no answer. And so, a loud, peremptory, his taking-no-refusal-knock came, but yet no answer. Bobby then ventured to turn the knob and open the door inch by inch, peeping in gingerly. Is the man perhaps dead? Has he cut his throat? What ghastly sight am I doomed to see? He opens the door a little more. There is no one. It is a little room of about eight feet by three feet. Yet he examines carefully. Behind the door? No. Under the chair? No. He gets wild and excited. He examines sponges and towels. Under these, perhaps? No. Where, then? Bath and water, soap and towels are there, but where the bather? Consternation is now changed into panic.
>
> The gaoler is called; the guard is alarmed; there is bustle and confusion.

(Right) Young Winston in a sailor suit, aged 7 years.

(Above) The beautiful Miss Jennie Jerome (Lady Randolph Churchill), Winston Churchill's mother.

(Right) Lord Randolph Churchill (aged 30) Winston's father. He died from advanced syphilis.

(Left) Lady Churchill with her two sons, 1889.

(Right) Winston — a Gentleman Cadet at the Sandhurst Royal Military Academy.

(Left) Winston in the full dress uniform of the 4th Hussars.

(Right) Winston, a subaltern in the 4th Hussars at Bangalore, India.

(Below) Polo in India.

Below) The charge of the 21st Lancers against the Dervishes at the Battle of Omdurman n which Winston Churchill took part. It was the last cavalry charge of the British Army. This artistic impression was by R Caton Woodville.

(Left) Winston Churchill as the Tory candidate for Oldham, 1899. He lost but would make a comeback later.

(Right) Winston Churchill, war correspondent, South Africa, 1899.

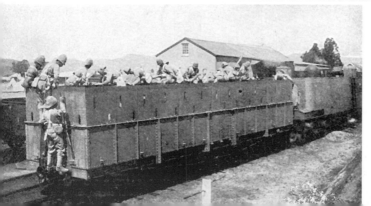

(Left) Troops of the Dublin Fusiliers climb aboard the armoured train at Estcourt to conduct a reconnaissance mission. It would end in disaster.

(Right) An artist's impression of the armoured train as it advanced towards Chieveley.

(Above) The armoured train under ambush by Boers at Chieveley. An artist's impression.

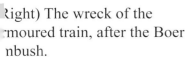

(Right) The wreck of the armoured train, after the Boer ambush.

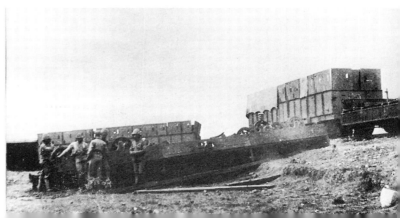

(Left) General and Mrs. Louis Botha. Churchill was convinced that General Botha had personally taken him prisoner at Chieveley, but this appears unlikely.

(Right) British POWs arriving in Pretoria from Estcourt by train. Taken from a French postcard.

Arrivée à Pretoria des prisonniers du train blindé d'Estcourt (Lord Churchill à gauche en casquette).
La Guerre Anglo-Boer

Ed. Nels, Bruxelles. Serie Transvaal III

(Left) Crowds gather at Pretoria Station, some even climbing on roofs and railway wagon to get a better view to watch the arrival of a train carrying British POWs.

(Left) Officer POWs arrive in Pretoria. Winston Churchill, wearing a fusilier's forage cap, stands apart from the others on the right.

(Above) British POWs being marched through Pretoria.

(Below) The State Model School where British officer POWs, including Churchill, were detained. Churchill managed his famous escape from there.

(Above) Another view of the State Model School.

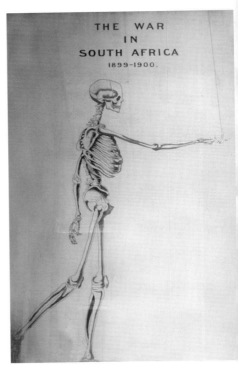

(Right) Lieutenant Frankland's drawing of skeleton on a wall at the State Model School. It was a reminder of the senseless killings caused by a needless war.

(Left) The Apies River bridge, Pretoria, which Churchill crossed on his way to freedom.

(Right) An artist's impression of the vulture seen by Churchill while on-the-run from the Boers.

(Left) Churchill arrives in Durban by ship from Lourenço Marques after his escape from Pretoria.

(Right) Churchill addresses an enthusiastic crowd in Durban after his escape.

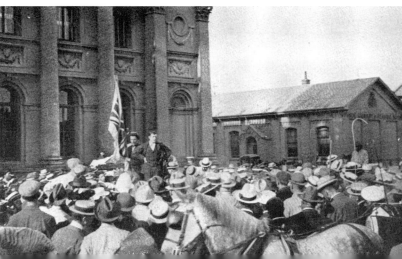

(Left) Following Churchill's escape the British officer POWs were moved from the State Model School to the more secure 'Bird Cage'. When the officers were leaving under escort, Captain Haldane and his two fellow escapees remained hiding beneath the floorboards awaiting their chance to go on-the-run.

(Right) An artist's impression of the Bird Cage POW detention centre.

(Left) Lieutenant Winston Churchill in the uniform of the South African Light Horse.

(Above) The South African Light Horse parading through Cape Town, early 1900. Inset, General Lord Roberts.

(Above) Winston Churchill returns to the scene of the ambush of the armoured train at Chieveley.

(Right) General Buller looks on as naval guns open fire at Colenso. His later continual unsuccessful attempts to get his army across the Tugela River earned him the nickname of 'the Ferryman' amongst the troops.

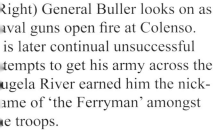

(Left) The Relief of Ladysmith. British troops march into town and break the Boer siege. Winston Churchill and the South African Light Horse were amongst the first to enter the town.

(Left) General Sir Redvers Buller who was replaced as commander-in-chief by General Lord Roberts after the relief of Ladysmith.

(Right) General Lord Roberts who became the commander-in-chief for the British Army's march on Pretoria.

(Left) General Lord Kitchener who took over as commander-in-chief after the occupation of Pretoria and during the guerrilla war.

(Right) President Paul Kruger arrives in Holland after Queen Wilhelmina sent a warship to Lourenço Marques to collect him.

(Above) Illustrating the slaughter at Spion Kop where the British and Boer dead lay intermingled.

(Below) This shows the main trench where the dead were piled three deep and more. During the heavy fighting Winston Churchill climbed Spion Kop three times while under fire.

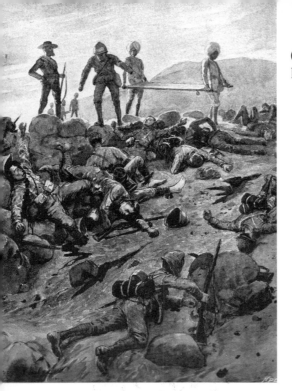

(Left) Dawn on Spion Kop. A truce while the living are sorted from the dead.

(Right) The British Army occupies Johannesburg. Winston Churchill and a French companion rode through the city on a bicycle many days before the arrival of the main army.

(Left) Winston Churchill and his cousin the Duke of Malborough reached the Bird Cage prison camp first and released 136 British officer POWs, many of them his former companion in captivity.

(Right) General Lord Roberts reads the proclamation regarding the annexation of the Transvaal, at Pretoria, 25 October, 1900.

(Below) The South African War was the first war to be intensively covered by journalists from all over the world. This group, of British and US journalists was taken in Pretoria. Churchill, second left in middle row.

(Right & below) Two views of one of the engraved gold watches that Winston Churchill gave to the men at Witbank who assisted with his escape to Lourenço Marques.

(Above) The Hon Winston Churchill, Member of Parliament for Oldham.

(Below) Winston Churchill and his wife Clementine, with whom, in his own words, he 'lived happily ever after'.

We are all asked when we saw Churchill last. 'Last night' was naturally the universal answer. So cocksure had the authorities been all along of the utter impossibility of escape, and of their superior intelligence, that they never even called a roll. Our chief gaoler, who naturally was in a great stew, was sure that he had seen the fugitive out under the verandah as late as 10:30pm the evening before, which, to put it mildly, was a cram, for the grand coup had come off at 7:15pm.[1]

Meanwhile, Dr Gunning arrived to enquire about Churchill's whereabouts. He reluctantly accepted an explanation, but shortly after, at 9:30am he returned and ordered a roll call. Churchill's absence could no longer be hidden from the authorities. A cup of coffee was still standing on a chair next to the bed and on the pillow there was a letter addressed to the Under-Secretary for War.

WSC to L. de Souza
11 December 1899
State School Prison
Pretoria

Dear Mr de Souza,

I do not concede that your Government was justified in holding me, a press correspondent and a non-combatant, a prisoner and I have consequently resolved to escape. The arrangements I have succeeded in making [in] conjunction with my friends outside are such as to give me every confidence.

But I wish, in leaving you this hastily and unceremoniously, to once more place on record my appreciation of the kindness which has been shown to me and the other prisoners by you, the Commandant and by Dr Gunning, and my admiration of the chivalrous and humane character of the Republican forces.

My views on the general question of the war remain unchanged, but I shall always retain a feeling of high respect for the several classes of burghers I have met and, on reaching British lines, I will set forth a truthful and impartial account of my experiences in Pretoria.

In conclusion, I desire to express my obligations to you and to hope that when this most grievous and unhappy war shall have come to an end, a state of affairs may be created which shall preserve at once the national pride of the Boers and the security of the British and put a final stop to the rivalry and enmity of both races. Regretting the circumstances have not permitted me to bid you a personal farewell, believe me.

Yours very sincerely
Winston S. Churchill

Commandant Opperman couldn't accept that Churchill had actually escaped. He ordered an immediate search of the building and the grounds but this was to no avail.

Ranting and raving, he waited for the inspector of police to arrive. He kept on insisting that he had seen the prisoner late the previous night, and escape could only be possible with the help of some corrupt guard. He presented a hand-written report to the secretary of the Commandant-General's office, confirming that Winston Churchill, the correspondent of The *Morning Post*, had escaped. A translation of this report, in the Government Archives, reads as follows:

13 December 1899

RWL Opperman to L. de Souza
Guard Office,
State Model School,
Pretoria.

I have the honour to inform you that one of the prisoners of war escaped during the night (WS Churchill, correspondent of *The Morning Post*). During the past four or five days his behaviour was most unusual. He hardly spoke to any of the other prisoners and dreamily wandered alone around the building.

In my view the only way he could have escaped was by bribing one or more of the guards, because the guards were so placed that it would have been impossible for him to escape without their knowledge.

I have the honour to be
Your Excellency's obedient servant

RWL Opperman [2]

On the same day Advocate Schagen van Leeuwen and HW Zeiler, a judicial commissioner, were appointed to investigate the circumstances of the escape. Rumours were rife. It was suggested that Churchill had been disguised as a woman. 'A nurse in the hospital, a young lady from the Cape Colony, who had never even seen Churchill, was suspected of having supplied him with a nurse's uniform. She was put over the border and sent home'.

Another popular rumour was that a small dog brought in a letter in its mouth; and a policeman had sold Churchill a uniform which enabled him to escape to Delagoa Bay as a Zarp.

Adrian Hofmeyr wrote: 'For us the whole thing was a great pantomime — a screaming farce. The authorities did act so foolishly over the whole matter, and their two brave handy men, their beautiful newspapers, making them out to be even greater fools than they were. Our poor gaoler could not, and would not, believe that the escape was a fait accompli.'[4]

Commandant Opperman — the gaoler Hofmeyr refers to — was trying to divert the blame of exercising poor control, continued to insist that the only way Churchill could have got out was by bribing guards. 'The big, blustering field-cornet went so far as to say, "Churchill is a blackguard; he gave his parole, and that is the way he keeps his English word of honour." Well, Churchill was not the blackguard. Somebody else was — a baffled official who took refuge in lies! The idea! A man gives parole, and yet he is guarded by men armed to the teeth! But, you see, with some of these officials anything will do for a fig leaf'.[5]

Even Dr Gunning fell under suspicion. The fact that he was married to an Englishwoman was cited as a reason for him being too lenient with the prisoners. Further, he was in charge of the library, and the last book issued to Churchill was John Mills' *On Liberty*. That pretty much confirmed his collusion.

When General Joubert learned that Churchill had escaped 48 hours after he signed his unconditional release, he shook his head. 'I wonder whether it would not be a good thing to make public the correspondence about the release of Churchill to show the world what a scoundrel he is,' he said to FW Reitz. But the State Secretary advised against this. In his letter of 8 December, Churchill had offered de Souza 'any parole that may be required not to serve against the Republican forces or to give any information affecting the military situation'.

Although General Joubert was fully aware of the part Churchill had played at Chieveley, he accepted the Englishman's word 'in preference to all the journalists and reporters'. Joubert cited this as his reason for no longer objecting to Churchill's release. He was in any case under the impression that a parole had been promised with no conditions attached.

Joubert's letter leaves no doubt that he had agreed to the release of the famous but troublesome son of Lord Randolph in the hope that he would return to England and report only the truth of his experiences. This, Joubert believed, would be of greater value to the cause of the Boers than keeping Churchill incarcerated in Pretoria. It was just unfortunate that the letter arrived after he had escaped. Although he was never given the opportunity to accept the parole he had suggested, it led to political opponents causing him considerable trouble for many years to come.

As far as General Joubert was concerned, the matter was no longer worth troubling about. He remembered President Kruger saying that Churchill was merely a journalist who could not do any harm and should rather be released, and thus gave instructions not to bother looking for the man, because he was just *'n klein koerantskrywertie* — a little newspaper writer. Nonetheless, the situation was considered an embarrassment by the authorities in the capital, and Commandant Opperman had to bear the brunt of the blame for the escape.

The Standard and Diggers News of Johannesburg, in its report on Churchill's escape had no doubt that the fugitive would be caught. Under the banner: 'Mr Winston

Churchill. His Escape from Custody. Melodramatic Journalism. A modern Prince Charlie', it stated:

> A description of the melodramatic descendant of the great Marlborough was furnished to the local station authorities and the Detective Department, but the popular impression is that Mr Churchill is in hiding in Pretoria, and that he is being surrounded by English sympathisers. There is really nothing to be gained by Mr Churchill from the latest journalistic exploit save 'copy'. Though he successfully eluded the vigilance of the State Model School guard, any attempt to return to the British Forces must be rendered abortive by the strict passport system now in force; and though every credit should be given to the enterprising young gentleman for his latest newspaper exploit, it will be some considerable time before his glowing narrative of how he escaped from Pretoria reaches his friends.

Opperman and the sentries on duty on the night of Churchill's escape had to sign sworn statements and some of the imprisoned officers were interrogated. According to Celia Sandys, one of the guards on duty, Stephan Schotel, would harbour a resentment of Churchill for the rest of his life. He never tired of telling his wife that Churchill made his getaway by horsecart, hiding himself in one of the containers used for emptying the latrines. 'Was Schotel, I wonder, the guard who, turning away to light his cigarette, gave Churchill the few seconds he needed to scramble over the fence?'[6]

A written report, supported by three sketches, revealed that there were supposed to be nine sentries on duty in the building and its grounds, and additional guards were on call. The afternoon and evening watches were from 4.00pm to 8.00pm, from 8.00pm to midnight and midnight to 4.00am. The sketches were called the 'Zeiler plans' (after the joint convenor of the commission of inquiry) and showed that there were only eight guards on duty at the time Churchill scaled the fence. No sentry manned the corner entrance of Meyer's property. Only at 8.00pm did Jan H Montgomery, *Polotie* No 94, take up his position at this strategic point. Another sentry, CFC Landman, stated that he saw Lieutenant Grimshaw and two others near the fence at 7.50pm . When he saw Grimshaw trying to look over the fence, he shouted: 'Go back you bastard!' Captain Lonsdale of the Royal Fusiliers admitted that he had looked over the fence and had seen Churchill crouching in the garden.

One could, of course, speculate that Churchill might have bribe a guard. Why were there only eight guards on duty when there should have been nine? Why did Schotel — or whoever the sentry was who lit the cigarette might have been — turn away at precisely the moment that Churchill scaled the fence but was fully alert when Haldane attempted to do the same? Why was there no guard on duty at the Skinner Street entrance to Meyers's property before 8:00pm? And why did the sentry who took up his position at 8.00pm pay no attention to Churchill when he passed him at five paces?

Although these questions have never been satisfactorily answered, the Zeiler Inquiry made it clear — and it has never been contradicted — that no bribes were offered or accepted. It is true that the rather casual approach of the guards towards their duties left much to be desired. They were veteran members of the Zarps who were considered too old or unfit for commando service. That general lack of discipline, however, should not be blamed on inexperience or age. It was the commander who didn't bother with rollcalls and allowed sentries to smoke and chat on duty. He alone was responsible for the appallingly poor discipline.

It emerged at the inquiry that Churchill, who complained about the heat in his room, had taken to sleeping on the verandah, but not before the small hours in the morning. Corporal ZJ Scheepers reported that a restless Churchill always walked at night until three or four in the morning. There was another startling disclosure. The guards had previously thought it inadvisable to report the escape of Troopers Cahill and Bridge earlier in the month using the same route that Churchill had taken.

Lieutenant Frankland, who kept a diary while imprisoned at the State Model School had this to say about Churchill's escape under the entry of 15 December:

Tempus fugit, and it has not been quite so dull as usual. First, and most important of all, Churchill has escaped. Whether he has made it good or not is still uncertain; but he has now been gone two days and I have great hopes. Apart from the excitement there has been a very amusing side to the affair. Of course Churchill was the very last person who ought to have gone. He was always talking and arguing with the officials, and was therefore well known, and, indeed, scarcely a day passed without Dr Gunning or Mr de Souza inquiring for him. His plans for escape were primitive; but, being still in prison, I must not write anything about this part of the affair. Let it suffice that Churchill got away without any trace left behind. Next morning, as it chanced, it was the day for the barber to come and shave him, and having only just woken up I put the barber off rather feebly by saying that Churchill had gone to the bathroom, and, finding no Churchill, began to suspect. Gunning then came upon the scene, closely followed by Opperman, both asking and seeking anxiously for their captive. Their distress at finding him gone was really pathetic. They immediately put on all kinds of restrictions.[7]

As was to be expected, immediate changes to spruce up discipline and tighten security at the prison were introduced by the fuming Commandant Opperman. A twice-daily rollcall was announced; no one was allowed in the yard after eight in the evening when the prisoners were confined to the main building. The luxury of beer and newspapers they had enjoyed was immediately cancelled. The privilege of visiting the hospital adjoining the school, where both English and Boer war casualties were nursed, was cancelled.

The grounds were thoroughly inspected and palings which connected offices at the

This translated as:

Warrant to Search a House

To all Constables and Officials authorised to carry out the instructions contained in a Criminal Warrant.

In consequence of information attested under oath before me, Field Cornet, this day, there is reason to believe that Mr Churchill — a Prisoner of War — who escaped from the building of the Model School is hidden in a certain house in this town inhabited by certain parties, to be pointed out by Detective Donovan.

You are hereby authorised in the name of the Government of the South African Republic to enter the said house during the day, and there to thoroughly search the house for the said Mr Churchill and if any articles are found there to bring the same together with the party in whose possession they are found, before the Landdrost to be dealt with according to law.

Given under my hand at Pretoria this 13th day of December 1899
Confirmed signed
P. Maritz Botha

back of the yard with the fence were removed so that the sentries could pass behind, making further escapes more difficult. Trees in the vicinity of the latrines were trimmed and reflectors on the electric lights were re-positioned so the entire area was illuminated.

A newly appointed German inspector of police ordered his officers to inspect the sentries every nightly to ensure that rifles were loaded at all times. The letter Churchill had addressed to de Souza was, of course, misleading, but the Under-Secretary of State for War did not realise that. The reference to friends outside the prison made him think the prisoner had been given sanctuary by Pretoria residents.

A *Lastbrief tot Huiszoeking* (a warrant for searching houses) was issued in the name of the government by Magistrate P. Maritz Botha.

Some houses were searched and how this was carried out can be gleaned from the notes of a Mrs TJ Rodda who was an English resident in Pretoria. While walking through town, Mrs Rodda heard a man telling her in a whisper: 'Churchill has escaped'.

Rodda felt excited at hearing the news, but did not show her emotions and simply nodded her head. Later, when having lunch at home, she noticed a shadow fall on her. Looking over her shoulder at the glass door that opened onto the stoep, she saw two men 'fully, very fully, armed standing at the door'.[8] She recognised them as Boers and whispered to her father, who could not speak Afrikaans, that he shouldn't move or speak.

Rodda rose, opened the door and in high Dutch said: 'Well, gentleman, what can I do for you?'

One replied: 'One of the English prisoners has escaped, and we have reason to believe that he is hidden in your house, so in the name of the State we demand an entrance.' She turned to her father, translated the request into English and asked the men to follow her. She walked to the bedroom and, while expressing her surprise at the escape of a prisoner, threw open the doors in a 'rather dramatic fashion' saying: 'Enter gentlemen.'[8]

Rodda returned to her chair, but a friend, an Irishman by the name of Aitkinson had arrived on a visit to see her father. They both stood at the door of the smoking room and watched the proceedings. A few minutes later the two Boers reappeared and said they would search the rest of the house. They went into the nursery and thrust their swords through two gowns hanging under a curtain in the doorway ripping large holes in them.

They then went to the coachman's room. The occupant, surprised at people entering without knocking, demanded: 'What the hell do you want here?

The men told him to watch his tongue and left the house through the dining-room.

When they were halfway across the garden Rodda called them back and out of sheer devilment, asked if they would like to check behind a bookcase. The men obviously felt foolish but they returned to the house and pushed the bookcase aside. Rodda then pointed out that there was a hatch in the ceiling. She told the coachman to bring a ladder.

The men just stalked off in disgust leaving the bedroom in chaos. 'The bed was stripped, sheets, blankets all on the ground, mattresses partly so, the slips off the pillows, every drawer and shelf of the wardrobe turned over, the small trinket drawers in the dressing table had been emptied on the tables, those in the washing stand the same — all to find Churchill — who was on the coal train on his way to Delagoa Bay'.[10]

16

Hiding out in a coalmine

Churchill waited out the day amongst the trees near Balmoral. He waited impatiently for the sun to set and watched the shadows of the hills gradually reach out across the valley. A wagon drawn by a full team of oxen slowly made its way to the kraal and the kraal dwellers were rounding up their stock to put it in kraals for the night. When darkness fell Churchill knew it was time to return to the railway line to a spot where during the day he had observed trains crawling up a gradient. There was also a curve that would again hide him from the view of the engineer while he clambered aboard the train.

But this time luck was not on his side. Some eight hours passed since he had last seen a train rumbling by. According to his account in *My Early Life,* he had waited for about seven hours in bushes near the track when, well after midnight, he came to the realisation that the 11:10pm train from Pretoria was the only one running that night. 'I might well have continued to wait in vain till daylight',[1] he grumbled, and decided to continue walking. His progress was slow because armed men were guarding every bridge that he came across.

Every few miles he encountered huts and stations with tin-roofed houses clustered around them. Churchill must have been thinking of the English countryside when he penned this part of his adventurous escape because except for Brugspruit and Balmoral, there were — and are to this day — no stations or villages in the countryside he traversed. 'All the veld was bathed in the rays of the bright moon',[2] he wrote.

He found himself walking in a very sparsely populated area during the small hours of the morning and he felt compelled to 'avoid these dangerous places' by making wide detours and even crawling along the ground. 'Leaving the railroad, I fell into bogs and swamps, brushed through high grass dripping with dew, and waded through streams over which bridges carried the railway.'[3]

He was soaked to the skin and dog-tired. He blames his tiredness on a lack of exercise during his imprisonment and because he had had little sleep or food. When he reached Brugspruit station he saw there were three long good's trains laid up at a siding that looked inviting. But he had no idea of their destinations and he feared they might be unloaded at Witbank, so he decided to check the consignment labels on the wagons.

As he crept between two of the trains up to the platform, he heard loud voices rapidly approaching him. Some Africans were laughing, and a voice he thought belonged to a white man was giving orders.

He left the siding as quickly as he could. Churchill re-commenced his walk but by then he was plodding on 'in an increasingly purposeless and hopeless manner'[4] as he observed lights burning in houses and thought of the warmth and comfort within. In the far distance he could see a row of lights belonging to what he thought was Witbank station and he knew there was a colliery there. However, as he descended a dip near the Brugspruit, the lights were lost to view and instead he saw fires burning away to his left.

He thought they were kraal fires and believed the Africans watching over them probably disliked the Boers and would be more well disposed towards the British,[4] he made his way towards them. The locals would provide him with food and shelter, he told himself as he marched on. The money in his pocket would open doors where his knowledge of the local language failed. 'I just felt quite clear I would go to the Kaffir kraal. I had sometimes in former years held a "Planchette" pencil and written while others had touched my wrist or hand. I acted in exactly the same unconscious or subconscious manner now', he wrote in *My Early Life*.[5]

'Psychics have sometimes claimed Churchill for one of their own, and in later life he would say that he would die on the anniversary of his father's death',[6] Celia Sandys wrote in *Churchill Wanted Dead or Alive*. (Winston died on 24 January 1965, 70 years to the day after Lord Randolph's death.) Atkins, referring to his compulsion to join Haldane on the ill-fated train at Colenso, had wondered if Churchill was accompanied by a demon that told him things..

Violet Bonham Carter, the daughter of Prime Minister YH Asquith and a friend of Churchill, had also frequently asked herself that question before she wrote:

> Again and again, watching his life and fortunes, it has seemed to me that Winston had a private wire with Fate. His course appeared to be shaped either by accident or impulse. It was always unpredictable in terms of reason, yet, following it, it is hard not to believe that it was directed by that beam which some call destiny and others instinct, by a Power which intervened between him and events and which, not once but many times, preserved his life to serve its purpose. What he called intuition was in fact obedience to the beam, which shaped his course. On this occasion, as on many others, the beam proved a true guide. That helpless, vulnerable and incongruous vehicle, the armoured train, turned out to be the Iron Horse on which he rode to fame.[7]

Churchill continued walking in an almost trance-like state for more than an hour towards the fires of what he believed was a small African village. As he got closer, they appeared to resolve into the furnaces of railway engines, but they finally turned out to be burning slag heaps so characteristic of coalmines in the area. He came to a group of houses. He hesitated for a while, toying with the idea of continuing his walk but then 'a small but substantial house two storeys high'[8] caught his eye. He remembered having been told that a number of Englishmen lived in the Witbank district keeping the mines going. This improved the chance that a countryman of his occupied the house. He knocked on the door, but there was no response. Growing impatient, he banged on the door with his fist. A light went on above him and a window opened.

'*Wer ist da*?' bellowed a man's voice.

'I want help; I have had an accident', Churchill replied.[9]

It seems strange that Churchill described the dwelling as a substantial stone house two storeys high, when in fact it was a small tin-roofed cottage surrounded by a verandah — the typical design of houses on the Highveld at that time. Strange, too, that the voice Churchill claims he had heard called out in German.

In *My Early Life* he gives a detailed account of the man coming down the stairs, opening the door abruptly and asking him in English what he wanted. Churchill told him that he was a burgher on his way to join his commando at Komatipoort. He had, however, fallen off the train while skylarking. He claimed to have been unconscious for hours and thought he had dislocated his shoulder. The tall man with a pale face and dark moustache listened intently to the explanation. When Churchill paused, not knowing what to say next, he was asked to elaborate on his accident.

Churchill knew there was nothing for it but to tell the truth. He admitted his identity and that he had escaped from the State Model School two nights earlier. He said he had plenty of money and would gladly part with it if he was helped to reach the border safely.

'Thank God you have come here!' the man said after a long pause.

He locked the door, placed the revolver — which Churchill had not noticed — on a table and told the nocturnal intruder that his was the only house within 20 miles where he would be safe. 'We are all Britishers (sic) here, and we will see you through', he added before introducing himself as John Howard, manager of the Transvaal and Delagoa Bay Colliery at Witbank.[10]

Howard invited Churchill to take a seat in a room that served as a dining room cum office.

'The Field Cornet was round here this afternoon asking about you. They have got the hue and cry out all along the line and all over the district', he said.[11]

It was quite possible that Theus Pretorius, the field cornet living in Brugspruit at the time of Churchill's escape, had paid Howard a visit to enquire about the escaped prisoner.

However, this could hardly have been 'this afternoon', because it was probably about 2.00am in the morning when Churchill related his escapades to Howard. What the latter must have said, if Churchill's account in *My Early Life* is correct, is that the field cornet came 'yesterday afternoon'. It may be argued that Churchill, exhausted from the ordeal he had been through, had muddled the time.

Churchill later lectured on his escape in England and the USA, and wrote elaborately about his adventures in South Africa. Since he was known for having a phenomenal memory, one would have expected him to have carefully worked out the details of his encounters and conversations, so as to avoid being questioned later on matters of fact.

The Commissioner of Police in Pretoria had no doubt that Churchill would be captured in due course. Commandant Opperman had been asked to give a description of the fugitive, and according to Hofmeyr, 'The Transvaal Zarps had his picture in their windows'.[12]

A warrant for Churchill's arrest was issued. On 20 December 1899 the office of the Commissioner of Police in Pretoria issued the following description:

> Englishman, 26 years of age, about 5 feet 6 inches in height, medium build, stooping gait, fair complexion, reddish brown hair, almost invisible slight moustache, speaks through his nose, cannot give full expression to the letter 's', and does not know a word of Dutch. Wearing a suit of brown clothes, but no uniform — an ordinary suit of clothes.

A copy of a photograph of Churchill taken some 18 months before, accompanied the letter, with the request 'to be good enough to show the public (as far as possible) the photograph'. Burghers were 'to keep a sharp lookout for the fugitive'. If he was identified, he should be placed under arrest and the acting commandant in Pretoria informed. The field cornet in Brugspruit — and indeed in all districts crossed by the railway line — were notified of the escape.

But this clearly could not have been so, for the 'day before' was 13 December, and the letter was dated 20 December. When it reached the field cornet in Brugspruit, the fugitive was already hidden among bales of wool and on his way to neutral Portuguese East Africa.

If Howard had been given Churchill's description, he would have instantly recognised the travel-worn fugitive who knocked on his door in the small hours of 14 December. And we may assume that his reaction would have been somewhat different.

According to a newspaper article in *The Star* of Johannesburg on 11 December 1923, Howard used to meet an English friend at his place once a week to discuss war matters. On the evening in question they played cards until about 1.00am. It was a warm night and, at about 1:30am while lying on his bed in his pyjamas, he heard a knock on the bedroom door which opened on to the verandah. He seized his revolver and opened the door. 'I saw a man below medium height, and dripping with water from the waist. His hair was red, his eyes blue, and his face inclined to be freckled.'[13]

The visitor asked him whether he was an Englishman, and Howard in turn asked him what he wanted and who he was.

Churchill replied: 'I am Dr Bentick. I have fallen off the train and lost my way.'[14]

Howard, thinking the stranger was a Boer spy, kept him covered with his revolver and ordered him into the dining room. 'He seemed very much knocked about and agitated, and he was no sooner in the dining room than he sank into a chair that was at the head of the table,'Howard recalled.

He stood at the other end of the table with revolver in hand and told him that it was an insult to his intelligence to say that he had fallen off a train and lost his way on a bright moonlit night.

After some word sparring, Howard told him that he would not allow him to leave the room and advised him to play open cards.

Churchill looked beaten into submission. His expression changed at intervals, doubt eventually giving way to determination. He finally exclaimed: 'I am Winston Churchill.'

Howard promptly put down his revolver, introduced himself and shook hands with the wet, weary and footsore man. He offered Churchill a whisky and soda and listened while he related the story of his escape.

He explained how he had scaled the fence at the State Model School and had managed to scramble into one of the rear trucks of a train passing through Sunnyside, 'somewhere near the spot at which Pretoria College now stands at the foot of the Rissik Station'.[16]

When he arrived at Wilge River station he realised that it would soon be daylight and he decided to leave the train and hide in the nearby hills. In the evening he continued his journey along the railway line until he reached Brugspruit. There he climbed a signal post and read the name of the station. He knew that the next station after that was Witbank and seeing lights about six miles away he walked towards them. There was no mention of detours to avoid guards, but when he came to a dip in the ground, he lost sight of the lights.

'Like most people', Howard said, 'he failed to march in a straight line — for he had deviated to the left where he sighted the lights of the Transvaal and Delagoa Bay Colliery, and fortunately he struck my house first.'[17]

Churchill was virtually starving and while Howard arranged something for him to eat he explained that he lived alone in the house. He was himself the son of a soldier, the late Captain K Fioard Howard of the Royal Engineers, and had come to South Africa to work on a mine.

When hostilities between Great Britain and the Boers reached its peak, he was already manager of the Transvaal and Delagoa Bay Colliery. The mine itself, known as the Brugspruit Mine on the farm De Witklip, had been opened in 1897 after Johannesburg financier Sigismund Neumann and his associates bought the land for the purpose of supplying the Witwatersrand gold fields with coal. A railway station called Witbank — after the white sandstone reef under which the coal lies buried — was established. It was only in 1903 after the war that the town of Witbank itself was established.

When war was declared the output of the mine was fairly limited and the shaft was barely 60 feet deep. Howard and a few of his fellow countrymen who had taken the oath of neutrality, were permitted by the Boer government to remain on the property to keep production going.

According to Churchill there were four Britons on the mine: an engineer from Lancashire, two Scottish miners and the mine secretary, John Adams. Howard had become a naturalised burgher of the Transvaal some years before the war. There were two Afrikaner servant maids who slept in the house and a number of black miners were housed elsewhere. Churchill was well aware that his host, whether he was a burgher or not, was committing treason and that he would be liable to be shot if it came out that he had helped an enemy escapee. So staying at Howard's house was risky, but Churchill was in need of a good rest.

He later wrote that he had asked Howard to give him food, a pistol, a guide, and if possible, a pony so that he could make his own way to the sea. He would march cross-country by night and stay far away from the railway line or any habitation. Howard was not convinced that this was the answer to Churchill's predicament.

'Never mind, we will fix it up somehow', he said as he looked at Churchill. 'But you are famished,' he added and invited his visitor to help himself from the whisky bottle while he went to the kitchen to get him more solid refreshment.[18]

Churchill had been on the run for almost 30 hours with only a couple of bars of chocolate for sustenance as well as some stream water. He'd had little exercise during the weeks he was in prison, but even for a fit man the journey he described would have been difficult. Walking throughout the night while on the lookout for armed sentries guarding imaginary stations and bridges, making wide circuits and wading through streams required a good deal of stamina.

Much has been made of Churchill's courage, but it has been amply demonstrated that he had a way with his pen that matched the skill and determination he exhibited when fighting for glory.

Howard 'returned after an interval with the best part of a cold leg of mutton and various other delectable commodities'.[19] Howard then left the house through the back door and returned an hour later.

'It's all right', he assured Churchill. 'I have seen the men, and they are all for it. We must put you down the pit tonight, and there you will have to stay till we can see how you can get out of the country.'[20] There was a small problem that had to be taken care of first. 'The cook will want to know what has happened to her leg of mutton. I shall have to think it all out during the night. You must get down the pit at once. We'll make you comfortable enough.'[21]

By Howard's account the scenario was not quite as Churchill described it in *My Early Life*. 'I then sent one of my servants to the secretary of the mine, Mr John Adams, requesting him to come at once to my house and on his arrival arrangements were made to enlist the services of the engineer, Dan Dewsnap, the mine captain, Joe McKenna, and a miner named Joe McHenry. Dr Gillespie, the mine's doctor, was also included in the friendly circle that was, if at all possible, to befriend Mr Churchill, and keep the secret of his whereabouts.'[22]

Churchill tells us that Howard led him across the yard to the mine's headgear. The mine was situated on bare ground that sloped gently to the west. The, headgear over the shaft and the plant straddled railway tracks that ran north-south. To the east was the boiler house, the workshop, the store and the office. A little farther away were the residences and a trading store. To the west of the line was the burning slag heap that had first attracted Churchill's attention and Howard's house.

On reaching the lift cage they were greeted by the mining engineer whom Howard introduced as Dan Dewsnap of Oldham — the constituency where Churchill had been defeated in a by-election only five months earlier. Dewsnap shook Churchill's hand. 'They'll all vote for you next time,' he said as he opened the cage door.[22] The mine captain, Joe McKenna, and a miner were waiting at the bottom of the shaft. Within an hour of being woken by Howard and notified of their unexpected visitor, they had brought a pillow, blankets, a mattress and a couple of candles into the mine. 'We walked for some time through the pitchy labyrinth, with frequent turns, twists and alterations of level, and finally stopped in a short chamber where the air was cool and fresh.'[23]

Howard must have been pleased indeed that Churchill had knocked at his door for he thought it worthwhile to bring along a bottle of whisky and a box of cigars to make the fugitive's stay in the 'bowels of the earth' as comfortable as he possibly could.

Alexander Graham of Salisbury, Rhodesia (now Harare, Zimbabwe) compiled a booklet entitled *The Capture and Escape of Winston Churchill during the South African War* which he published in 1965. In the foreword he wrote:

> All previous accounts of the escape of Winston Churchill during the South African War have been incomplete and partially incorrect; incomplete in that they gave only Churchill's own account and not those who assisted him; incorrect in that owing to wartime security risks Churchill had to omit full details of his experiences or alter names of persons concerned for their own safety. Unfortunately, these errors and omissions have been perpetuated from book to book and no complete account has ever been published.[24]

In his account, Graham wrote that it was Joe McKenna who suggested hiding the escapee in the new and so far unused underground stables. These were designed to stable horses used to haul loaded coal trucks up steep inclines to the hoisting cage. Graham reproduced a map which originally appeared in the *Witbank News* of 6 October 1944. It shows the location of the stables as being far removed from the mineshaft, and according to this sketch, it was unnecessary for Churchill to go down the mine at all. Howard was also somewhat apprehensive that mine workers might discover him underground, but he finally agreed to the proposal as a temporary measure.

Howard confirmed to *The Star* that having taken him underground, 'exercising every precaution in the process, [we] accompanied him to a new stable that had never been used, and in which, under the circumstances, he was made as comfortable as possible.'[25]

While Churchill's escape had come to a temporary halt at the Transvaal and Delagoa Bay Colliery, the news of his getaway had made international headlines. Speculation as to what might happen to him if he were recaptured fired the imagination of readers who had been enthralled by reports of his courageous conduct at Chieveley a month earlier.

The *Daily Telegraph* of London was of the opinion that, if caught, he would not enjoy the privileges of a prisoner of war again. 'He cannot be shot unless he uses arms to resist capture, but he may be subjected to confinement rigorous enough to control the innate daring and resourcefulness of which he inherits his full share.'[26]

The *Daily Nation* of Dublin was less complimentary about his resourcefulness and character:

> Mr Winston Churchill's escape is not regarded in military circles as either brilliant or an honourable exploit. He was captured as a combatant, and, of course, placed under the same parole as the officers taken prisoner. He has, however, chosen to disregard an honourable undertaking, and it would not be surprising if the Pretoria authorities adopted more strenuous measures to prevent such conduct.[27]

Churchill was unaware of the controversy surrounding his escape. Of more immediate interest was that Howard gave him some essential supplies in the form of a bottle of whisky and a box of cigars.

'Don't you move from here, whatever happens. There will be Kaffirs about the mine after daylight, but we shall be on the look-out that none of them wanders this way', Howard warned him. [28] This again makes it clear that he was not deep down in the mine because Africans would not just 'wander around' such an area.

Celia Sandys pointed out that there are strict rules in mines to prevent explosions caused by the ignition of gas. 'But with typical insouciance, Churchill continued lighting cigars underground. Their smell, drifting through the workings, aroused the curiosity of a coloured mine worker who traced it to the stable, where he came face to face with its temporary occupant'.[29]

On seeing Churchill he was supposed to have run off as if being chased by the devil himself, shouting that he had seen a *tokoloshe* — believed by Africans to this day to be a hairy dwarf with evil intent and it caused quite a furore. Howard embellished on the sighting of the *tokoloshe* and spread the word to prevent superstitious black workers from showing curiosity in that part of the mine.

Of course, if pockets of combustible gas had collected, a burning candle would have proved just as dangerous as Churchill's cigar. If there was truly any danger it is highly unlikely the manager would have given him a generous supply of candles and cigars.

Churchill lay there wondering where fate might next lead him. 'Viewed from the velvety darkness of the pit, life seemed bathed in rosy light', he later recorded. 'After the perplexity and even despair through which I had passed I counted upon freedom as certain. Instead of the humiliating recapture and long months of monotonous imprisonment, probably in a common jail, I saw myself once more rejoining the Army with a real exploit to my credit, and in that full enjoyment of freedom and keen pursuit and adventure dear to the heart of youth'.[30]

With these thoughts, he lay back and fell asleep.

It was late afternoon when he awoke. The candle was not just out — he couldn't find it at all. Wide-awake with apprehension, he decided to lie quietly in anticipation of further developments. Hours passed before he saw the shimmer of a light moving towards him. It was Howard, carrying a roasted chicken, some books and half a dozen candles.

The disappearance of the burning candle (in *My Early Life* he wrote that Howard handed him a couple of candles) was blamed on a horde of white rats with dark eyes that turned pink when exposed to daylight. Howard made no mention of the rats. The chicken, he told Churchill, had come from the kitchen of an English doctor who lived about 20 miles away and added that 'if he could not get another chicken cooked for the next day, he would have to take double helpings on his own plate and slip the surplus into a parcel while the servant was out of the room'.[31]

The English doctor turned out to be James Gillespie, the mine doctor who lived in Brugspruit only four miles away. Other food was, according to Howard's account, provided from the workers' hostel at the mine which was managed by two English women, Ada Blunden and Ellen David, who had only just moved to the mine.

The servants had already questioned the disappearance of the cold mutton that Churchill had feasted on earlier. Howard could have claimed that his compatriots had eaten it while playing cards, but instead — according to Churchill — he said it had been eaten by his dog. To add credence to this, he had thrown the remains of the joint on the floor after returning from settling his visitor in the mine shaft. The fact that neither of the servants sleeping in the house, nor the dog, had been disturbed by Churchill beating furiously at the door after midnight was ignored by the storyteller.

Churchill told his readers that it was not only the cook whose suspicions had to be allayed. 'Enquiries are made about you all over the district by the Boers', Howard told him, 'and the Pretoria Government makes a tremendous fuss about your escape'.[32] Some of the English miners in the district were suspected of harbouring the escaped prisoner. Churchill once more offered to be on his way but asked to be provided with an African guide and a pony.

Howard refused to discuss the matter. 'Here you are absolutely safe', he assured Churchill, and added that McKenna knew all the disused workings and places that no one else could dream of.

'There is one place here where the water actually touches the roof for a foot or two', Howard said. 'If they searched the mine McKenna would dive under that with you into the workings cut off beyond the water. No one would ever think of looking there'. Speaking of the black mine workers he said: 'We have frightened the Kaffirs with tales of a ghost, and anyhow, we are monitoring their movement continually.'[33]

When Howard left Churchill stored the candles under his pillow and mattress and settled down to sleep. Several hours later he was woken up by something pulling on his bedding. The rats, of course. One of the rodents proceeded to cheekily 'gallop' right over him. 'Luckily for me', he wrote, 'I have no horror of rats as such, and being reassured by their evident timidity, I was not particularly uneasy'.[34]

There is evidence, however, that he was not quite so indifferent to the antics of rat antics as he maintained in 1930 so much later. Perhaps he was anxious to move on so that he could escape the attention of these frightening creatures.

'The next day — if you can call it day — arrived in due course', Churchill continued with his reminiscences. 'This was December 14 and the third day since I had escaped from the State Model School'.[35]

But 'the next day' couldn't have been 14 December. In retracing Churchill's steps from the time he scaled the fence at the State Model School at about 7:15pm on Tuesday 12th, to his going down the mine, 'the next day' must have been Friday, 15 December — his third day on the run.

He was visited on that day by the two Scottish miners who told him that the mine was only 200 feet (60 metres) deep. 'There are parts where one could see the daylight up a disused shaft', he was told.[36] He was invited to walk around and investigate. He was probably delighted to get away from the dark and rat-infested hole where he claims to have been confined. He happily spent 'an hour or two wandering round and up and down these subterranean galleries, and spent a quarter of an hour near the bottom of the shaft, where grey and faint, the light of the sun and of the upper world was discerned'.[37]

It is difficult to imagine that the stable where Churchill was actually accommodated could only be reached by going down to the bottom of the shaft, then following a labyrinth — with frequent turns, twists and alterations of level — before reaching his rat-infested chamber. A stable, whether in a barn or underground, is associated with warmth and a certain amount of light. The image Churchill paints conveys the opposite and suggests neither a safe and healthy environment for horses, nor a practical coalmining operation.

The location of the stables at the Brugspruit Mine of the Transvaal and Delagoa Bay Colliery is shown on the map of the mine compound drawn in 1944. Whether it was situated underground is not indicated.

On 15 December Howard told Churchill that the hue and cry seemed to be dying down and it was quite safe for him to walk in the veld that night. If all was quiet, he could move into Howard's office and be concealed behind packing cases in an inner storeroom.

Churchill eagerly took advantage of the suggestion. When darkness fell, he was taken 'out of the mine'. He had complained about the rats and 'declared he would

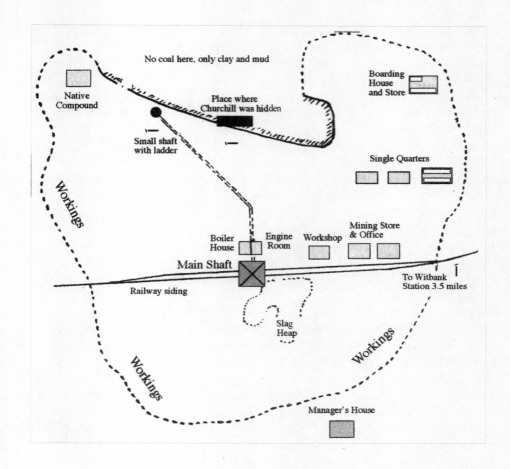

Plan of the Transvaal and Delgoa Bay Colliery

rather be captured than spend another night underground with thousands of white rats'.[38] He told Dr Gillespie while enjoying 'a fine stroll in the glorious fresh air and moonlight',that his health had suffered and that Howard had no choice but to accommodate him in his office.[39] A special signal was agreed to guard against him opening the door to a stranger. Before midnight he was safely ensconced in his new quarters in the storeroom.

On 22 December 1923, ten days after Howard's version of Churchill's stay at the colliery was published, Charles A Burnham related his version. It appears that Burnham thought that Howard had not given him the credit he deserved in relation to Churchill being smuggled out of Witbank to Portuguese East Africa. Indeed, Burnham was a major role player, who probably took greater risks than anyone else on the mine in making Churchill's escape a success.

Burnham ran a concession store on the mine in partnership with a Mr Bourhill. He claimed in *The Star* that he ran also the mine hostel. As a sideline he bought in wool on behalf of a German firm that he railed to Delagoa Bay.

It was the mine secretary, John Adams, who had introduced Burnham to Churchill so that arrangements could be made for his meals to supplied from the hostel. Burnham writes: 'I approached my partner's wife, Mrs JA Bourhill, and insisted that had it not been for the loyal silence of Mrs Bourhill and the assistance of Mr Adams, the plan would not have been successful'.[40]

He didn't explain why Mrs Bourhill was sworn to secrecy, but it seems that she was in charge of the hostel and had given instructions for food to be provided by the two young women, Ada Blunden and Ellen David. After Churchill refused to go back into the mine his presence at the colliery became a problem for Howard. He sent for Adams, Dewsnap, Dr Gillespie and Burnham for an emergency meeting to discuss the situation. Burnham had proposed a possible solution to the problem.

The meeting was 'held in the sitting room of the mine office at which we discussed the question of devising means to get Churchill out of the country'.[41] Burnham claims that he suggested hiding him amongst bales of wool that he intended railing to Delagoa Bay.

'The plan I had conceived in that connection appealed to me', he told a reporter of *The Star* in 1923, 'and as I did not doubt the feasibility I decided to unfold it to the meeting. Mr Churchill was present and after other schemes had been turned down I laid mine before my friends and it was accepted'.[42]

However, according to Howard's story in the same publication it was his idea and not Burnham's. 'One evening, while conversing with Mr Churchill, discussing ways and means for his escape, it occurred to me that Mr Charles Burnham was loading six trucks of wool for Delagoa Bay. I thought we must be able to smuggle Mr Churchill into Portuguese territory in one of these, and mentioned the matter to him, telling him I would see what I could do in that direction'.[43]

It no longer matters who thought up the idea. The fact is that merely being associated with Churchill's capture and escape would carry its own glamour and cachet as his fame spread. This explains why no one ever publicly contradicted the somewhat embroidered claims made by Churchill concerning his escapades in South Africa. Audiences in England and the USA paid large sums of money to listen to the entertainingly embellished account of his adventures.

The idea put forward in Howard's office was simple and proved to be practical at the same time. The mine was connected to the main Pretoria-Lourenço Marques railway line by a branch line some four miles long. At the siding were the six trucks loaded with wool. Burnham, who was referred to by Churchill in *My Early Life* as 'a Dutchman, Burgener by name',[44] had purchased the wool from local farmers.

All he needed was a permit from the field cornet to allow him and his consignment to leave the country. He invited Churchill to accompany him to that official's office. 'There is no fear of my going to a field cornet', Churchill allegedly said when Burnham told him he would pass him off as his assistant. But it seems Burnham changed his mind.

'In order to expedite the delivery of the wool I made representation to the railway people that it was essential to have it delivered at once, as there was a likelihood of a fall in the market'.[45] Burnham also informed his partner's wife of his intention and told *The Star*:

> In view of the fact that I was running a big risk, and did not know what the consequences would be, I felt it incumbent on me to take Mrs Bourhill into a confidence, and I must say she loyally respected it. When I communicated my intentions to her, she expressed a wish to see Churchill before he left the property, and I myself took her to the mine. Mrs Bourhill had a conversation with Mr Churchill and wished him success in his venture. Were it not for her silence we would not have succeeded.

Churchill would be hidden among the bales and a tarpaulin pulled over everything. It was agreed that Burnham would accompany the transport. The train was due to leave the mine siding at 11.00am on 19 December.

Seven goods wagons were waiting at the siding, but there was only sufficient wool bales to fill six. Howard, in his interview with *The Star,* says that he persuaded Burnham to offload the six full trucks and redistribute the bales over all seven, leaving enough space in one to make a concealed nest for Churchill. Burnham needed three days to re-arrange the bales and get clearance. Adams volunteered to assist, ensuring that the work was done without arousing suspicion.

Meanwhile Churchill remained hidden in the spare room. After dark he walked outside in the open with his new friendsand conspired with them how to get 'Dr Bentick' — his new temporary identity — safely to the coast.

How Howard dealt with the two Dutch maids who slept in his house is not mentioned. And why the two English women were not taken into his confidence about the food being taken to the fugitive, was left unanswered.

Another point that may puzzle the observant reader concerns Churchill's ablutions. Bathing was an important part of his daily ritual and in later years, on long flights, a portable canvas bathtub was always part of his luggage. When he arrived at Howard's house he was in a sorry state. Not only had he slept on used coal bags, but wading through swamps, trudging for hours through long wet grass and lying low in the veld must have added to his bedraggled appearance. Two days and a night in the underground stable must have also added to his hygienic woes. It seems odd that he only mentions having had a bath and a change of clothes after nine days on the run, only when he had reached the safety of the British consulate in Lourenço Marques.

18 December, the day before his planned departure, was not incident free. During the morning, a cleaner who was sweeping the stoep either dropped his broom by accident or banged it on the door behind which Churchill was hiding. Churchill interpreted it as a signal. He unlocked the door and found himself staring into the face

of a terrified African. He ran off and told Howard that a stranger was hiding in the back room. He was persuaded to keep quiet by the promise of a new suit of clothes.

That afternoon Churchill was faced with another nerve-wracking experience. He was engrossed in reading Robert Louis Stevenson's *Kidnapped*. 'Those thrilling pages which describe the escape of David Balfour and Alan Breck in the glens awakened sensations with which I was only too familiar. To be a fugitive, to be a hunted man, to be "wanted" is a mental experience by itself ... the need for concealment and deception breeds an actual sense of guilt very undermining to morale.'[46]

His thoughts were suddenly punctuated by rifle shots being fired at irregular intervals close to his hiding place. The Boers had come to arrest Howard, was his first thought, and the mine manager and his compatriots were fighting them off. He had been instructed that he was not to leave the storeroom under any circumstances whatsoever, and he obeyed, anxiously awaiting the outcome of the shoot-out. When he heard voices approaching — interrupted by laughter — he guessed there was little to fear.

Howard walked in, looked around and locked the door behind him. 'The Field Cornet has been here', he said. 'No, he was not looking for you. He says they caught you at Waterval Boven yesterday. But I didn't want him messing about, so I challenged him to a rifle match at bottles. He won two pounds off me and has gone away delighted'.[47]

Churchill was primed and ready to set out on the next leg of his escape.

17

Churchill wanted, dead or alive

By now Churchill's notoriety had been broadcast far and wide in the Boer community. He knew that the pressure was building to find and arrest him and he had to get out of the danger area as soon as possible.

> Telegrams with my description at great length were dispatched along all the railways. Three thousand photographs were printed. A warrant was issued for my immediate arrest. Every train was strictly searched. Everyone was on the watch. The worthy Boshoff, who knew my face well, was hurried off to Komatipoort to examine all the sundry people 'with red hair' travelling towards the frontier. The newspapers made so much of the affair that my humble fortunes and my whereabouts were discussed in long columns in print, and even in the crash of the war I became to the Boers a topic all to myself.[1]

The warrant of arrest alerted police officers to be on the lookout for Churchill and to apprehend and remand him. But it is not clear what would have been done to him after he was remanded. President Kruger had stated that the journalist was of no use to the Boers and that he should be set free. General Joubert felt the same and there is little doubt that he would have been happy to be rid of him.

Adrian Hofmeyr, who wrote in detail about Churchill's escape in his book, *The Story of My Captivity during the Transvaal War 1899-1900,* mentions that Commandant Boshoff was asked to describe Churchill, but there is no indication that Boshoff left the State Model School to join the search. Churchill published extracts of Lieutenant Frankland's diary under the heading 'Held by the Enemy' in his book, *Ian Hamilton's March*. Frankland didn't seem to be aware of the publicity the escaped prisoner claims to have received.

In *My Early Life* Churchill no longer boasts about the importance of his status as an escaped prisoner. There is no mention of photographs being circulated or of the supposedly lengthy newspaper columns. He is silent too about Boshoff being sent to Komatipoort to watch out for people with red hair. Churchill had accepted the proposal of being concealed among bales of wool on a railway truck but 'I dreaded in every fibre the ordeal which awaited me at Komatipoort and which I must impotently endure if I was to make good my escape from the enemy'.[2]

'I could have been still more anxious if I had read some of the telegrams which were reaching English newspapers, or if I had read the description of myself and the reward for my recapture which were now widely distributed or posted along the railway line. I am glad I knew nothing of all this'.[3] He quotes four of the telegrams, two of which gave him little chance of crossing the border and the other two claiming that he had already been captured. The official description of him included the request to find him, apprehend and remand him. This warrant, however, carried no reward.

Malcolm Thomson, in *Churchill, His Life and Times,* believed that Churchill's escape from prison in Pretoria was perhaps the most fantastically dramatic episode in a life holding many vivid moments and thrilling experiences. 'He retold it often, in print and in lecture; and others, too, have recounted it — not without reason, for it is one of those true stories which are stranger than fiction. It seems to have been written in Winston's stars that, whenever he captivated popular imagination by some brilliant stroke, he should at the same time stir up a storm of detraction from envious or hostile critics'.[4]

But although Churchill was a target for criticism, he also — like many public figures — had his fair share of admirers. The admirers of his escapades in South Africa far outweighed his opponents. It is accepted that stories repeated often enough change until they become almost unrecognisable. However, few writers have felt the need to exaggerate the tales of his escape, because the story as told by Churchill himself is in itself stranger than fiction.

One of the most puzzling issues concerning Churchill's escape is the reward note for his recapture referred to in *My Early Life.*

Below this an explanatory note which says: 'The original reward for the arrest of Winston Churchill on his escape from Pretoria, posted at Government House in Pretoria, was brought to England by the Hon Henry Meshem and is now the property of WE Burton.'

What the pamphlet does not reveal — and has never been pointed out by historians reproducing the document to illustrate their accounts on Churchill's escape — is the certainty that the original note comprised only the handwritten part, and that the typed translation was added much later.

The fact that nowhere on the 21 x 32cm 'poster' do the words *Zuid-Afrikaansche Republiek* appear, and nor is any government office mentioned, should have caused suspicion concerning its authenticity as an official document. There is no date or stamp or any other indication that the note was issued on behalf of the Boer government.

There is only the signature of a certain Lod D de Haas, secretary of the sub-commission for Ward V. Yet, since Churchill's autobiography was published in 1930, the note — or 'poster' as it became known — has been reproduced in numerous books

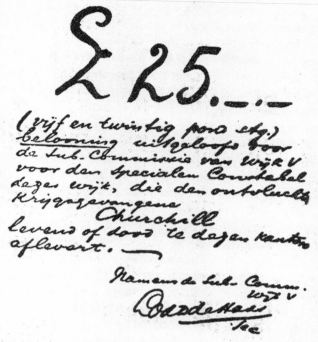

The reward notice was not sanctioned by the Boer authorities and the £25 reward apparently only applied to constables of the sub-commission for Ward V in Pretoria. Some doubt remains regarding the authenticity of the 'Dead or alive' part.

with the added translation invariably appearing as an integral part as if it were a single official document.

When Churchill wrote of a warrant that had been issued for his immediate arrest in his dispatch of 22 December 1899, he made no mention a reward being offered. Celia Sandys notes that on the 18th, a handwritten poster offering £25 for his recapture 'Dead or Alive', was displayed at Government House, Pretoria.[5] If this was indeed the case, Churchill could not have known about it because well before sunrise on that day he had exchanged his hiding place in Witbank for a railway truck bound for Lourenço Marques.

Churchill may have heard of the note before W Roby Burton of North Finchley wrote a letter to him on 27 September 1904 explaining that he was in possession of the document. As he had fallen on hard times he was, unfortunately, compelled to part with it. He suggested that the note, framed in plain oak, could assist Churchill's political campaign.

Churchill was delighted. He asked Burton to issue a receipt certifying that he had been paid for the war memorabilia. Burton complied, writing on a piece of paper the words: 'Received from Winston S. Churchill, Esq the sum of five pounds, for document framed in oak'. He attached a one penny revenue stamp and dated the receipt 17 October 1904.

The author of the poster, Lodewijk de Haas, was a Dutch immigrant who had joined the Hollander Corps at the outbreak of war. This volunteer unit comprised immigrants from the Netherlands who were not naturalised citizens of the Transvaal. One section saw active service and the other was part of the *Garnizoendienst*, or guard force known as *Subcommissie voor the bescherming van Rust en Orde te Pretoria en Voorsteden* (Sub-commission for the protection of peace and order in Pretoria and suburbs). The man behind the formation of the corps was a former state attorney of the Transvaal Republic, Hollander, Dr Herman Coster.

The Hollander Corps was dedicated to defending 'the cause of the South African republics — the cause which the people of the Netherlands had come to regard as that of liberty and justice'.[6] De Haas was a member of the mounted commando that had captured Newcastle. Although later defeated at Elandslaagte, the men remained certain of final victory. But then De Haas had received a telegram recalling him for police duties in Pretoria.

The police force of the combined Boer republics, the Transvaal and the Orange Free State, amounted to 1 695 men. The largest part of the force was needed to serve at the front, which made it necessary for the remainder to be supplemented by a special night guard force or sub-commission, which was responsible for maintaining peace and order in urban areas. Although official documents refer only to 'Pretoria and suburbs', sub-commissions also existed in Johannesburg, Klerksdorp, Potchefstroom and other towns in the Transvaal.

Regulations and other provisions for this special guard force were approved by the Executive Council of the South African Republic and published in a special edition of the *Staats Courant* (Government Gazette) on 18 November 1899. It comprised 22 clauses, the first of which declared: 'The town Pretoria and suburbs shall, for the purpose of peace and order, be divided into as many wards or sections as the Head of the Commission will deem necessary'.

Represented on the commission was the temporary town council comprising *Burghermeester* (mayor) Potgieter, chairman Richard Kelsey Loveday, secretary

Bosch and nine officials.

Instructions were passed from the head of the commission to the First Lieutenant of the Republican Police Force, who was in overall command of the sub-commissions.

Seven wards were identified, Ward V being situated at the corner of Church and Du Toit Street. Every sub-commission was ordered to keep a book, in the front of which appeared a form with the oath of loyalty to the South African Republic. Members and specially appointed constables had to take the oath and sign and date the form.

This is relevant because it emphasises that not even a stamp appeared on the 'dead or alive' note. The special constables were subject to the laws and regulations pertaining to the police. While the majority were Dutch immigrants to the Transvaal there were also men of other nationalities, as well as burghers who by reason of age or physical condition, were considered unsuitable for service at the front.

It was the duty of every sub-commission to report each morning in writing all incidents which had occurred in their wards during the previous night to the First Lieutenant of the Police. In addition to their prime function of protecting lives and property, they kept files on the various buildings and their occupants, noting who had left town and the reason.

Anyone abroad on the streets between 6:30pm and 5.00am had to be in possession of a permit. The constables, equipped with revolvers, whistles and usually bicycles, had the authority to question any suspicious looking individuals about their movements or what they were doing. If anybody refused to answer, or their explanations proved unsatisfactory, the constables had the authority to arrest them.

Lodewijk de Haas was assigned to Ward V and appointed secretary. The commission for the ward was headed by the Postmaster-General, Isaac van Alphen, with Minnaar, the registrar of deeds, and RTN James, an old farmer of English extraction, in support.

'These gentlemen were all fully occupied with their own affairs and, apart from attending short meetings every day at which reports were read, they left the running of the office to me and my two assistants, a bright Boer lad, even younger than myself, and a Hungarian musician. There was also, of course, the inevitable kaffir boy'.[7]

Their office was in an old school building the commission had requisitioned and converted for the purpose. Amongst the furnishing was a piano that the Hungarian played, often accompanied by the Boer boy singing sentimental songs. A large garden with innumerable fruit trees was at the back of the building.

This idyllic setting was rudely disrupted when, on the morning of 13 December, a telephone call from the head of the commission informed De Haas that Winston Churchill had escaped from the State Model School. De Haas had never heard of him and he enquired about the importance of the fugitive. This brought him a reprimand for his ignorance. In a near hysterical voice, De Haas was told that Churchill was a non-combatant who had sabotaged an armoured train in Natal. He was a 'Jingo' and moreover, the son of the Duke of Marlborough. He should be arrested on sight.

De Haas didn't believe the missing man could be the son of a duke, and not being personally responsible for guarding prisoners of war, he dismissed the call. He nevertheless informed his colleagues of the escape. The Boer boy thought the prisoner on the run could well be important. The sons of dukes were dukes themselves, he argued — except, of course, when they were illegitimate, which made them marquesses.

De Haas pondered this piece of wisdom and decided that the matter was not worth bothering about. Then the telephone rang again. The voice demanded to know what they were doing about Churchill. De Haas assured the caller that they were attending to the matter and that he was certain they would catch the fugitive before the end of the day.

Thinking of how to tackle the problem, De Haas remembered that he had read somewhere of prices being put on the heads of wanted desperadoes in America, and suggested they should do the same with Churchill. The question was how much of a reward should be offered.

The Hungarian suggested £100 as he felt sure this would get him back before evening. De Haas didn't have £100 and reasoned that £25 would be sufficient. He took up his pen and wrote the 'proclamation' on a sheet of paper and pinned it to the door in his office.

Towards evening the commission convened for De Haas to report on the action he had taken. Van Alphen told him that house searches of some British subjects had already been conducted by the special constabulary. He was told to get some men together and organise house-to-house searches in his own ward. The Anglican Bishop of Pretoria, Henry Bourgham Bousfield, was pointed out as a prominent British sympathiser.

De Haas stuck a huge revolver in his belt and accompanied by his two assistants, he called on the bishop. A large oak chest caught his eye, but apparently the key had been lost. The bishop looked pointedly at the revolver, but De Haas shrugged and insisted that he was only following orders. The bishop had little choice but to agree that the lock on the chest should be prised open.

In another house the trio was told not to touch the clothes hanging in a deep wardrobe. They needed no more prompting and they attacked the garments feeling sure that Churchill was hiding behind them. All they found was a large cache of whisky and gin. A large stock had been laid down to see the family through the expected lean years ahead.

The next morning one of the constables, a Frenchman who was confident he had earned the reward, brought in a young man he had arrested in his garden. In appearance he corresponded with the description of the escaped prisoner, but to everyone's disappointment he turned out to be a Swedish national.

As the days passed Churchill's escape dropped from being the main topic of conversation. As far as the members of Ward V were concerned, he had already crossed the border and was out of their jurisdiction. This was confirmed by the acting commissioner of police on 28 December after an announcement by the British consul in Lourenço Marques that Churchill had arrived there.

When Churchill reproduced De Haas' note in *My Early Life*, he knew it was merely an official document issued by the authority of the Boer government, and that it had never been distributed or posted outside of Pretoria. He regarded it merely as a curiosity of the South African War to be kept as a souvenir. It was also clear that the translation pasted below the handwritten note was not contemporaneous with it.

Churchill's account of his escape published in *Strand Magazine* in December 1923 makes no mention of the 'poster' at all. It was his statement in *My Early Life* published in 1930: '... the description of myself and the reward for my recapture which was now widely distributed or posted along the railway line',[8] that caused the 'dead or alive' warrant becoming widely accepted as a genuine official document. When Churchill acquired it there was no translation attached.

Six years later De Haas happened to be in London and he read about the forthcoming marriage of the President of the Board of Trade, the Rt Hon Winston Churchill, to Miss Clementine Hozier. He sent him a note expressing his best wishes for his future happiness. In thanking De Haas Churchill commented: 'I think you might have gone as high as £50 without an overestimate of the value of the prize — if living.'[9]

On 23 November 1944, 36 years after he had first written to Churchill, De Haas addressed a letter to Mrs Kathleen Hill, the personal private secretary of the British Prime Minister. De Haas by then was living in Twickenham in Middlesex and working as a Reuter's correspondent. He asked for an appointment so he could present documents of importance about which he wanted a decision. These papers, he assured Mrs Hill, would greatly interest her. She was unable to meet him but asked him to write about the matter he had in mind.

On 13 December he sent her a photograph of his poster and explained that he was contemplating embodying the letter that Churchill had sent him in 1908 into an article he intended publishing either in England or America. On 23 December he was told that Churchill had no objection to him publishing his letter of 24 August 1908.

The correspondence did not end there and on 27 December De Haas addressed yet another letter to Mrs Hill. His first point was that he believed the original notice he had written was amongst the papers of the late Sir Algernon Methuen. He was not sure whether the handbill still existed, but the executors of Methuen, Messrs. Russel Cook & Co, solicitors, II Old Square WC might be of assistance.

It was not clear to which handbill De Haas referred. If it was the reward notice, he was obviously unaware that Churchill had acquired it.

According to Celia Sandys, 'Some doubt has been cast on the authenticity of the handwritten poster. This seems to have arisen as a result of the appearance of bogus printed posters which purported to be the original reward notices and which included a translation into English — in a typeface which was not designed until 1928.'[10]

If this was the case, one must ask why the explanation added at the bottom of the poster read: 'The Original Reward for the arrest of Winston Churchill after his escape from Pretoria, posted on the Government House of Pretoria, brought to England by the

Hon Henry Meshem, and is now the property of WR Burton.'

Churchill had acquired the poster in 1904 — 24 years before the typeface attesting to Burton's ownership was, by Sandys account, created.

Under item 2, De Haas wrote that the photo of the poster he had sent to Mrs Hill was rather indistinct and he would either like to have it back or alternately obtain a specimen from the printers. Failing this, he asked Mrs Hill to let him know where he could buy a copy of Churchill's book.

The next point refers to an erratum slip which he enclosed. It concerned a mistake in the translation of the poster, and said that if it was not too late to have this corrected in the second edition of *My Early Life*, he suggested that the handwritten note be inserted in Churchill's personal copy. This note, dated London, 26 December 1944 read:

> The correct English rendering is not 'on behalf of the Special Constable to anyone' but 'to the Special Constable who'. ... In other words my offer was made to the police and not to the general public.

The fourth point in De Haas' letter was to the effect that he would like to visit 10 Downing Street to write an article on Churchill for *Envoy*, the Ministry of Information's Dutch illustrated review. For this he requested certain documents and one or two photographs taken by a professional photographer.

De Haas was certainly tenacious in pursuing his contact with Churchill's office and, no doubt, trying to gain his personal attention. However, there is no evidence that he was ever actually inside 10 Downing Street.

World War II was at its climax and it is unlikely that the hands-on Premier would have made time to discuss relatively frivolous matters. It is, of course, quite possible that De Haas merely walked past the official residence of the Prime Minister and conjured up a plan to write about it in the hope of gaining entry and meeting Churchill personally.

Returning to the poster, there are a number of aspects that are of interest when scrutinising the now historic document with translation added. The wording is an obvious starting point, with the accuracy of the translation being vital for a full understanding of its meaning. In closely examining the text, a discrepancy becomes evident.

When De Haas pointed out the incorrect English interpretation, he overlooked two words: *dezen wijk*, which mean 'this ward'. Thus the English translation should read:

> ... Reward offered for the Sub-commission of Ward V to the Special Constable of this ward who delivers the escaped prisoner of war Churchill, alive or dead to this office.
> In the name of the Sub-Comm. Ward V.
> Lod D de Haas, Sec.

The inclusion of *desen wijk* leaves no doubt that the reward was intended only for the constables of Ward V. Whether he was serious about the reward is another matter. De Haas had never heard of Churchill and was not particularly concerned about an escaped prisoner of war for whom he had no responsibility, and the circumstances under which he penned the 'warrant' indicate that he did so lightheartedly.

If he had posted the proclamation at 'Government House' (the *Raadsaal*, or House of Assembly on Church Square), the reward would have caused him serious trouble with the Boer authorities. By that time, five days after Churchill's escape, it was generally accepted that the correspondent had already reached safety. If he had been recaptured, however, the police would doubtless have interrogated him in order to establish who had helped him escape. The military authorities would have decided what to do with him, and there is little doubt that he would have been set free, for his official release had been signed well before he climbed over the prison fence. There was no point in the Boers trying to save face by keeping him.

In the unlikely event that a special constable of Ward V had killed Churchill, De Haas would have been responsible for his death and liable for prosecution. With no sign of governmental approval on the piece of paper he had written, and with the limitations set, there are no grounds for further speculation about its validity.

Having established beyond doubt that Churchill was aware that the note was written by an individual who had no authority to do so, the obvious question that arises is: why did Churchill pass off the poster as genuine? The possibility that De Haas could have exposed his statement as a deliberate distortion of the facts must be considered.

If an official reward for Churchill's recapture had been issued by the Boers, and if this had been 'widely distributed or posted along railway lines', it seems very strange that no copies of the poster can be found in archives or museums in South Africa. One would also expect that copies of the note would have been discovered in private collections or at auctions of South African war memorabilia. The same can be said about the 'bogus posters' that are supposed to have appeared in England. If this had been the case, there should be some examples in existence. As far as the poster Churchill acquired from Burton is concerned, the Churchill Archives of the National Trust in Cambridge — deposited there at the end of 2004 — state that it is the only poster they are aware of.

Another aspect about the poster story that has never been explored is the fact that 'wanted dead or alive' warrants were totally alien to the Boers. Churchill knew that they did not resort to such practices to apprehend fugitives, whether black or white — whatever their crime might have been. The Boers would certainly not have issued such a warrant for an escaped prisoner of war.

James Ambrose Brown, in his foreword to the reprinted edition of Haldane's book, *How we escaped from Pretoria*, writes:

> It has taken two world wars and a decade of professional terrorism to fully
> illustrate how fortunate these British prisoners were in Boer captivity. They

175

were in the hands of men who hesitated from extreme measure, to whom firing squads and torture and the whole hideous business of political manoeuvring at the expense of captives was unknown. Even in their escapes, British prisoners in South Africa were in no great danger. Neither were those of their civilian population who had sympathy with the prisoners risking much from the police of the republic. Execution for what would now be regarded as fifth column activity would have been unthinkable in a Pretoria where Paul Kruger, seated on his stoep, did not neglect to return the salutes offered him by officer-prisoners returning from the funeral of a comrade.[11]

It is understandable that General Joubert and State Secretary Reitz would have been annoyed that the son of Randolph Churchill — who had been anything but complimentary about the Boers on his visit to southern Africa eight years earlier — had escaped the night before he was due for release. It also stands to reason that they had more important things to worry about than a man who, at worst, was a nuisance to them.

One would believe that Churchill, in turn, had more things to worry about at the end of 1944 than a Hollander seeking publicity with the 'dead or alive' warrant he had written almost a half a century earlier. But the 14 items of correspondence that passed between De Haas, Mrs Hill and Churchill during the period 27 September 1944 to 5 January 1945 suggest otherwise. For well over three quarters of a century the poster first reproduced by Churchill in *My Early Life* has, in good faith, been accepted as an authentic document issued by the Boer authorities during the South African War. Moreover, it has been included with a wrong translation in almost every book dealing with Churchill's escape. It is a legend that is long overdue for laying to rest.

18

Among bales of wool to Delagoa Bay

At 2.00am on the morning of 19 December Howard came to collect Churchill from his hiding place in the mine office. Not a word was spoken as the two headed for the siding where the goods train for Portuguese East Africa was still being loaded. A gang was busy lifting an enormous bale into the rearmost of three large bogie trucks. Dewsnap and the two Scottish miners were walking around in an effort to distract attention from the scene of action. Howard walked past the first truck and pointed with his left hand. Following the finger Churchill saw a hole between the wool bales just wide enough for him to squeeze into. This led to a narrow tunnel in the centre of the truck. 'Here was a space wide enough to lie in, high enough to sit up in. In this I took up my abode'.[1]

Burnham was already on board, riding in the rather more comfortable accommodation of the guard's van.

Churchill felt certain he would be safe. He lay there patiently waiting for the first rays of the sun to find their way through the many crevices on the sides and bottom of the truck. He felt around him to check his stock of provisions. He had the revolver he had asked for to give him moral support. There were also two roasted chickens, some slices of cold meat, a loaf of bread, a melon, and three bottles of cold tea — enough to sustain him for the journey which should take 16 hours at the most.

Feeling pleased himself he crawled to the end of the truck. Through a large chink he would be able to check on the progress the train was making. He had learned the names of the stations he would have to pass while at the State Model School. 'I can remember many of them today', he wrote thirty years later, 'Witbank, Middelburg, Bergendal, Belfast, Dalmanutha, Machadodorp, Waterval Boven, Waterval Onder [Watervalonder], Elands, Nooitgedacht, and so on to Komatipoort'.[2]

The train remained at the siding for what seemed like an eternity but finally, at 11.00am it started to move. It had hardly reached full speed when it was shunted into a siding at Middelburg station. Burnham enquired why and was told the trucks would have to remain at the siding for the day, but 'a few tips to the shunter soon put him in a good frame of mind, and we went on after a short delay', he wrote in a letter to Churchill on 8 March 1908.

At Waterval Boven there was another delay. The guard told Burnham that they would have to wait because a passenger train was expected and that had priority. A bottle of whisky overcame that problem, too, and the wool trucks were coupled onto the passenger train. While Burnham was smoothing their passage, Churchill realised that it was likely that he often snored and that this could give him away. He had been up since 2.00am. 'Indeed, I did not think I could possibly keep awake. But if I slept I might snore! And if I snored while the train was at rest in the silent siding, I might be heard ... I decided in principle that it was only prudent to abstain from sleep, and shortly afterwards fell into a blissful slumber from which I was awakened the next morning by the banging and jerking of the train as the engine was again coupled to it'.[3] Needless to say, if he had snored it was unlikely the sound would have penetrated the heavy bales of wool to be heard outside.

They stopped at Waterval Onder. Burnham doesn't mention any incidents that occurred there in his letter to Churchill, but Brian Roberts has it that 'the trucks were detached, and the guard, who was then leaving the train, held out little hope of persuading his relief to take them on further unless another bottle of whisky was forthcoming'.[4]

Burnham went off to buy whisky in the village and also ordered dinner at the local hotel. He must have been highly amused when the proprietor informed him that 'Churchill had passed that way two days before, dressed as a Roman Catholic priest'.[5]

The train reached Kaapmuiden the next morning where the station was swarming with armed Boers. One, an elderly fellow, was leaning on the truck that Churchill was hiding in and he was looking suspiciously at the tarpaulin covered bales of wool. Burnham, who was watching from his compartment, had a strange feeling about this peculiar character. Something told him to pry the man off the wagon as quickly as he could. He rushed over to him thinking only of asking directions to the buffet — which happened to be right opposite them.

The man looked at Burnham in disbelief and told him it was staring him in the face. Burnham kept calm. He thanked him and invited the stranger to join him for a cup of coffee which was accepted.

While this was going on, Churchill must have been sweltering in his woolly nest in the subtropical heat of the Lowveld summer. During the long hours of the stop-start journey, his mind frequently turned to the pleasures of freedom and the excitement of rejoining the army. Despite this he was still dreading that the train might be searched before it crossed the border.

Eventually the train clanked into Komatipoort. Churchill crawled back to the end of the wagon and peering through the chink, he observed several trains and numerous people moving about with much shouting and whistling. As the train came to a halt he retreated to his hiding place, covered himself with a sack and anxiously awaited further developments.

This was where the cross-border trains were thoroughly searched. Burnham, however, had a few words with his acquaintance, Morris, who was the chief detective at Komatipoort. He issued strict orders that nothing belonging to the merchant was to be touched and that the wool was to be sent on to Lourenço Marques without delay. Despite this, the train was only cleared to proceed into Portuguese territory at 11.00am the following day.

There was no way for Churchill to tell whether they had crossed the border or not until they pulled into the next station. Then, peering through the chink in the slats he saw the unfamiliar uniforms of foreign railway officials and the name of the station Ressano Garcia, painted on a board.

He had arrived in neutral territory. The long, dangerous trek was over! He could hardly control his excitement, but waited until the train was on the move again before he pushed his head out from under the tarpaulin to shout with joy and sing at the top of his voice. 'I was so carried away by thankfulness and delight', he wrote, 'that I fired my revolver two or three times in the air as a *feu de joie*'.[6]

At Ressano Garcia, Burnham was ordered off the train because Portuguese regulations did not allow individuals to travel on a goods train. He offered the stationmaster £20 if he would allow the trucks carrying his wool to be coupled to the passenger train, but he turned out to be the only official during the entire journey who was not susceptible to a bribe. Burnham had no choice but to transfer to a waiting passenger train, but not before he had extracted a promise from the stationmaster that his cargo would be on its way within half an hour of his own departure.

The train pulled into the Lourenço Marques' goods yard late that afternoon. As labourers approached the wagons to unload them, Churchill managed to slip out of his hot and no doubt smelly hole without being detected. He had already thrown out every vestige of food and removed all traces of his occupation. He then 'mingled unnoticed with the kaffirs and loafers in the yard — which my slovenly and unkempt appearance well fitted me to do'.[7] Considering that he had probably not bathed or changed his clothes since breaking out of the State Model School, he must have been so filthy that he stood out among the loafers like a scarecrow on a potato patch.

Burnham was waiting at the gate. He claimed that a policeman wanted to arrest him for 'loitering with intent', but yet another bribe saw that he was not inconvenienced. It does seem somewhat strange that a respectable wool dealer awaiting the arrival of his merchandise should be charged with loitering.

Churchill recorded that he and Burnham exchanged glances and the latter walked off with Churchill following 20 yards behind him along several streets and around a number of corners. He does not say why these precautions were necessary, although it may have been for the protection of Burnham who had to return to the Transvaal and could not afford to be seen in the company of a fugitive; Lourenço Marques was full of Boers and their sympathisers.

They presently came to a house and on the flagpole was the welcome sight of the Union Jack fluttering in the breeze. It was the British Consulate. But no one had warned the staff of Churchill's likely arrival so he was not allowed to pass the front door. They could hardly be blamed for thinking that the scruffy unkempt individual was a tramp looking for a handout. The secretary invited him to return at 9.00am the following morning. Angered at this unexpected reception, he repeated his demand to see the consul immediately 'in such a loud voice that the gentleman himself looked out of the window and finally came down to the door and asked me my name'.[8]

He turned out to be Ross and he immediately apologised for having mistaken Churchill for a fireman off one of the ships in the harbour. Once the misunderstanding had been cleared up, the unexpected visitor was offered hospitality and every resource available. Understandably, his first priority was a hot bath and clean clothing.

After Churchill had washed off the stains of his adventures, he saw to it that his mother and Pamela Plowden were telegraphically informed of his safe arrival in Lourenço Marques. He then asked Burnham to accompany him 'to buy a rigout and a cowboy hat'.

On returning from their shopping spree, an enormous dinner awaited them. But there were still anxious moments in store for Churchill. The news of his arrival 'had spread like wildfire through the town'.[9] While he was having dinner with the consul and Burnham, rumours were reported that he was about to be kidnapped and returned to the Transvaal. A large number of people armed with rifles started to gather outside the consulate.

But how had the news of his arrival in town a few hours earlier been leaked to the enemy? Had he not bothered to take precautions when he went shopping with Burnham? A cleaned-up Churchill was surely more easily recognisable than the filthy looking fugitive who had strolled from the railway yard to the consulate. Was it the cowboy hat that had given him away? Or was there perhaps a leak in the security system at the consulate? On the other hand, what was the point of kidnapping a relatively unimportant war correspondent while he was in the sanctuary of the British consulate in a neutral country? Such speculations are, of course, futile.

Churchill must have been relieved when he was told over coffee and cognac that the armed men mingling in the garden of the consulate were not sinister Boers or their sympathisers, but Englishmen 'determined to resist any attempt at my recapture'.[10] Less comforting were the newspaper reports on the state of the war. 'Great events had taken place since I had climbed the walls of the State Model School. The Black Week of the Boer War had descended on the British Army. General Gatacre at Stormberg, Lord Methuen at Magersfontein, and Sir Redvers Buller at Colenso, had all suffered staggering defeats and casualties on a scale unknown to England since the Crimean War. All this made me eager to rejoin the army, and the Consul himself was no less anxious to get me out of Lourenço Marques'.[11]

Luck was again on Churchill's side. The weekly steamer *SS Induna* was and due to sail for Durban at 1.00am the following morning. A hasty booking was made and later that evening a tired but immensely proud Churchill boarded the vessel.

At about this time the *Natal Mercury* informed its readers of their strong belief that Churchill had arrived in Lourenço Marques incognito, but had already left the town. 'It is believed that Mr Churchill was disguised as a woman and it has good authority that even if captured he will be leniently treated, and after it is discovered who assisted him to escape he will probably be released'.[12]

Before the *SS Induna* reached Durban harbour on 23 December 1899 everyone there was talking about Winston Churchill. A special correspondent of the *Natal Mercury* compiled a highly imaginative account of his eventful escape from the Boers under the headlines: 'Winston Churchill. Makes Good His Escape. Will Arrive in Durban Today.' The informant confessed: 'I am not able to say how he managed to elude his guards and get out of Pretoria, but the story of his journey afterwards is sufficiently exciting to win general admiration.'[13]

The people of Durban wanted to give the hero of Chieveley — he who had shown outstanding courage coupled with supernatural strength and endurance while making his way through dangerous enemy territory — a rousing welcome on his arrival. As the *Mercury* correspondent put it:

> Few people thought that he could possibly get through, considering the long distance and the careful watch that would be kept throughout the Transvaal, and particularly on the border, at Komatie Poort [Komatiepoort]. Only under clever disguises, most difficult to obtain under the circumstances, was it believed possible for him to reach a haven of safety. As will be seen, he was disguised, but not in any orthodox way, or by any means that had previously been contemplated. Nevertheless, his appearance was such that his most intimate friend would not have readily recognised him. Disguise alone, however, would probably not have availed him, and he got through by the exercise of indomitable pluck and sharp wit. [14]

The paper then went on to say that Churchill managed to elude his guard at the State Model School, and after getting out of Pretoria walked unaccompanied to Middelburg. There, seeing a coal train coming his way, he determined to travel by it somehow, and effected his purpose by hanging on to the buffers. At the siding he managed to get under the sacks of coal, and there he remained for 36 hours, the drivers and guard little thinking what company they had. At Waterval Onder the train was shunted, and Mr Churchill was still in the enemy's country. Waiting patiently till the coast was clear, he left the train and walked on for a considerable distance, having to keep eyes and ears acutely alive against detection. At length he saw another coal train, and, repeating his tactics, got on board and was conveyed as far as Komatiepoort. Here, as he was well aware, was the greatest risk and danger. The train was examined, the officials even turning over the sacks, but he luckily escaped detection. The train came forward, and Mr Churchill arrived here as black as a kaffir. He suffered great privations, being for sixty hours without food. [15]

It is obvious that the special correspondent was given basic details of Churchill's escape, such as hiding under coal sacks on the train, and making his way to Lourenço Marques. But who was the informant? Was it Churchill himself who, with the help of the secretary to the British consul, contacted the Lourenço Marques-based correspondent of the *Natal Mercury* before his departure on the *SS Induna*? No one stood to benefit from the incredible story but himself. His hiding in the coalmine had to be omitted to protect Howard and his men. But with his gift for embellishing a story and his insatiable desire for publicity, Churchill found ways to compensate for this detail. The grossly exaggerated tale further sensationalised by an eager reporter led to his hero's welcome in Durban. Nonetheless, the subject of this adulation must have been amazed when he read the accounts of his feat.

The telegram Churchill sent to the Johannesburg-based *Standard and Diggers' News* was short. He had seen the article at the British consulate in which the pro-Boer newspaper had featured his escape. He laughed at the prediction that he would not succeed getting out of the country, but realised that there was no point in elaborating on his escapades.

On Christmas eve 1899 Churchill's note was published under the heading 'Message from the Missing'. It read:

We were last evening in receipt of the following telegraphic message from Lourenço Marques:

> From: Churchill
> To: Editor *Standard and Diggers' News*.
>
> Am now writing 'How I escaped from the Boers', but regret I cannot for obvious reasons disclose many interesting details. Shall be happy to give you any you may require when next I visit Pretoria, probably third week in March.

The editor was fuming at this rather cheeky note and he could not hide his resentment in an open letter to Churchill that he published on Christmas Day:

> Mr Winston Churchill
>
> The *Standard and Diggers' News* has been honoured by Mr Winston Churchill's evident desire to become a contributor to its columns, where in or about the third week of March, he would relate his experiences under the title: 'How I Escaped from the Boers.' We are sorry indeed to have to disappoint so promising a youth, but unless Mr Churchill can offer us something much more interesting to the general public, we must decline the promised contribution. Mr Churchill is a very young man who has his way to make in the world, and we would from our maturer experience venture to suggest that it would be advisable to bear in mind the old adage 'A still tongue maketh a wise head'. And to demonstrate to our journalistic fledgling the true appreciation of his particular desire we would recommend that he

alter the title of his publication to 'How I was allowed to escape from the Boers', a précis of which would read: A moonlight night, easygoing guards, Netherlands Railway Station. A coal truck. Ressano Garcia station. Begrimed and miserable objects. Arrived at Lourenço Marques. Admittance to British Consulate. Departure by French steamer. Typewritten telegrams. And the key to the whole scene: Pretoria War office: 9.00am Mr Churchill reported missing: orders of arrest issued to police authorities 11.00am Receipt of official letter by morning's mail from Commandant General Joubert, dated Volksrust, December 15th, 1899, ordering release of Mr Churchill as non-combatant. Orders to police authorities not to execute warrant of arrest.

Durban's harbour was decorated with bunting and flags. Twenty troopships and supply vessels lay at anchor, and three more were waiting for pilots to guide them into the docks. A band was playing and an enormous crowd was looking forward with eager anticipation for the hero to disembark. Churchill was 'detected on the captain's bridge', the *Natal Mercury* reported, 'his round boyish face shielded by a large brimmed hat. The instant he was recognised a rousing cheer went up from the crowd which had gathered and as Mr Churchill bowed his acknowledgments he became the cynosure of all eyes, and all voices joined in one loud acclaim of welcome'.[16]

Durban harbour was so cramped that the *SS Induna* had to triple berth, but as he finally walked down the gangplank, the crowd again broke into loud cheers. Churchill thought of the October day when the crowd at Southampton cheered for 'their general', 59-year-old Sir Redvers Buller. But the war was not progressing as expected. The British had suffered nearly 1 000 killed and 2 000 wounded at the battles of Magersfontein, Stormberg and Colenso. Churchill doubted whether Buller, at his age, was still in possession of the 'military capacity, or the mental and physical vigour, or the resource of ruthlessness, which his duty required'.[17] He questioned the fact that a man who had gained the Victoria Cross for bravery as a young officer was still fit to command an army 20 or 30 years later. 'I have noticed more than one serious misfortune which arose from such assumption',[18] he wrote in *My Early Life*.

But this was not the time to entertain such thoughts. Today the cheers were not for the general but for the 25-year-old non-combatant everyone was talking about. The *Induna* had hardly tied up when some of the men in the crowd jumped on board to seize Churchill and carry him on their shoulders around the deck. 'I was nearly torn to pieces by enthusiastic kindness',[19] he said. As the gangway was lowered, the mayor of Durban strode up the gangplank, followed by an admiral and a general to take turns in embracing him.

A group of men carried him shoulder high through the harbour before they placed him on a box at the main wharf and demanded a speech. The *Natal Mercury* reported his words as follows:

We are in the midst of a fierce struggle with vast military power, which has grown up in the heart of this country, which is resolved at all costs to gratify its reckless ambition by beating the British out of South Africa. (Cries of 'Never!' and a voice: 'Never while we have such fine fellows as you!') When I see around me such a crowd as this, such determination and such enthusiasm, I am satisfied that, no matter what the difficulties, no matter what the dangers and what the force they may bring against us, we shall be successful in the end. (Cheers and a voice: 'God bless you, my boy!') ...

You will see in this country the beginning of a new era, when peace and prosperity shall reign, so that the Cape may be in fact as well as in name a Cape of Good Hope.[20]

The cheering crowd demanded more from their hero. Again he was seized and forced into a rickshaw, to be conveyed to the town hall together with a Reuters' correspondent and the editor of the *Natal Mercury*. The crowd followed as they sang 'Rule, Britannia' and 'Soldiers of the Queen'. Many of his enthusiastic supporters shook hands with him and tried to say a few words. Churchill loved the spectacle but he kept his emotions under control. He politely answered questions and thanked each and every one for their complimentary remarks and good wishes. But there were also critics in the crowd. The rumour that he had broken his parole had begun to circulate and someone shouted and asked whether this was true.

'No it is not true', Churchill replied. 'I was in exactly the same position as all the other prisoners'.[21]

The crowd at the town hall was even larger than at the docks. Again the cheers went up and he could not ignore the demands for another speech. Standing on a small cart he waited for the assembly to quieten. It took some time and 'Rule Britannia' was sung again before he could finally express his gratitude for the reception given to him:

I need not say how grateful I am for the great kindness you have done in your welcome to me. When I see this great demonstration I regard it not only as a personal kindness to me, and as a demonstration of hospitality to a stranger (Cries: 'You're not a stranger!'), but as a token of the unflinching and unswerving determination of this colony to throw itself into the prosecution of the war. (Cheers) ... with the determination of a great Empire surrounded by colonies unprecedented loyalty we shall carry our policy to a successful conclusion, and under the old Union Jack there will be an era of peace, purity, liberty, equality and good government to South Africa. (Cheers) I thank you once again for your great kindness. I am sure I feel within myself a personal measure of that gratitude which every Englishman who loves his country must feel towards the loyal and devoted colonists of Natal.[22]

A tremendous cheer broke out at the end of his speech and everyone jostled to exchange a few words with him. He could only break free with the help of the town commandant, Captain Percy Scott, who took him to his office and handed him congratulatory telegrams — some of which said that they were naming their children after him. Outside, the well-wishers were undeterred and waited until he reappeared to ask him to pose for more photographs.

Churchill told the gathering that he wanted to return to the front as soon as possible. Only when he insisted that he had to take the next train to Pietermaritzburg — where he was invited as a guest of the governor of Natal, Sir Walter Hely-Hutchinson — did the good-natured crowd agree to let him go. Again a rickshaw, this one draped with the Union Jack, was placed at his disposal to take him to the station where yet another crowd awaited him.

Churchill was overwhelmed by the reception given to him in Durban. He must have had difficulty controlling his emotions as the crowd broke into 'Goodbye, Dolly Gray', as the signal was given for the train to depart. The gloom that prevailed as the century drew to a close was turning into a mood of hope and confidence that victory was around the corner.

19

Controversial issues

Churchill arrived in Pietermaritzburg on the evening of the 23 December 1899, and probably slept over at Government House. He continued his journey to Frere the following morning. In a dispatch from there, he wrote: 'It was still dark as we passed Estcourt, but morning had broken when the train reached Frere, and I got out and walked along the line inquiring for my tent, and found it pitched by the side of the very same cutting down which I had fled for my life from the Boer marksman, and only fifty yards from the spot on which I surrendered myself as a prisoner. So after much trouble and adventure I came safely home again to the wars.'[1]

If this was indeed so then the tent must have been moved from the shunting triangle of the railway station in Estcourt to Frere after his capture almost six weeks earlier. Was Churchill told that the tent had been moved? Who occupied it while he was away? Why did he have to look for it? With his spreading fame, there must have been someone to welcome him and take him to his tent so that he did not have to walk along the line asking for it. Or did Churchill not stay in a tent at all? The question is justified, for in *My Early Life* he made no mention of a tent. 'I took up my quarters in the very platelayer's hut within one hundred yards of which I had little more than a month before been taken prisoner, and there with the rude plenty of the Natal campaign celebrated by dinner to many friends my good fortune and Christmas Eve.'[2]

When discarding the discrepancies in Churchill's reports rather generously as minor details, one should remember that variations of his interpretation of events occur frequently in his writing. It may be argued that details — such as whether he slept in a tent in Frere on Christmas Eve 1899, or if he indeed took up his quarters 50 yards from where he surrendered — are of little consequence. But then it can also be argued that it doesn't matter whether it was Louis Botha or Sarel Oosthuizen who captured him, or whether he hid 'in the bowels of the earth'[3] in a rat-infested mine, or bedded down for two days and a night on a mattress with a pillow and blankets in a new, clean stable at ground level at the colliery in Witbank.

Indeed, the frequent contradictions of detail, coupled with generous embellishments which are not necessary to achieve literary effect, may lead to the ask what is the truth?

Henry Labouchere in his newspaper *Truth* of 23 November 1899 published the following on Churchill's conduct during the train ambush:

> ... The train was upset and Mr Churchill is described as having rallied the force by calling out 'Be men! Be men!' But what can officers have been doing who were in command of the attachment? Again, were the men showing signs of behaving otherwise than as men? Would officers in command on the battlefield permit a journalist to 'rally' those who were under their order?[4]

Durban's *Phoenix* had this to say: 'That Mr Winston Churchill saved the life of a wounded man in an armoured train is very likely. Possibly he also seized a rifle and fired at a Boer. But the question occurs: 'What was he doing in the armoured train? He had no right to be there whatsoever.' Churchill, according to the reporter, was no longer a soldier and, for that matter, no longer represented the *Morning Post*. 'Whoever commanded this ill-fated armoured train overstepped his duty in allowing Mr Churchill to be a passenger on the train, or Mr Churchill took the unwarranted liberty of going without permission, thereby adding to the already weighty responsibilities of the officer in command'.

The article expressed the sincere hope that Churchill would not be shot. Nonetheless, the paper found it necessary to point out that as a non-combatant, Churchill had no right to carry arms and the Boer general ordering his execution could not be blamed for doing so. 'In the Franco-Prussian War non-combatants who carried arms were promptly executed when they were caught; and we can hardly expect the Boers to be more human than were the highly civilised French and Germans', the *Phoenix* concluded.[5]

People wrote to him from all over the world. 'One gentleman invited me to shoot with him in Central India', he mentioned in a dispatch from Frere, while 'another favoured me with a poem which he had written in my honour, and desired me to have it set to music and published'.[7] An American wanted him to plan a raid into Transvaal territory along the Delagoa Bay line to arm the prisoners and seize the president.

A member of the Natal parliament wrote: 'My heartiest congratulations on your wonderful and glorious deed, which will send such a thrill of pride and enthusiasm through Great Britain and the United States of America, that the Anglo-Saxon race will be irresistible.'[8]

On Boxing Day the *Westminster Gazette* published the following:

> ... we confess that we hardly understand the application which Mr Churchill is reported to have made to General Joubert asking to be released on the ground that he was a newspaper correspondent who had taken no part in the fighting. We rubbed our eyes when we read this — have we not read glowing (and apparently authentic) accounts of Mr Churchill's heroic exploits in the

armoured train affair? General Joubert, apparently, rubbed his eyes too. He replied that Mr Churchill — unknown to him personally — was detained because all the Natal papers attributed the escape of the armoured train to his bravery and exception. But since this seemed to be a mistake, the General would take the correspondent's word that he was a non-combatant, and sent an order for his release — which arrived half a day after Mr Churchill had escaped. Mr Churchill's non-combatancy is indeed a mystery, but one thing is clear — that he cannot have the best of both worlds. His letter to General Joubert absolutely disposes of the probable VC with which numerous correspondents have decorated him.

The question of a Victoria Cross has already been discussed, but when Churchill read the report in the *Westminster Gazette* he must have been disappointed. He stated in *My Early Life* that he could not but think the comments ungenerous, saying that he had already explained his reasons for travelling on the train and taking part in the fight. He also found it odd that General Joubert's order for his release should only have been given publicity after he had escaped. 'The statement that I had broken my parole or any honourable understanding in escaping was of course untrue', [10] he wrote. But what is the nature of truth? He maintained:

> No parole was extended to any of the prisoners of war, and we were all kept as I have described in strict confinement under armed guard. The lie once started, however, persisted in the alleys of political controversy, and I have been forced to extort damages and public apologies by prosecution for libel on at least four separate occasions. At the time I thought the pro-Boers a spiteful lot. [11]

For many years Churchill was stigmatised for having behaved unfairly towards his brother officers who had reluctantly accepted his plea to escape with them. To have broken parole, however — of which the *Daily Nation* accused him on 16 December and the *Westminster Gazette* on 26 December — was another matter. Even the legal actions he instigated during subsequent years could not eradicate the persistent rumours that his conduct was dishonourable.

As late as 1964, the former Labour Home Secretary, Herbert Morrison, in a 90th birthday television tribute to Churchill, made reference to the incident. In reply to a question, Morrison said: 'I think I remember his name in the Boer War where he was taken prisoner and then was put on parole and he broke his parole.' [12] And still later, when Celia Sandys was researching her book on her grandfather, she was asked by 'an eminent British newspaper editor' how she would deal with 'the matter of Churchill breaking his parole and leaving his friends in the lurch'. [13]

An indignant Randolph S Churchill commented on the *Daily Nation's* attack on Churchill that General Joubert's wish to have the character of his father maligned 'was thus gratified sooner than he could ever have expected'.[14] In reference to Lord Morrison's remarks, he expressed his displeasure thus:

> There has of course always been a noisy pacifist or nationalist element in Britain, which is ready to traduce the conduct of their fellow countrymen who are helping to fight their country's battles. Naturally, being silly billies they know nothing of the traditions of the British army nor in their passionate hatred of their own country do they mind what lies they tell. British officers and troops are not allowed to give their parole — it is indeed laid down that it is their plain duty to escape. It is true — though this was not the point of the *Daily Nation* — that Churchill did not hold a commission and was a civilian war correspondent; he could have given his parole. Indeed, he offered it if he were released. But since his suggestions were rebuffed, all bets were off. Churchill was not to know that at the very time he was escaping, the authorities were considering in a more favourable light the possibility of his release.[15]

As far as the actual escape was concerned, Churchill insisted that the three had never discussed the question of them climbing the fence together. He had taken the lead and when he realised that the others were unable to follow him, he carried on alone. But barely 30 hours later he handed himself over to Howard after he had covered only covered a quarter of his long road to freedom. If it were not for that helpful Englishman to whom chance had directed him, one wonders what chance he would have had of completing his flight to Delagoa Bay?

Lord Rosslyn who, like Churchill, had come to South Africa as a war correspondent, was attached to Colonel Thorneycroft's Mounted Infantry. Like Churchill he was taken prisoner and escaped. He was recaptured and taken to the State Model School. In his book titled *Twice Captured,* he wrote that Churchill was persona non grata with his fellow prisoners. As far as he could make out, Churchill did not play fair with Haldane and Brockie who 'concocted the plot but according to them followed the principle of *sauve qui peut* rather than shoulder to shoulder'.[16]

Churchill was not impressed. He sent a copy of the page of Rosslyn's book to Haldane and enclosed his interpretation of the events. There is no record of Haldane's reply, but in 1935 he wrote that Churchill's version 'threw quite an unexpected light on the matter, and I replied that I laid no blame on him for departing when he did'.[17]

Whether Haldane blamed Churchill or not, the damage was done. Later, many of his ex-fellow prisoners were abusive about Churchill for having adopted the law of every man for himself. Rosslyn confirmed their sentiments.

Churchill ranted and raved about 'the enormous liars in the world'. Blackwood & Sons stopped the distribution of the book and agreed to delete the offending passage from further editions, but the matter did not rest there.

In October 1900, Churchill was invited to speak as guest of honour at the annual dinner of the Pall Mall Club in London. 'Twice captured', he proclaimed in the opening to his speech, 'is a curious title; it is not a very difficult thing to be captured. A man might just as well call his book, "Twice bankrupt". I think it intolerable that a person who, by his own fault or folly has fallen in the mud, should endeavour to hide his own ignominy by splashing mud over other people'.[19] Churchill beamed with satisfaction at the favourable reaction shown by his audience.

The revenge of publicly humiliating Rosslyn for having dared to cast doubt on his integrity — however slight — was sweet but there was more to come. In 1907, when Churchill was scheduled to speak in support of a Liberal candidate at a by-election, an attempt was made to discredit him for having cowardly deserted Haldane. Major Sandham Griffith, an acquaintance of Haldane and a supporter of the Liberal's opponent, did not agree with such tactics. He asked Haldane to send a telegram stating that he denied having ever said that Churchill deserted him in Pretoria.

In a letter to Churchill, Griffith explained that a friend had heard the 'cowardly desertion' story from a lady, who claimed to have heard it from Haldane himself and she told him. Haldane agreed to the request and sent a copy of his letter to Churchill with a note suggesting that the enclosed correspondence might amuse him.

It is unlikely that Haldane's letter actually amused Churchill, nor that Haldane, although giving the impression — and wisely so — that he was on Churchill's side, was really in agreement with him.

Finally, in 1912, when Churchill was First Lord of the Admiralty, the recurring accusations came to a head. Blackwood & Sons had again suggested, in *Blackwood's Magazine*, that he had broken his parole when imprisoned in Pretoria in 1899. Churchill sued the publishers for libel. The hearing was scheduled for 20 May and Blackwood requested Haldane to give evidence against Churchill, but he refused.

On 25 April Haldane, by then a brigadier in command of an infantry brigade, was summoned to the admiralty. Churchill, who was First Lord of the Admiralty, asked him to testify that he had behaved 'quite fairly and properly' and had given a detailed and favourable account of the escape that would leave no doubt that he had acted correctly on that fateful evening in Pretoria 12 years earlier.

Haldane replied that he believed Churchill to be a man of honour and asked if he would be prepared to go into the witness box and testify that, having heard his (Haldane's) statement which, although it differed from his own view, he would accept his word in the matter and assume that he had escaped without realising that he was behaving unfairly towards Brockie and himself.

In his opinion Churchill should not have gone on alone as he had made it quite clear that he, Haldane, was in charge of the escape and all three had to be considered, but Churchill had thought only of himself. Having made it clear that he refused to have words put in his mouth that he did not agree with , he asked Churchill to send him his proposed statement. After scrutinising it he would let him know if would be prepared to testify accordingly.

Churchill had spoken to Haldane as an old friend and he did not like his reply. Ted

Morgan wrote: 'According to Haldane, Winston assumed a browbeating air, and said that if Haldane did not support him, he would state in court that he and Brockie had funked going'.[18] Winston was indeed 'a chip off the old block,' as General Joubert had put it, resorting to threats and blackmail in a fit of temper towards an officer who had helped him and shown him his friendship on more than one occasion. 'Haldane felt nothing but regret that a man of such splendid ability and brilliant parts, whom he had once regarded as a friend, but could never trust again, had allowed himself to commit an action that he had then lied about'.[19]

Realising that crossing swords with the powerful minister running one of the departments of war could be detrimental to his career, Haldane consulted a lawyer. He was advised that if Churchill spoke out against him in court, he should write to *The Times*, stating that Churchill had threatened to call him a coward. As it turned out, Blackwood decided not to defend the case so Haldane being unable to attend the hearing was of no importance.

Churchill must surely have been relieved.

Although quick to lose his temper when his reputation was at stake, he showed no ill feeling towards Haldane. In 1920, when he was Secretary of State for War, he appointed Haldane to the highest military command he would ever hold — Commander-in-Chief of British forces in Mesopotamia, 'and he worked with him through critical times on the best of terms'.[20]

20

Back to the front

Immediately after returning to Frere Churchill cabled the *Morning Post*. 'More irregular corps are wanted. Are the gentlemen of England all foxhunting? Why not an English Light Horse? For the sake of our manhood, our devoted colonists, and our dead soldiers, we must persevere with the war'.[1] General Buller had already sent for him, questioned him on his experiences and sought information about conditions in the Transvaal.

There was little of importance that Churchill could tell him, but he still had his own opinion about how the war should be conducted. This he had already outlined in a telegram he had written on the *SS Induna* and sent to the *Morning Post* when he arrived in Durban. He repeated the gist of his comments to Buller, stressing that 'It is foolish not to recognise that we are fighting a formidable and terrible adversary.' He praised the high qualities of the burghers, saying that 'the individual Boer, mounted in suitable country, is worth from three to five regular soldiers. The power of modern rifles is so tremendous that frontal attacks must often be repulsed ... the only way of treating the problem is either to get men equal in character and intelligence as riflemen, or, failing the individual, huge masses of troops. The advance of an army of 80 000 men in force, covered by 150 guns in line, would be an operation beyond the Boer's capacity to grapple with ... it is a perilous policy to dribble out reinforcements and to fritter away armies'.[2]

With regard to costs Churchill believed it would be much cheaper in the long run to send more troops than was necessary. 'There is plenty of work here for a quarter of a million men, and South Africa is well worth the cost in blood and money.'[3]

His telegram caused serious resentment in England. His statement that an individual Boer was worth three to five regular soldiers was considered an insult to the army, and his contention that an army of quarter of a million men was necessary to fight the Boers was shrugged off as simply ridiculous. The retired generals and colonels of what he called 'The Buck and Dodder Club' expressed their contempt by sending him a cable saying: 'Best friends here hope you will not continue making a further ass of yourself.' The *Morning Leader* sarcastically commented: 'We have received no confirmation of the statement that Lord Landsdowne has, pending the arrival of Lord

Roberts, appointed Mr Winston Churchill to command the troops in South Africa, with General Sir Redvers Buller, VC, as his Chief of Staff'.[4]

General Buller, however, did not share the opinion of the retired senior officers in England. 'Winston Churchill turned up here yesterday having escaped from Pretoria', he wrote to Lady Theresa Londonderry.

'He really is a fine fellow and I must say I admire him greatly. I wish he were leading irregular troops instead of writing for a rotten paper. We are very short of good men, as he appears to be, out here'.[5]

'You have done very well,' he said to Churchill, 'is there anything we can do for you?'

'Yes', Churchill said, 'I would like a commission in one of the irregular corps now being improvised'.

'What about poor old Borthwick?' Buller asked, referring to Sir Algeron Borthwick, afterwards Lord Glenesk, who was the proprietor of the *Morning Post*.

'I am under a definite contract and cannot possibly relinquish this engagement', Churchill replied.[6]

Buller knew that officers were — as result of the War Office ruling after the Nile expedition — no longer permitted to double as correspondents. Churchill's own dispatches had prompted the ruling, now he was himself asking for an exception to it. His pay as a journalist was 12 times more than he would make as an officer and Buller feared that if a solution was not forthcoming, the conversation would end there. Churchill could not be expected to give up his lucrative job as an opinion-making journalist after his sudden jump to fame.

'All right', Buller said and stopped pacing the room. 'You can have a commission in Bungo's regiment. You will have to do as much as you can for both jobs, but you will get no pay for ours.'

'To this irregular arrangement', Churchill wrote in *My Early Life*, 'I made haste to agree.'[7]

Bungo was the nickname of Colonel Julian Byng, commander of the South African Light Horse, comprising six squadrons with over 700 mounted men and a battery of galloping Colt machine-guns. It was part of Lord Dundonald's cavalry brigade. The regiment had been raised by Byng when he was a captain of the 10th Hussars in the Cape Colony. Churchill saw in Colonel Byng an officer from whom great things could be expected. In fact, he later became Field Marshal Lord Byng of Vimy and Governor-General of Canada.

In South Africa his *Uitlander* regiment was generally known as 'Bingo's Own', or the Cockyoli Birds, after the coloured plumes of the sakabula bird his troopers wore in their slouch hats.

Churchill joined the Cockyoli Birds on 2 January 1900 in the position of assistant-adjutant with the understanding that he could go where he liked when there was no fighting taking place. He was reunited with his valet, Thomas Walden, who had joined the regiment when Churchill was captured at Frere, and 'lived from day to day in perfect happiness'.[8]

Borthwick was also happy with the arrangements, for since Churchill's escape, his newspaper circulation had soared beyond all expectations. Churchill thus became the first man to break the regulations preventing an officer from acting as a correspondent for the press. But because his commission was authorised by Buller himself, no one was prepared to complain about this 'curse of modern armies', as Lord Wolseley had described Churchill the journalist.

In a letter to his mother, Winston wrote that he felt the privilege extended to him may have been done to qualify him for some reward they might care to give him, but his son Randolph, in *Youth*, thought this expectation came to nothing because 'he had already acquired too many enemies'.[9]

Churchill's dual role of serving officer and correspondent did not work out altogether satisfactorily. 'Taken as a whole, Churchill's youthful war correspondence reveals a remarkable grasp of strategy and tactics and an admirable readiness to criticise senior officers. He felt indebted to Buller, however, and here, as in Cuba, gratitude warped his judgement'.[10] An example of his sometimes biassed reporting was when he wrote: 'If Sir Redvers Buller cannot relieve Ladysmith with his present force we do not know of any other officer in the British Service who would be likely to succeed.'[10]

In early January 1900 Buller set out to cross the Tugela River at Colenso intending to advance along the railway line to rescue General Sir George White and his 16 000 men, many of them dying of typhoid and dysentery within the besieged town. The Boers were entrenched in the hills and each time Buller crossed the river, he was chased back.

'The ferryman', as he sometimes came to be called, decided to wait his moment until his army was reinforced to a strength of 19 000 infantry, 3 000 cavalry and 60 guns. Once up to strength he ordered his army to cross the Tugela 25 miles up-stream of Colenso. On 18 January about 16 000 troops successfully crossed the river.

Lieutenant-General Sir Charles Warren, in command of the operation, was eager to press on over open ground to Ladysmith. Buller and his staff, however, deemed it necessary to shorten the route by climbing the rocky heights west of Spion Kop, a prominent hill rising 1 400 feet above the Tugela.

On 20 January the first attempt to storm the heights was unsuccessful. Churchill was one of those who reached the flat top where the Boers were entrenched. The British lost 300 men before the attack was called off and another 170 when they tried for a second time to seize the position.

Eventually, on the night of 23 January, Buller gave the order for an infantry brigade led by General Woodgate and Colonel Thorneycroft's dismounted regiment to seize Spion Kop. Scouts had reported that there were only a few Boers on the summit. In the event some 2 000 British infantry made it to the top.

The next day they were attacked by 1 500 burghers commanded by General Schalk Burger. Woodgate was one of the first to fall. Buller and his army of 30 000 remained on the far side of the Tugela River while their comrades were slaughtered by the Boers.

During the afternoon of 24 January Churchill and another officer climbed the mountain. 'The severity of the action was evident. Screams of wounded, some carried or accompanied by as many as four or five unwounded soldiers, trickled and even flowed down the hill, at the foot of which two hospital villages of tents and wagons were rapidly growing.'[12]

On the plateau a reserve battalion waited in anticipation of things to come. Here Churchill learnt that Colonel Thorneycroft, who had not been on a campaign since his early youth, was in command of all the troops at the summit. He had beaten down a white flag when he arrived and was fighting desperately to keep his position.

As the sun set, Churchill and his companion reported back to Sir Charles Warren at headquarters and reported what they had seen. Warren appeared worried. There had been no communication with the summit for several hours and the news did not please him. His staff officer said that fresh troops would be sent up. Meanwhile, they should dig in for the night, and hold the position with a much smaller force the next day. Churchill was requested to pass this information on to Colonel Thorneycroft. He asked for the message to be put in writing, and although it was dark by then he once more climbed the mountain.

On reaching the top he was horrified to see the large numbers of dead and wounded lying around. When he finally found Thorneycroft and handed him the note, the colonel had already made up his mind. Order or no order, he and his men were going to evacuate the plateau. At the bottom of the hill a long column of men with picks and shovels were ready to ascend. The officer at the front had another note for Colonel Thorneycroft. Churchill was asked to read it. 'We are sending 400 sappers and a fresh battalion. Entrench yourself strongly by morning', it said, but Thorneycroft ordered the troops to return to camp.

On the following day, 25 January, the Boers re-occupied the position. They displayed a flag of truce inviting the British to tend to their wounded and to bury their dead. Throughout that and the following day Buller withdrew his wagons across the bridges. On the dark and rainy night of the 26th, Buller himself supervised the retreat and on the following day he was able to proclaim that he had effected his retreat 'without the loss of man or a pound of stores'.[13] The 1 600 British soldiers killed or wounded during the past 16 days were replaced by a fresh draft of 2 400 men.

In his column for the *Morning Post,* Churchill wrote that he had often seen dead men, killed in war, but the Boer dead aroused the most painful emotions. He then described the sight of a dead Boer as 'a grey-haired Veld-Kornet, clutching a letter from his wife, lying next to a 17-year-old boy, shot through the heart'. Close by lay 'the dead and injured, smashed and broken by the shells, littering the summit till it was a bloody, reeking shambles'.

He concluded by saying: 'Ah, horrible war, amazing medley of the glorious and the squalid, the pitiful and the sublime, if modern men of light and leading saw your face closer, simple folk would see it hardly ever.'[14]

On the day his mother arrived in Durban, Winston wrote to Pamela Plowden, saying: 'The scenes on Spion Kop were among the strangest and most terrible I have ever witnessed.' He claimed to have gone through five very dangerous days and had been 'continually under shell and rifle fire and once the feather in my hat was cut through by a bullet. But in the end I came serenely through'.[15]

21

Relief of Ladysmith

Unlike the Boers, on whose side volunteers from all over the world fought, it would have been unthinkable for imperial Britain to seek outside help, either materially or financially. Besides that, American sympathy, on the whole, was on the side of the Boers. A voluntary effort on behalf of the British was nonetheless made by a group of wealthy American women married to Englishmen. Lady Randolph Churchill led the group, followed by the Duchess of Marlborough and Mrs Joseph Chamberlain.

The committed anti-imperialist, Andrew Carnegie, declined to give them assistance, but his employees gave £500, which raised the total donation to £41 579. The millionaire Bernard Nadel Baker, founder of the Atlantic Transport Company in Baltimore, donated the use of one of the company's transport ships to the British Government for the duration of the war in South Africa. The fact that the vessel was an old cattle boat posed another problem for Jennie. To convert it into a hospital ship required more capital. Jennie's name was not on the list of subscribers. She was, as always, short of money and was thus unable to contribute to the costs. But she did manage to persuade Baker to maintain the ship and the crew to the tune of well over £3 000 a month. Jennie named it *SS Maine*, after the US warship that had been blown up in Havana harbour.

President McKinley was less generous. He was approached to present the Stars and Stripes but politely declined. A purchased American standard was thus hoisted in the forecastle, alongside the Union Jack readily supplied by Queen Victoria.

Jennie learned of her son's safe arrival in Lourenço Marques the day before she sailed from England. At Las Palmas the 46-year-old was told that her young admirer, George Cornwallis-West — a 25-year-old Scots Guards subaltern who had come to South Africa a few days after Winston arrived — was on his way home. For some time Cornwallis-West had bombarded her with marriage proposals. She finally agreed to accept and looked forward to a reunion with her future husband.

Unfortunately, during the three weeks Cornwallis-West spent at the front, he was seriously afflicted by sunstroke. He was hospitalised, but failed to recover and was sent back to England on the *SS Pannonia*. He asked Jennie in a letter to postpone her departure until he arrived in England or they would miss each other — a thought she found too awful to contemplate. But she had already left when the letter arrived, passing the *Pannonia* somewhere on the high seas.

The *SS Maine* docked in Cape Town on 22 January for a two-day stopover en route to Durban. It was a busy time for Jennie. She was entertained at Government House by Sir Alfred Milner, the High Commissioner, and she indulged herself on strawberries. She enjoyed walking in the lovely gardens of the Mount Nelson Hotel at a reception given by a committee of American ladies. Besides all this, her 19-year-old son Jack was in town and he would accompany his mother to Durban. Winston, believing that the worst fighting would be over before he arrived, had obtained a commission for him in the South African Light Horse.

The passage in the small trans-Atlantic steamer was rough and the heavy swell did not allow the *Maine* to enter Durban harbour until the following day. Jack wasn't waiting until then, so he and one of the ship's officers set off in a small steam launch to be met by a tug. Jennie was glad to hear that a midshipman on board the tug had delivered   a message from Captain Percy Scott 'to the effect that my son Winston was in Durban, having come on a two days' leave from Frere to meet me'.[1]

When the *Maine* docked on 28 January, Winston was waiting on the quay. He took up quarters on the *Maine*, living 'as on a yacht'. Captain Scott, the commander of *HMS Terrible,* was 'the greatest swell' in Durban. He invited the Churchills to inspect the armoured cruiser and 'lavished his courtesies upon us and showed us all the wonders of his vessel'.[2] Jennie asked to fire a test round on the 4.7 inch gun he had mounted on a railway truck. Scott named the artillery piece after her before it was railed to the front.

Churchill had met Scott before when he had arrived in Durban from Lourenço Marques after his escape. After this second meeting the commander wrote to Churchill, saying how very proud he was to have met him. 'Though I did not shake hands with you before I left PMB [Pietermaritzburg] I feel certain that I shall someday shake hands with you as Prime Minister of England. You possess the two necessary qualifications, genius and plod', he added.[3]

Winston and his mother had much to talk about, and 'after they had killed a bottle of '25 brandy', as William Manchester puts it in *The Last Lion*, 'Jennie mounted a wild horse, tamed it, and rode into the regiment's camp'.[4] She discussed her relationship with George Cornwallis-West with Winston — who was a mere two weeks older than George — and was delighted by his indifference. She wanted everyone to know how happy she was 'to have so much fun'.

Brian Roberts does not subscribe to the brandy story and the taming of the wild horse. He wrote that Lady Randolph 'had an invitation to stay with the Governor of Natal, Sir Walter Hely-Hutchinson, and Winston had arranged for the necessary passes which allowed her to travel up country. That evening she left for Pietermaritzburg, accompanied by her chief assistant, Eleanor Warrender, and her two sons'.[5] They spent two days at Government House. Jennie intended to stay on for a while, but on the third day a telegram from the *Maine* informed her that the first patients had arrived from the front. She returned to Durban by train to give instructions to her staff concerning the wounded and to make arrangements for strict visiting hours.

At the front, the battle was concentrated on the ridges running eastward from of Spion Kop. 'In spite of the vexatious course of the war, the two months fighting for the relief of Ladysmith makes one of the most happy memories of my life',[6] Churchill wrote in *My Early Life*.

News from the besieged town was that Sir George White's men were on starvation rations. They could survive for another six weeks on the horses and mules, but they no longer had the mobility to co-operate with Buller's army. Churchill continued dispatching letters and cables to the *Morning Post*.

'We lived in great comfort in the open air, with cool nights and bright sunshine, with plenty of meat, chickens and beer.'[7] Reporters from Natal newspapers irritated him by getting into the firing line at lunchtime and awaiting his party when they returned from excursions among the hills. 'One lived entirely in the present with something happening all the time. Carefree, no regrets for the past, no fears for the future, no expenses, no duns, no complications, and all the time my salary was safely piling up at home!'[8]

Winston enjoyed Jack's company. He had written to him about the battles he had taken part in and he looked forward to introducing him to the real war. But the time with his brother at the front was short-lived. On 12 February, two weeks after Jack had joined Buller's army, Winston was out with a squadron scouting the wooded area they called Hussar Hill. 'I could often feel danger impending from this quarter or from that, as you might feel a light breeze on your cheek or neck. When one rode, for instance within rifle shot of some hill or watercourse about which we did not know enough, I used to feel a draughty sensation.'[9]

His sixth sense proved correct. A shot rang out, followed by a hail of bullets from two or three hundred Mauser rifles, 'emptying a few saddles and bringing down a few horses'. The squadron spread out immediately and reached a nearby crest beyond which they took cover. The Boers were out of sight and Winston felt safe with Jack lying next to him.

Suddenly Jack jumped and crawled back a yard or two from the line. A bullet had hit him in the calf. It was his first skirmish. Winston helped him get to an ambulance. The following day, after having received the necessary attention at a field hospital, Winston sent him with a letter to his mother saying that the colonel and the squadron leader spoke highly of his conduct, and that his wound, although not officially classified as such, was slight. Lady Randolph 'received her younger son as the very first casualty treated on board the hospital ship *Maine*',[10] Churchill wrote in *My Early Life*. But this was not really so.

In a letter to Pamela Plowden on 21 February, he described the incident as follows: 'Here is an instance of Fortune's caprice. There was a very hot fire — bullets hitting the ground or whizzing by the dozen. Jack — whose luck was fresh — was lying down. I was walking about without any cover — I who have tempted fortune so often. Jack was hit. I am glad he is out of harm's way honourably for a month.'[11]

John Atkins of the *Manchester Guardian*, with whom Winston had travelled to South Africa, had a point when he wrote: 'Mr Jack Churchill was hit in the leg. He had just arrived from England, and this was the first day's fighting he had seen. It seems as though he had paid for his brother's debts.'[12]

The fight to relieve Ladysmith continued and heavy losses were incurred on both sides. Slowly General Buller pushed forward. Major-General John French relieved Kimberley, 240 miles to the west. Botha's Boers fought on bravely, trying the defend Hlangwane Hill, then Pieter's Plateau, Railway Hill and Hart's Hill.

27 February was the anniversary of Majuba. Buller was ready for his final attack. First Barton's Hill was stormed, then Railway Hill and finally Inniskilling Hill. The men were ready to cross the river and storm Ladysmith lying six miles distant. Buller met them at the bridge.

'Damn pursuit!' he said and ordered them back.

Churchill was outraged. 'Damn reward for sacrifices! Damn the recovery of debts overdue! Damn the prize which eases future struggles.'[13]

Churchill would have his rewards. In his dispatch to the *Morning Post* he told his readers:

> Never shall I forget that ride. The evening was deliciously cool. My horse was strong and fresh, for I had changed him at midday ... beyond the next ridge was Ladysmith, the goal of all our hopes and ambitions during weeks of almost ceaseless fighting. Ladysmith, the centre of the world's attention ... within our reach at last. We were going to be inside the town within an hour. The excitement of the moment was increased by the exhilaration of the gallop ... presently we arranged ourselves in military order ... so that there might be no question about precedence, and with Gough, the youngest regimental commander in the army, and one of the best, at the head of the column, we forged the Klip River and rode into the town.[14]

According to Churchill, the two squadrons of the South African Light Horse were not allowed to ride into Ladysmith until evening. He was with them and was fired at by a few Boer guns as they rode across the veld. 'Suddenly from the brushwood up rose gaunt figures waving hands of welcome. On we pressed, and at the head of a battered street of tin-roofed houses met Sir George White on horseback, faultlessly attired. Then we all rode together into the long beleaguered, almost starved-out, Ladysmith. It was a thrilling moment'.[14]

In fact, despite the eye-witness description, Lieutenant Winston Churchill was not there to witness the meeting of Sir George White and his rescuers, led by Lieutenant-Colonel Gough.[16] He was miles away, riding with the commander of the 2nd Mounted Brigade, Lord Dundonald, along with Major William Birdwood and their orderlies.

200

They arrived well after dark, long after the public celebrations were over. True to form, when Churchill did arrive he made sure he was noticed. A group of subalterns were engaged in conversation with White when Churchill pushed his way through to the front. To the astonishment of the general, Churchill addressed him in a loud voice as if they were equals, then went on his way.

'Who on earth is that?' an older officer asked Sir George.

'That's Randolph Churchill's son Winston', was the reply. 'I don't like the fellow, but he will be Prime Minister of England one day.'[17]

The real meeting between Gough's column and Sir George White 'had a quality of pathos that is missing from Churchill's imaginative account'.[18] White was a broken man looking 'ten years older than the trim, taut soldier of his official photograph; a stooped, patient, almost pathetic figure, walking, cane in hand, through the streets of Ladysmith'.[19]

'That night', Churchill recorded, 'I dined with Sir George White ... and was placed next to Hamilton, who won the fight at Elandslaagte and beat the Boers off Wagon Hill'.[20] Seated next but one was Sir Archibald Hunter, White's chief of staff 'whom everyone said was the finest man in the world. Never before had I sat in such brave company nor stood so close to a great event'.[21]

Churchill mentions jealously preserved bottles of champagne being uncorked — which he expected to accompany an entree of horseflesh. But horseflesh was not to be. The last trek-ox had been slaughtered in honour of the occasion. 'Our pallid and emaciated hosts showed subdued contentment', he remembered, and 'having travelled so far and by such rough and devious routes, I rejoiced to be in Ladysmith at last.'[22]

Whether Churchill did indeed meet Sir George when he entered the town, and whether credence should be given to the general's prediction, is of little importance. That Churchill arrived 'long after the public celebrations were over', Celia Sandys attempts to disprove in her book *Churchill Wanted Dead or Alive*. She travelled to South Africa to visit the sites where her grandfather had seen action and to meet people who could tell her tales of Churchill that were passed onto them by previous generations. Sandys came across the diary of Lieutenant-Colonel BW Martin in the Ladysmith Siege Museum:

> I, personally, was fortunate enough to secure standing room ... opposite the City Hall ... I therefore enjoyed an uninterrupted view of the official meeting between General Sir Redvers Buller and General Sir George White ... I stood alongside and conversed with a young man of somewhat untidy appearance ... He wore the slouch hat with Sakabula feathers ... he asked me my name and then told me he was Winston Churchill, and that he was a War Correspondent attached to the South African Light Horse.[23]

Martin's entry in his diary clearly refers to the public celebration that took place on 3 March when the relieving army made its triumphant entry into Ladysmith. Buller himself entered the town on 1 March, the morning after Churchill claimed to have sat next to Ian Hamilton at Sir George's banquet. The banquet in fact took place on 1 March, at the headquarters at Convent Ridge. It was there that Buller, commenting on the abundance of food, caught the wrath of White.

In his dispatch to the *Morning Post* of 10 March, Churchill described the proceedings that Lieutenant-Colonel BW Martin had diarised: 'Before the Town Hall, the tower of which, sorely battered, yet unyielding, seemed to symbolise the spirit of the garrison. Sir George White and his staff sat on their skeletal horses. Opposite them were drawn up the pipers of the Gordon Highlanders. The townsfolk, hollow-eyed but jubilant, crowded the pavement and the windows of the houses. Everyone who could find a flag had hung it out, but we needed no bright colour to raise our spirits'.[24]

What Churchill doesn't mention is that the victory parade, first proposed by Colonel Sir Henry Rawlinson, was only agreed to reluctantly by Buller and was highly criticised by his senior officers. Some members of the relief column regarded it as a cheap stunt and an insult to both relieved and relievers — which led to resentment between White and Buller.

In Durban, too, the victories over the Boers were celebrated in style. On the day before General Cronjé surrendered to Lord Roberts at Paardeberg, the band didn't stop playing in the streets until well after midnight. On 29 March Jennie was dining with Captain Scott aboard the *Terrible* when news of the relief of Ladysmith came. The celebrations in Durban reached a climax with crowds cheering and singing in front of the town hall.

In his dispatch of 4 March Churchill wrote: 'Now the great event over, the long and bloody conflict around Ladysmith has been gloriously decided, and I take a few days' leisure on the good ship *Maine*, where everyone is busy getting well, to think about it all and set down some things on paper.'[25] In his earlier dispatches to the *Morning Post* he had avoided all reference to his mother arriving on the *Maine* and welcoming her in Durban.

In *My Early Life*, he was equally silent about the *Maine* until after Jack was wounded. He then creates the impression that this led him to take a few days' leave during which he was, 'by curious coincidence',[26] reunited with his mother and her younger son.

Jennie, who visited the front while wounded soldiers filled up the *Maine*, is just as vague about Winston being in Durban when she arrived there on 28 January. In an article for the *Anglo-Saxon Review* — a magazine she had ambitiously started a few months earlier and of which there were only saw 11 issues published before her finances dried up — she remarked that everyone was very depressed about Spion Kop. The retreat, she claimed, had taken place 'the night before'. Brian Roberts says: 'This is either a mistake or deliberately misleading, for the retreat from Spion Kop occurred three days before the *Maine* arrived at Durban.'[27]

According to Roberts: 'It might well be that neither of them was anxious to broadcast the fact that the correspondent of the *Morning Post* had left the front at a critical stage in the fighting.'[28]

Jennie had made it known that she was anxious to see the front. The Governor of Natal was happy to oblige. He offered her his own railway carriage and the military supplied her with a pass. 'Provided with much food ... armed with Kodaks and field glasses, not to mention a brown holland dress (my substitute for khaki), in case we should meet the enemy and wish to be invisible, we started on our journey.'[29]

Accompanied by chief assistant, Miss Warrender and the officer commanding the *Maine*, the party travelled by night train to Estcourt. The following morning the visitors were shown the derailed train her son had so gallantly defended and taken around the camp at Chieveley. There Jennie again admired the naval gun on which Captain Scott had her name painted in white letters. In the distance the white tents of Colenso could be seen and guns could be heard as they unloaded their deadly cargo onto the enemy. 'It was thrilling', Jennie noted, 'I longed to be a man and take some part in the fighting, but then I remembered my Red Cross.'[30]

4 March was the date that Churchill officially arrived in Durban to spend the last few days of his leave with his mother and Jack. After attending to his dispatches he invited his mother to see Ladysmith. Sir Redvers Buller arranged passes for them. With Miss Warrender and one of the officers of the *Maine* as company, they took the train to Colenso and crossed the Tugela. As there was no train running into Ladysmith, the group continued the journey in an open trolley pushed along the rails by some local people.

Jennie was enthralled by Winston's explanations of the battles and seeing the places along the line where the fighting had taken place. At the station they hired a Scotch cart drawn by six mules and Winston piloted the rig through the deserted town. There was no hotel to spend the night, but Buller had kindly arranged beds in the convent that served as his headquarters. He also placed a cart with a driver at their disposal. They enjoyed tea 'out of bottles and tin mugs' at Churchill's camp before they were taken back to have dinner with Buller in his tent.

The next morning Jennie and her companions returned to Durban on a Red Cross train to sail for London later that month.

Churchill was kept busy in Ladysmith for another month. He read the first reviews of his novel, *Savrola*, which he had written three years earlier in Bangalore. The book was published in February in both New York and London. More than half of the 65 books he was to write during his long life dealt with war and warriors. His first book, the two-volume *The River War* and the *Malakand Field Force,* had been well received and was financially successful. *Savrola*, his only novel, also dealt with war and revolution. Its author is the leader and hero of the fictitious plot. 'Presented as a romantic adventure, *Savrola* was in fact a fantasy in which Winston worked out his Oedipal problem in a purely intuitive manner, for there is no indication that he had ever heard of Freud, whose *Three essays on the theory of sexuality* — in which it was first suggested that children had sexual urges involving their parents — was only published in 1905, five years after *Savrola*.'[31]

Bryan Magee states: 'Every writer, whatever his subject, reveals more about himself in his writing than he intends or even realises. However skilfully he may try to project a certain image he can no more entirely determine the impression his readers form of him than he can jump on his own shadow. The young Churchill was no exception.'[32]

Savrola, the cultured philosophic hero of the story, leads the people of imaginary Laurania against the military dictator Antonio Moralo in a revolt to overthrow the government, which had refused to enfranchise its citizens. Moralo shows many of the unpleasant traits Winston had not wanted to recognise in his father. There are gory scenes of fighting and bloodshed and the mob shooting the dictator as he defends his palace. Savrola falls in love with Moralo's beautiful but unfaithful wife Lucile. He believes that his supporters will turn against him if he is seen with the adulteress whose husband had begun to ignore her. Further, his insistence on a fair trial of the prisoners taken is turned down by the citizens and he and Lucile are forced to flee the country. 'In Winston's fantasy, the character representing his idealised self won the mother away from the father. Savrola and his beautiful consort lived happily ever after.'[33]

On finishing his manuscript, Churchill sent it to his grandmother, the Duchess Fanny, for comment. 'It is clear that you have not yet attained a knowledge of women', the Duchess replied. It is true that Churchill had not been in a close relationship with a member of the opposite sex and years would pass before he considered marriage. 'Even in his early thirties he would have difficulty establishing relationships with young women.'[34]

Bryan Magee provides the following insight: 'Any number of things about Savrola, from the books he reads to his way of preparing a speech, are exactly like Winston Churchill. He is the only character with whom the author identifies so completely that no criticism of his is uttered or even implied.'[35] Ted Morgan puts it thus: 'The novel depicted the classical Oedipal situation of the son's instinctive need to slay the father and win the mother, but in the style of a chaste Victorian romance, full of notions of chivalric honour. Savrola was Winston as he would have liked to have been.'[36]

He also thought of writing a play about the Boer War, to be performed in London. In the autumn he wrote to Pamela Plowden, asking her to approach Herbert Beerbohm Tree, the actor-manager of Her Majesty's Theatre in the Haymarket. He was going to 'have the people talk and act as they would in a real war', he wrote to his mother, but when he would find the time to write the script, he did not say. As it turned out, his mother talked him out of the idea, and once again he had to face the real war happening around him.

The royalties Churchill received from the sale of his books, together with the cheques from Oliver Borthwick of the *Morning Post*, were used to finance his entry into politics. Already the conservative electorate of Southport had invited him to run in their constituency, but he had not yet made up his mind.

While Churchill was waiting in Ladysmith for further developments, an American lecture agent, Major James Pond, wrote to him and offered to set up a lecture tour in the United States. This was an exciting prospect. International fame would secure him the finance he needed to fuel his political ambitions. He wrote to his mother asking her to find out if Major Pond was the most suitable agent available, and cautioned her not allow this opportunity to be thrown away.

Before the year was out Churchill indeed toured the United States, but his acceptance there was not quite what he had anticipated. The reason for this was partly because of the strong pro-Boer feeling and partly because of Pond — 'a vulgar Yankee who had poured a lot of very mendacious statements into the ears of the reporters'. He met President McKinley and dined with Theodore Roosevelt. Mark Twain introduced him to his first American audience, at the Waldorf Astoria in Manhattan; he spoke in Baltimore, Boston and Chicago, and felt that a fee of £5 000 for the months' lecturing was not excessive. He must have been disappointed when total American earnings amounted to only £1 600.

22

Rejoining the 4th Queens Own Hussars

After the relief of Ladysmith, Field Marshall Lord Roberts of Kandahar replaced Sir Redvers Buller as Commander-in-Chief. Lord Kitchener, the conqueror of the Sudan, was his Chief of Staff. Roberts had his eyes set on Pretoria, and so determined was he to get to the capital of the South African Republic that his army marched from the Orange Free State at an average rate of 17 miles per day, reaching Pretoria in less than two months.

Impatient to step into the main theatre of the war, Churchill wanted to join the British army in Bloemfontein, but there was a problem. He had offended Lord Kitchener and, after a church parade attended by some 5 000 soldiers in a little village between Spion Kop and Vaal Krantz, he also offended the deeply religious Lord Roberts.

Churchill took exception to what he considered a totally inappropriate sermon preached by an army chaplain about the siege of Jericho. Spion Kop had been a disaster and a new offensive was readying to be launched. To deprive the army of confidence by taking 'a ridiculous discourse on the peculiar and unconvincing tactics by which the Israelites were said to have procured the downfall of the walls of Jericho' was unacceptable.[1] He remembered the inspiring sermon Father Bindle, a highly respected Roman Catholic priest had given at Omdurman, and this led him to complain in his dispatch to the *Morning Post* about the foolish formality in Natal, and 'wondered whether Rome was again seizing the opportunity which Canterbury denied — the opportunity of telling the glad tidings to soldiers about to die'.[2]

While the devout Lord Roberts was unable to forgive his outspoken critic, his Chief of Staff, the squint-eyed misogynist Lord Kitchener, didn't even consider giving Churchill more than a sideways glance of disapproval. He hadn't wanted Churchill in the Sudan two years earlier, and he still didn't want him because he had offended him by criticising his campaigns in *The River War*.

That Roberts turned down his application still came as a surprise. However, as usual, Churchill would have his own way. Not only was his good friend Ian Hamilton in Roberts' entourage, but his father had also been a great friend of the commander. Fifteen years earlier Lord Randolph, as Secretary of State for India, had insisted on placing Roberts at the head of the Indian Army. Winston had frequently met 'Bobs' — as he was affectionately known — and had great admiration and respect for him.

While Churchill awaited the outcome, he took indefinite leave of absence from the South African Light Horse. He took a train to Durban, arriving just in time to travel on a coaster, the *Guelp*, to Port Elizabeth. From there he continued his journey by rail.

'In Cape Town the visitor stays at the Mount Nelson Hotel, if he can be so fortunate as to secure a room', he wrote in a dispatch of 13 April. 'At this establishment he finds all the luxuries of a first-class European hotel without the resulting comfort. There is a good dinner, but it is cold before it reaches him; there is a spacious dining-room, but it is overcrowded; there are clean European waiters, but they are few and far between.'[3]

The hotel, just over a year old, had come about as a result of fierce competition between the Union and Castle companies before they finally merged in 1900 to become the Union Castle line. In 1894, the new and fashionable Grand Hotel in Strand Street, the pride of the Union Steamship Company, was within walking distance of the docks. It agitated its competitors at the Castle Company to such an extent that they determined to establish an even grander hostelry on a historic site below the majestic Table Mountain. The Mount Nelson estate — named by two Englishmen after the hero of the Battle of Trafalgar — was unrivalled in scenic beauty but at the same time was within walking distance of Cape Town's main thoroughfare.

On 4 March 1899 the four-storey 150-roomed mansion set in seven acres of luxuriant gardens opened its doors to the public. A week before the inauguration the *Cape Times* said: 'Such a triumph of construction, of decoration, so perfect a blending of a first-class modern hotel, South Africa would try vainly to even distantly imitate, and there is no exaggeration in the statement that London, the capital of the world, would not be able to produce anything superior.'[4]

It was perhaps the wartime conditions that led Churchill to complain about the overcrowded dining-room and the state of the food. A war is not an affair which attracts the type of clientele the hotel was aiming for. Yet the large influx of people to South Africa at the turn of the century — the politicians and soldiers, adventurers and financial speculators from every corner of the globe — made the hotel a success long before its fame as a truly great hotel could spread in more peaceful times.

'At the hotel, in its garden, or elsewhere in the town, all the world and his wife are residing — particularly the wife', Churchill observed.[5] Indeed, with the soldiers' women flocking to South Africa during the war, either seeking adventure in the true or in the romantic sense, they became such a nuisance that a complaint about them was made to Sir Alfred Milner.

Sir Redvers Buller stayed at the Mount Nelson and Lords Roberts and Kitchener made it their headquarters before they proceeded to the front. However, common soldiers, were not permitted to stay there, although they were strongly attracted to its elegant bar. To avoid lesser ranks crowding the hotel's facilities and possibly causing disturbance among the celebrities, the manager introduced an 'officers only' rule.

This, of course, was much resented by the soldiers of the British expeditionary force. A Canadian private, extremely annoyed that the hotel's luxuries were denied him, shot his way into the bar and its well-stocked shelves.

Lord Kitchener even refused officers the luxury of the hotel. He announced that 'a baggage train would remove them from the Helot's Rest' to the lesser delights of Stellenbosch. They were to be 'Stellenbosched'. But even the ruthlessly efficient general couldn't keep them away for long.

Churchill soon grew tired of the spectacle at the hotel, and indeed of Cape Town itself. 'Let no one stay long in Cape Town, now who would carry away a true impression of the South Africans', he wrote in a letter to the *Morning Post* on 13 April, and added: 'There is too much shoddy work there at present.'[6]

It was obvious that the restless Churchill needed a different kind of stimulation to keep his adrenaline pumping. The *Morning Post* made the necessary application for their principal correspondent to be accredited to Lord Roberts' army. Ian Hamilton and Sir William Nicholson, Churchill's friends from India, did their best to convince the commander-in-chief that he would be valuable in forthcoming campaigns. When he was finally notified, on 11 April, that Roberts had agreed to allow him to accompany his force as a correspondent 'for your father's sake', he immediately set off for Bloemfontein.

Meanwhile the Boers had started to disrupt railway lines and were busy cutting off supplies to the British. Roberts had to despatch troops to the troubled areas, and Churchill accompanied them. 'Equipped by the *Morning Post* of a munificent scale with whatever good horses and transport were necessary', he wrote, 'I moved rapidly this way and that from column to column, wherever there was a chance of fighting'.[7]

Churchill was once more in his element, but it was his self-assured arrogance that the generals resented. They also believed that the interloper, who wrote articles that could be as critical as they were popular, was not to be trusted. But Churchill couldn't care less whether he was liked or not. He knew what he wanted and how to get it. He had friends and knew how to make other friends when he needed them.

One of his old friends was General Brabazon, the Commanding Officer of the 4th Queens Own Hussars, and he joined his column when the troops moved from Bloemfontein to Dewetsdorp.

After some skirmishes among the outlying hills in the vicinity of Dewetsdorp, the cavalry was sent to reconnoitre the enemy's left flank where a force of about 200 Boers was detected. When the British opened fire another group of Boers appeared. The first group had taken cover behind a hill and the second had made its way to another hill towards the cavalry's right.

Captain Angus McNeill, the officer commanding Montmorency's Scouts, was given permission to chase after the second group. He called Churchill to join him. 'So, in the interests of the *Morning Post*, I got on my horse and we all started — forty or fifty scouts, McNeill and I, as fast as we could ... '[8]

Churchill trailed behind the troop, catching up with them as they came to a barbed wire fence on the crest of a hill. They dismounted and started cutting the wire when 'grim, hairy and terrible heads and shoulders of a dozen Boers'[9] appeared from behind rocks a short distance from the fence. A Boer aimed his rifle at the two scouts cutting the fence. McNeill shouted as bullets started flying about. Churchill attempted to mount his horse, but the saddle slipped down under the belly of the frightened animal. The horse bolted and he once again became a prime target for the deadly Boer Mausers. Reaching for his own Mauser, he started to run for the nearest cover, about a mile away. Most of the scouts had already moved beyond the range of the Boer rifles. Churchill was not so lucky. He was alone. 'I turned and, for the second time in this war, ran for my life on foot from the Boer marksmen.'[10] But then, seemingly from nowhere, a lone horseman appeared. 'It was one of the scouts, a tall man, with skull and crossbones badge, and on a pale horse. Death in Revelation, but life to me!'[11]

Churchill called out and to his surprise the rider at once stopped and allowed him to mount the horse behind him. Bullets spat on the ground around them as they galloped off. Churchill held on, trying to reach the horse's mane as he stretched his arms around his rescuer's waist. When they reached safety, his hand was covered in blood. The horse, had already been hit when Churchill mounted it, 'but, gallant beast, he extended himself nobly'.[12] In a letter to his mother Churchill remarked that this encounter with the Boers was the closest he had been to death.

The tall man who had saved his life was Trooper Clement Roberts. But Churchill's well-being, it appears, mattered less to Roberts than the condition of his horse.

'My horse, oh, my poor bloomin' horse; shot with a dum-dum! The bastards! Oh, my poor horse.'

Churchill tried to console him. 'Never mind, you saved my life', he said, to which the rider replied 'Ah', but it's the horse I'm thinking about. And that', Winston wrote, 'was the whole of our conversation'.[13]

Unlike at Chieveley, where he had run for his life with bullets whistling around his head — to be finally captured by another tall man — his fellow troops had witnessed the result of the race with death.

'Virtually every event he [Churchill] described in South Africa, as in Cuba, on the North-West Frontier, and at Omdurman, was witnessed by others with whom recollections were consistent. The difference, of course, lay in interpretation.'[14]

In his dispatch of 22 April 1899 Churchill wrote: 'But it was with a feeling of relief that I turned the corner of the farthest kopje and found I had thrown double sixes again.'[15] He repeated this statement 30 years later when he wrote *My Early Life*. The rider had paused long enough for him to vault up behind him while 'the pursuing bullets piped and whistled — for the range was growing longer — overhead'.[16] In *My Early Life* the scout said to him: 'Yes, get up', and as they rode away the rider had urged him not to be frightened because the bullets wouldn't hit him.

They rejoined the troop without further ado where the officers agreed that: 'the man who pulled up in such a situation to help another was worthy of some honourable distinction', as Churchill put it in the *Morning Post*. 'Indeed, I have heard that Trooper

Roberts — note the name, which seems familiar in this connection — was to have his name considered for the Victoria Cross'.[17]

William Manchester commented, however: 'The difference lay in interpretation.' The way things turned out Trooper Roberts' gallant conduct was not regarded as sufficiently worthy by the authorities to warrant official recognition. Churchill was not prepared to comment on that decision, 'for I feel some diffidence in writing impartially of a man who certainly saved me from great danger'.[18]

Churchill harboured a deep-seated conviction that he had to pursue fame and recognition wherever and whenever an opportunity presented itself. This would explain his disapproval of Trooper Roberts being denied an 'honourable distinction' for rescuing him from harm in the South African veld.

Churchill, however, would find a way to remedy the perceived injustice. Seven years later when Churchill was the Secretary of State for Colonies, he was able to obtain a DCM (Distinguished Conduct Medal) for Roberts. Whether Churchill would have remembered the trooper's gallantry if he had rescued an ordinary soldier is questionable, but as he saw it, he had risked his life to save a very important person. By ensuring that Roberts was rewarded for an act expected of any soldier in a similar position, Churchill once again drew attention to his own bravery under fire.

23

By bicycle through Johannesburg

On 2 May 1900 Lord Roberts continued his march to the Transvaal. The day before they set off, Churchill wrote to his mother about the considerable undercurrent of hostile and venomous criticism he was experiencing, but he assured her that, on the whole, he had gained considerably from his experiences in South Africa. Realising that his behaviour had provoked much of the hostility, he decided to join Ian Hamilton's flanking column of 15 000 men some 50 miles to the east — rather than Lord Roberts's main column.

The disadvantage for Churchill was that Hamilton's column did not provide him as readily with an opportunity to be in the forefront of encounters with the Boers and shine as the star of battles, but 'by this time he knew that he was quite capable of attracting attention if and when he wanted it'.[1]

But there was another reason why he joined Hamilton's column. The Duke of Norfolk, the Duke of Westminster and the Duke of Marlborough — who was Winston's cousin Sunny — were all on Lord Roberts' staff. Jack Churchill, the new Assistant Military Secretary, had arranged Sunny's appointment. Senior officers had always been drawn from the ruling classes.

The radical press in England, however, had begun voicing severe criticism about the aristocracy being favoured. The Field Marshall, who was quite sensitive to public opinion, decided that Sunny should be retrenched. At this point Winston came to the rescue. He persuaded Hamilton, who was now an acting lieutenant-general, to take both himself and the duke as his aide-de-camp on the flanking march. Publicity in the *Morning Post* was assured.

With the formalities out of the way, Winston and his cousin stocked a newly acquired four-horse wagon, which had a raised floor 'beneath which reposed two feet of the best tinned provisions and alcoholic stimulants that London could supply'.[2]

By joining Hamilton, Churchill missed the relief of Mafeking conducted by two flying columns on 17 May. He would, no doubt, have played a major role in the release of his aunt Sarah and the commander of the garrison, Colonel Robert Baden-Powell. His columns in the *Morning Post* would once more have provided testimony to his own conduct; but Johannesburg and Pretoria were yet to be taken and this,

Churchill had no doubt, would provide him with opportunities to keep his name in the limelight.

Lady Sarah had been at Mosita for some weeks before she was finally noticed by the Boers and taken prisoner. They knew about her having acted as a spy by smuggling notes between Mafeking and the south. She was offered to the British in exchange for a Petrus Pretorius who had been fined £100 for inciting natives to rebel, and also jailed for six months for stealing a horse. The exchange was rejected by the British.

The *Daily Mail* was proud of its correspondent. 'Will it be that Lady Sarah will have to go to Pretoria to join her nephew, Mr Winston Churchill, and thus form the nucleus of a pleasant family circle on the Pretoria racecourse? We shall soon know,'[3] read the report.

But Pretoria was not to be her destination. Lord Edward Cecil convinced Baden-Powell that it would not do to leave an Englishwoman as a prisoner of the Boers. The plea from the son of the Prime Minister could not be ignored. He insisted, however, that Sarah's release would officially be in recognition of the intelligence services she had rendered. The Boers agreed to a short truce, endorsed by President Kruger, for the exchange to take place and Sarah was shortly reunited with her husband Gordon.

Winston must have known about Sarah's exploits in Mafeking, but nowhere does he mention his aunt. Instead he was looking forward to being in the vanguard of the column that would take Johannesburg and enter Pretoria with the victorious Bobs. It would be a fitting grand finale to the war.

On 29 May some 500 men led by the City Imperial Volunteers and supported by the Derbyshire and Cameronians, advanced on Johannesburg. They were covered by heavy artillery fire with the additional moral support by the thunder emanating from General French's guns in the rear. The battlefield in this quarter opened onto the very ridges which four years earlier had witnessed Jameson's disastrous defeat at Doornkop. The Gordons delivered the main attack on the right. The troops closed with the enemy and stormed the ridges. The firing of the 82nd Field Battery, which was pushed into the firing line, was devastating.

Churchill was once again in the midst of a hail of bullets. 'After the ridge had been taken by the Highlanders, General Smith-Dorien, who commanded one of Sir Ian Hamilton's brigades, wished to bring his artillery immediately on to the captured positions, and as time was short, determined to choose the place himself.'[4]

He asked Churchill to follow him. As the two rode across the rolling slopes, long lines of smoke obscured their view. The Boers, Churchill claimed, had lit the dry grass — as was their custom — to make way for new growth in spring. The veils of smoke obscured the view with the result that Smith-Dorien and Churchill missed the left flank of the Gordon Highlanders on the ridge. Instead of turning back or riding sideways to avoid being engulfed by the smoke that was fanned in their direction by a gentle breeze, the two cantered on. As the two came out of the smoke curtain, they found themselves 'only a few score yards distant from the enemy'.[5]

They must have presented a wonderful target of opportunity for the Boer sharpshooters, who wasted no time zeroing in on them. 'The air all around us cracked with a whip-lash sound of close-range bullets.'[6] But Churchill's legendary luck held again. They wheeled around and plunged back into the smoke curtain. A bullet, however, grazed one of the horses. It could not have been Churchill's for he made no further mention of this close encounter. The final skirmishes drove the Boers back in disorder and confusion upon the ridges of the Witwatersrand. By the end of the day, 150 men, mostly Gordons, had fallen but the battle was won.

Roberts' headquarters group should have arrived to the south of Johannesburg by the following day. Hamilton lay to the west of the town, which was still occupied by the Boers. As there were no telegraph wires, the only means of communicating with the commander-in-chief was by sending mounted messengers by a long and circuitous route. A faster means of communication had to be found. News from civilians leaving Johannesburg was not reliable. Certainly the Boers were on their way out, but no one had any idea how many of them were still there. 'The shortest, and perhaps the safest, road lay through Johannesburg itself',[7] Churchill observed in his dispatch of 2 June, but he wondered if such a venture was worth the risk.

He was relaxing on the verandah of the temporary headquarters when he met two cyclists who had arrived from the direction of the town. One, a Frenchman named Lautré who was connected to the Langlaagte Mine, convinced Churchill that he could easily move through the centre of the town by bicycle without being questioned — provided he wore civilian clothes.

This presented Churchill with another opportunity to find renewed excitement and again be in the forefront of developments. He would not only be the first Britisher to enter occupied Johannesburg, but he would get to Lord Roberts long before the riders who had left before him. Hamilton agreed to the proposal and Churchill armed himself with military dispatches and his own telegrams for the *Morning Post*. With Lautré at his side, he cycled straight down the main road into the city.

'Lautré, who knew every inch of the ground, avoided all highways, and led me by devious paths, across little private tram lines, through thick copses of fir trees, or between vast sheds of machinery, now silent and idle'.[8] They reached Langlaagte on the outskirts of Johannesburg within 45 minutes where they met a scout of the Rimington Tigers. He told them that the correspondent of *The Times* had passed through more than two hours earlier, which must have put Winston's nose somewhat out of joint. After a short briefing and being eager to get to his destination, he pushed on with the Frenchman.

Churchill was in his element. But he was also in grave danger. In *My Early Life* he recounts his thoughts on entering Johannesburg: 'Darkness was already falling. But numbers of people were about, and at once I was among the armed and mounted Boers. They were still in possession of the city, and we were inside their lines. According to all the laws of war, my situation, if arrested, would have been disagreeable. I was an officer holding a commission in the South African Light Horse, disguised in plain clothes and secretly within the enemy lines. No court-martial that ever sat in Europe would have had much difficulty in disposing of such a case.'[9] Lautré assured Churchill that most of the Boers had already left the town, and those remaining were so engrossed with their own affairs and problems that they wouldn't have time to be bothered with strangers.

As the two of them pushed their bicycles up a steep hill, a mounted Boer rode alongside them with his rifle slung on his back and a pistol at his side. The intrepid cyclists had agreed to converse in French so as to allay any possible suspicion. Churchill looked at the horseman trotting alongside and their eyes met. 'He was a Boer, sure enough', Churchill wrote in his dispatch two days later, 'and I think he must have been a foreigner'.[10]

To be a Boer and a foreigner is, of course, a contradiction in terms — unless Churchill

The opening paragraph of an original dispatch dated 29 May 1900 sent by Churchill to the *Morning Post* regarding the 'Battle of Johannesburg'.

believed him to be a member of one of the voluntary corps that had agreed to fight on the side of the enemy. His appearance did not inspire much trust in the two cyclists. 'He had a pale, almost ghastly visage, peering ill-favoured and cruel from beneath a slouch hat with a large white feather',[11] Churchill observed in his melodramatic fashion. 'The horse he rode carried a full campaigning kit on an English military saddle. Wallets, saddlebag, drinking-cup, holsters — all were there. His rifle was slung across his back, he wore two full bandoleers over his shoulders and a third round his waist — evidently a dangerous customer.'[12] Suddenly the sinister rider dug in his spurs and in an instant he was gone.

This turned out to be their most serious threat as they cycled through the near-deserted Johannesburg. One can only imagine Churchill's mixed feelings: of disappointment that his craving to expose himself to danger had not met with more challenges; combined with relief that all had gone well in Johannesburg. But according to a dispatch he wrote two days later, the adventure had only just begun.

As the two approached the south-eastern outskirts of the town, the streets became progressively more deserted until eventually no one at all was to be seen. The shops were shut and the windows of houses boarded up. 'The night was falling swiftly', Churchill wrote, 'and its shades intensified the gloom which seemed to hang over the town, on this the last day of its republican existence'.[13]

They met an old man who directed them to a sentinel on the top of a hill only five minutes away. Sure enough, they stumbled on three British soldiers of Maxwell's brigade. But there were no picket lines. The three complained about being on half rations and said they were looking for something to eat — and possibly a pint or two of ale. Churchill warned them that mounted Boers were still around and that they should take more care.

Churchill and Lautré continued on their way in their search for Maxwell's picket line. Eventually they walked right into a bivouac where Churchill was informed by a fellow officer whom he knew, that Roberts was not at Elandsfontein where they were heading, but had moved back to Germiston, almost seven miles away.

It was completely dark and there was no road to pedal on, but Lautré assured his companion that he knew the way. They traversed the countryside to get to the main road leading south, but they had to cross densely wooded areas and negotiate a number of fences, ditches, holes and high grass, so progress was slow. After an hour or so they reached a railway line and from there they could see campfires in the distance to their left. After another half mile they came to yet another bivouac. Nobody stopped them and a soldier they approached didn't even know to which brigade he belonged.

Churchill pushed his bicycle towards an enormous camp-fire that was surrounded by a group of officers, one of whom directed him to General Tucker's mess. He had known the general in India when he was the commander of the Seventh Division at Secunderabad, and meeting him again at night by a pine forest outside Johannesburg called for whisky and water.

Duly refreshed and with clear directions on how to reach Roberts' headquarters, 'two miles beyond Germiston, a mile and a half west of the road, in a solitary house on a small hill which stood beyond a large tank'.[14] The instructions appeared difficult to follow because of the darkness, but Tucker led them up a slope from where they could see the lights of the 11th Division's camp. With an assurance that Roberts' camp was close by and after 'a drink for the road' the two cyclists bade the general farewell.

Another half-hour's walk took them to a tarred road. It was a cold night and this made them realise that dinner time had passed. Churchill, however, was not unduly concerned about where he could get a meal and a bed for the night. They reached Germiston and found a hotel which could cater for their bodily needs. As it turned out, Lionel Jackson, the principal correspondent of *The Times,* was waiting there for his subordinate with Hamilton's force. Churchill told him his colleague had left two hours before him, which caused Jackson some concern and Lautré to show a 'heartless grimace'.

Why Lautré, who had never met Churchill before, showed so much concern for him and put himself out considerably to get him to Roberts' headquarters, we will never know. After a hasty and rather disappointing dinner, they carried on to the camp which was about two miles away. An officer directed them to the headquarters situated in a solitary house which they arrived at 10:30pm . Churchill handed Hamilton's report to an orderly, and shortly afterwards Lord Kerry appeared and took them to Roberts.

The Field Marshal was sitting at a large table with Sir William Nicholson, Lord Kitchener, Colonel Neville Chamberlain, Sir Henry Rawlinson and others. 'He jumped up from his chair as I entered, and with a most cordial air advanced towards me holding out his hand.'[15] Two Rimington's guides whom Hamilton had sent during the course of the morning had already briefed him, but Roberts wanted to know all the details of the previous day's action. After Churchill had related everything that he knew, Roberts, 'with his eyes twinkling bright with pleasure or amusement or approbation, or, at any rate, something friendly',[16] invited Churchill and Lautré to stay at his HQ for the night.

The next morning there was intelligence that the Boers under De la Rey, Viljoen and Botha had retreated to the north. Meanwhile, General French was finding little resistance while he was pushing on past Johannesburg for Driefontein. Ian Hamilton's column had entered Florida. Colonel Henry, commanding the Australian Mounted Infantry, had already taken the Germiston and Elandsfontein junction, where the branch railway from Springs joined the lines to Pretoria, Johannesburg, Bloemfontein and Natal. With the Boer's main force in confused retreat and in complete chaos, the chance of further resisting the advancing British Army was unlikely. Johannesburg, with its fabulous golden wealth, on which President Kruger's power had been built, was there for the taking.

On the 30 May the town was called on to surrender. Dr FE Krause, the Boer commandant who had been charged by General Botha with maintaining law order in Johannesburg, complied with the call.

However, he requested a 24-hour respite to allow for the withdrawal of armed burghers to prevent the horrors of hand-to-hand fighting in the streets. The respite was granted and with order restored, Lord Roberts accepted the surrender of the town from Dr Krause on 3 June. The Union Jack was hoisted, and the 11th and 7th Divisions paraded before the commander-in-chief of the British Army in an imposing array.

With the gold mines and the commercial capital of the Transvaal secured, Lord Roberts ordered a two-day rest to allow his men and horses to recover from the hard marching and continual skirmishes of the past week. Roberts settled down in pleasant headquarters at the Orange Grove Inn on the outskirts of Johannesburg on the road to Pretoria. The hostelry was owned by Franz-Joseph Ziegler, a German immigrant who had made a small fortune on the Griqualand West diamond diggings.

Roberts arrived with a large contingent of cavalry with several Long Tom canons in tow. He introduced Colonel Baden-Powell and General Smith-Dorien to the innkeeper. He said they would be staying at the inn for the next three days, and that his officers would pitch tents in the grounds. He asked for water for the horses and was directed to a bubbling stream behind the inn. Robert told Ziegler that his own Indian chef would take over the kitchen.

One evening a staff officer wanting to consult him on an important matter, found the Field Marshall with Ziegler's three-year-old daughter sitting on his knee. The little girl's 14-year-old sister Victoria watched as Robert tried to teach the child how to trace the letters of the alphabet.

'Bobs' looked at the staff officer and smiled. 'Don't come now', he said, 'can't you see I'm busy!'

Lord Roberts was in no hurry. He knew that Pretoria lay there for the taking.

24

Marching to Pretoria

Dismayed by the rapid advance of the conquering British army from the south, President Paul Kruger made arrangements to leave the capital on 29 May for Machadodorp, a little town in the Eastern Transvaal. The seat of Government of the Boer Republic had been transferred to Middelburg on the Delagoa railway line. He had called a meeting of the State officials at his house late that afternoon, where it was decided that, to prevent the sudden departure from attracting too much attention, he should go out by cart along the eastern road and take the train at Eerste Fabrieken.

In the confusion of President Kruger's departure and last farewells, 15-year-old Jimmy Smith, in the uniform of an American District Telegraph Company messenger, came to see him. Of the many odd things that occurred at the time, one of the oddest was this little-known meeting between the Boer patriarch and the youthful emissary of 29 000 American schoolboys.

A volume bound in black sealskin with heavy gold-edged pages had been prepared and a handsewn brown leather box had been made to contain it. Together they weighed 25 kilograms. Pages with signatures were sewn into a roll of heavy silk that hung from the messenger's side. James Francis Smith of New York, a bright youngster of Irish extraction who had given proof of his independence and character, was selected from 2 000 messenger boys to travel to South Africa to present the weighty memorial to President Kruger.

Young Jimmy at last stood in the President's drawing room, beneath the widespread wings of the golden bald eagle presented to the Boer leader by American sympathisers of the Boer cause.

Oom (uncle) Paul, as the President was affectionately known, took the boy's outstretched hand and shook it gravely.

'Your Excellency', Jimmy began, 'I have been chosen to convey to you this memorial signed by 29 000 American schoolboys, which I now have the honour to present'.

Jimmy held out the silken roll of signatures, and placed the box on the floor. All faces in the room were wreathed in smiles. Kruger fingered the roll, turning it over and over in his hands. The box captured the imagination of the onlookers. The

President stepped back warily and looked at it with some misgivings, fearful perhaps that it contained an infernal machine.

By then everyone there had become painfully conscious that Jimmy was struggling with the lock. There was a chorus of suggestions and advice. State Secretary Reitz sank to his knees beside Jimmy and wrestled with the lid. A penknife was inserted in an effort to force the lock, the score-marks of which are still visible to this day. The Secretary of War, Mr Grobler, produced a coin and attempted to prise open the lock. Jimmy suddenly recalled that the key was in his pocket. He turned the key and opened the lid. *Oom* Paul stepped forward and gazed down at the gold-and-vellum volume. He straightened up and smiled at Jimmy.

'It 's a Bible?' he asked, a note of real pleasure in his voice.

'No, it is a history of war', said Reitz who was standing at his side.

The book was an album containing press cuttings, pictures, drawings and photographs. The Secretary of State turned the thick pages and showed the President photographs of noted Boer generals, Creusot Long Toms firing shells into beleaguered Ladysmith, Winston Churchill standing moodily aloof from fellow British prisoners of war in Pretoria, shattered bridges, observation balloons, and heavily armoured trains.

Oom Paul shook his head and closed the book with a heavy sigh.

'Tell them, tell all the American schoolboys, that I thank them for their kind message, and for the history. Now it is time to go.'

Later that afternoon the old man, his shoulders bent by cares and worries — which had been particularly heavy during the last few years of his period of office — said farewell to his beloved wife of 54 years, never to see her again. He drove away from his residence in Church Street West in a dilapidated landau coach, and bid *totsiens* (goodbye) to Pretoria which he had known since the time when the first wattle-and-daub houses were built in Elandspoort. He was met by his bodyguard beyond Arcadia and escorted to Eerste Fabrieken (Heatherley) where he joined a waiting train that took him to the new temporary seat of government in the Eastern Transvaal. For five months he lived in his railway carriage at Machadodorp and in a house at Waterval-Onder.

On 19 October 1900 he sailed from Delagoa Bay for Holland on the *Gelderland*, a man-of-war sent by Queen Wilhelmina of the Netherlands to collect him. Less than four years later, Kruger died in exile at Clarens, Switzerland.

Only General Schalk Burger and State Attorney Jan Smuts remained in Pretoria to represent the Government. The British commander regarded the expected Boer stand at Pretoria and its capture afterwards as the final decisive battle.

The Boers themselves believed their men would come from all parts of the Transvaal to defend the capital and fight their greatest battle ever. Victory for the burghers would send the British back to their colonies of Natal and the Cape, never again to be so foolhardy as to covet territory that didn't belong to them. But neither Lord Roberts nor the weary Boers with their ever-diminishing resources knew that the inner circle of the Boer government had already agreed that Pretoria should not be defended — thereby avoiding bombardment and the destruction of the town.

Indeed, things looked bad in the capital. Streams of people were pouring out of the town on their way to the east. Virtually denuded of police and others who could maintain order, there were many robberies. Doubtful characters pestered people and the future was uncertain. Rumours were rife and people were nervous. Nobody knew what was happening because the newspapers, except for *De Volksstem*, had suspended publication. That, printed on oddments \ of pink, yellow and green paper, could still be obtained free of charge.

The prisoner of war camp at Waterval, 14 miles north of Pretoria on the main railway line to Pietersburg, held more than 3 000 British prisoners. They were guarded by about 300 inadequately armed Boers — young boys, old men and convalescents deemed unfit for active service. The prisoners had also heard rumours and were becoming increasingly agitated. The camp was surrounded with barbed wire and brilliantly illuminated — electricity was generated by a plant especially made in Pretoria for the purpose — but the guards despaired of keeping their charges in check. British officers imprisoned in the 'Bird's Cage' were requested to send 24 of their number to calm the men and assist in maintaining order.

Thursday 31 May was a black day in the history of Pretoria. The looting of Government stores which had started the previous night was getting completely out of hand. Everybody — not only burghers wanting fodder for their horses — was helping themselves to prevent supplies falling into British hands. The looters were using every kind of transport including wheelbarrows and prams. The unruly and criminal classes were rampaging through Pretoria like a swarm of locusts. They were smashing shop windows and looting with impunity.

It was left to Louis Botha, who had entered Pretoria with a force of between two and three thousand burghers, to restore the town to a semblance of order. From the steps of the *Raadsaal* he delivered an impassioned plea to the crowd, exhorting the men to do their duty, gather their rifles and get ready to advance towards Irene, an important point in Pretoria's line of defence. By that afternoon, the general's strong will had begun to tell and comparative quiet and order had set in, but horses were still being stolen. Burghers passing through Pretoria simply commandeered them, handing them back only if the owners protested.

On 2 June Botha, acting under the powers vested in him as the Republican Commander-in-Chief — which gave him absolute control over all areas falling within the 'front' — issued a proclamation appointing a triumvirate to maintain law and order. The three members of this 'chief commission' were the *Landdrost* of Pretoria, Commandant PF Zederberg, Jonkheer CGS Sandberg and Dr WJ Leyds, the former Secretary of State for War and by then acting military secretary to General Botha. In reality, however, only Sandberg was an active member of the commission.

On the same day, Lord Roberts gave the order to commence the march on Pretoria the following day. He had received reports about the capital being in a state of frightful panic and confusion.

They reached Six Mile Spruit within the day and they were opposed by a 500 strong contingent of Boer volunteers who had heeded Botha's call to intercept the advancing enemy near Irene. General Schalk Burger had taken ill, but veterans Lucas Meyer and State Attorney Jan Smuts were available to lead the volunteers. They occupied the hills sloping down to Six Mile Spruit, but when morning broke, the British had gone.

To force back the Boer line, Ian Hamilton had been ordered to turn eastwards and march to Elandsfontein some ten miles west of Pretoria, while Gordon on the right flank was directed to strain every nerve to get his horsemen astride the Delagoa Bay railway to cut off the Boers' last avenue of escape.

Meyer and Smuts returned to Pretoria with their men. Scouts were sent out to search for the enemy. Boer morale was low because many were not prepared to take the risk of being surrounded in the capital and being forced to surrender. 'Ridiculous as the whole affair may appear', Jan Smuts later wrote in his *Memoirs of the Boer War*, 'it must not be forgotten that a night march such as this was over and over again performed by the British columns in the later stages of the war and would have brought them to Pretoria that night, and but for the show of resistance which would have come from us they might have captured Pretoria without firing a shot'.[1]

Unfortunately, in its haste to leave the town the government had forgotten to confer authority on Schalk Burger and Jan Smuts. To make matters worse, Burger immediately left for Lydenburg with his family, leaving Smuts behind with only the civil authority enjoyed by a state attorney in times of peace.

There was the *Rust en Orde* committee, of which *Burghermeester* Piet Potgieter and Chief Justice Reinhold Gregorowski were prominent members, but they questioned Smuts' role instead of giving him support. Both were bitterly opposed to the war and believed that Pretoria would be defended to the bitter end. They realised that this would result in a bombardment of the town and they wanted to avoid this by hoisting the white flag of surrender. It was rumoured that various members of the 'surrender committee', as the organisation became known, argued about who would be given the honour of going out in a black coat and waving the white flag to welcome Lord Roberts and his forces.

Meanwhile, the British army advanced to the outskirts of Pretoria. Ian Hamilton had almost joined Roberts' force when they encountered shelling from the hills at the southern entrance to the town. The commander-in-chief, supported by Hamilton and Colonel Henry's mounted infantry, pressed forward. The artillery of the 7th Division came into action, but no guns were emplaced at Fort Schanzkop and Fort Klapperkop that could combat the onslaught. The republican forts around Pretoria had been built at a cost of £150 000 for just such an eventuality, but not a shot was fired from them. Indeed, it had been decided to not even man the forts. Perhaps this was just as well, because military observers regarded them as useless for defensive purposes.

The British were unaware that the forts were unmanned, however, and they soon had seven field and horse batteries and six or eight heavy guns bombarding them. A Boer pom-pom suddenly engaged the gunners and the infantry deployed for an assault, but the weapon was located and silenced by one of the Yeomanry's Colt guns. The British directed their artillery fire onto the ridges crowned by Fort Schanzkop and Fort Klapperkop on the opposite side, as well as onto the railway station and magazines below. So heavy was the artillery fire that the Boers hastily retreated through the town.

By 4.00pm the whole line of defence was in British hands. What they had not realised was that the dispirited Boers, less than 7 000 in number, were intent only on keeping the enemy out of Pretoria for just another day to give officials sufficient time to remove the government's money and bullion from the vaults of the National Bank and the Mint. They also needed to spirit out vast quantities of reserve ammunition and some guns that had been removed from the forts earlier.

The gold, its estimated value was between £2 500 000 and £3 000 000, had been moved from Johannesburg only a short time earlier. According to Smuts, whose task was to secure the bullion, the total value of the money and the gold there was between £400 000 to £500 000. Whatever its true worth might have been, he had for some time been negotiating with the bank's directors to take possession of it. When this failed, he returned with a posse of policemen and threatened them with arrest and criminal proceedings. The directors had no choice but to allow Smuts and his policemen to enter the bank and carry away the treasure. At the suggestion of Louis Botha, he also included a special war fund of £25 000 standing to the credit of the Commandant-General.

Smuts took the money and the bullion to the station where a special train in charge of a reliable force of police awaited him. Shells were bursting all round the station and howitzers were firing onto the trucks at Sunnyside. But Smuts, with the government treasure under his care, got safely away before sunset.

The train had hardly moved out of sight when Colonel de Lisle's corps of mounted infantry, composed mainly of Australians, galloped forward so furiously that they captured a Boer Maxim on their way to take a small hill west of the town. These were the first men to break through the defensive semicircle around the capital. It was 4.45pm when de Lisle crested the rise and looked down on the little town. The honour of having Pretoria surrender to him, he felt, was his for the taking. He told Lieutenant WWR Watson that, as he had done so well, he should take a white flag into Pretoria and in the name of Lord Roberts and the British army, demand that the Boers end all hostilities.

Watson beamed with delight as he tied a white handkerchief to a whip and set out to find the *landdrost's* office. He had not gone far when he was stopped by a Republican artilleryman whom he asked to escort him into town. The man obliged but Watson was unable to find either the *landdrost* or the *burghermeester*. The Commandant-General was still fighting in the hills, and Watson decided to go to his private residence near Burgers Park. Messages were sent everywhere to summon whoever was available to meet him at Botha's home.

Watson patiently waited while Mrs Botha entertained him with coffee and sandwiches. Eventually Botha's military secretary, Mr Sandberg — he of the law and order triumvirate — who had just returned from an inspection, was told to rush to the commander's residence where an Australian officer was waiting to demand the surrender of Pretoria. Sandberg at once rode to Botha's home, but nobody knew when Botha himself would be returning.

Eventually Watson became impatient, but with the help of whisky and sodas, Sandberg managed to persuade him to stay a little longer. When Botha finally arrived, Sandberg briefed him on developments.

Botha decided to ask Lord Roberts in writing to grant an armistice for the evacuation of women and children from Pretoria. Sandberg drafted the letter. An early reply was essential, so volunteers were called for to go to Robert posthaste. The Boers who had just returned from the fighting line were dropping from fatigue, so Sandberg decided to undertake the mission himself. General Sarel Oosthuizen, who happened to be in Pretoria, agreed to accompany him. It was a long, hard ride to the British headquarters, which had been established on a small hill, later named Roberts' Heights (subsequently Voortrekkerhoogte and now Thaba Tshwane).

'Lord Roberts', records Sandberg in his memoirs published in 1941, was in his little wagonette standing alone in the open veld [2] The staff officer in charge welcomed Sandberg. This officer, later General Lord Rawlinson, became Commander-in-Chief of the Army in India until his death in 1925. He also played a prominent command role during World War-I.

Henry Rawlinson took Botha's letter to Roberts but returned with the request that Sandberg translate it into English for the Field Marshal. There was no explanation why the letter had been written in High Dutch. Sandberg had been secretary to Dr Leyds, who in turn had been secretary to President Kruger, so he should have been able to write in English. The letter might also have been dictated to Watson. Be that as it may, Sandberg said that he had followed Rawlinson and inside a tent he found a 'little man with a white nightcap on his head lying snugly under blankets which were pulled up to his neck. I was face to face with Roberts of Kandahar, the grizzled veteran of army campaigns in far-flung corners of the Empire since he had joined the Army forty-nine years earlier'.[3]

Roberts kept the interview as brief as possible, intimating that he would speak to Botha the next morning only if the town was surrendered unconditionally. He said his troops had orders to advance at 5.00am. He had nothing further to say. Rawlinson took Sandberg to the campfire. He reminded him that when they had met on board ship when Sandberg was returning from a visit to Holland, they had agreed that if they should ever meet again, whoever could do so would treat the other to a whisky and soda.

Rawlinson was now in that position and the representatives of both warring nations put aside the war for a while and enjoyed a sociable drink or two in the middle of the night. It was only after 3.00am on Tuesday 5 June that Sandberg eventually arrived back at General Botha's home and passed on Lord Roberts' message. Botha at once issued orders that all commandos still in and around Pretoria were to immediately withdraw to Eerste Fabrieken. He and General Lucas Meyer would follow them before the British entered Pretoria.

In the absence of any government representative, Botha gave the dubious honour of surrendering the Boer capital to the *burghermeester*, PJ Potgieter. Dr Knobel, representing the appointed Pretoria committee of the Red Cross, called on Potgieter early on 5 June to ask if he could accompany him to see the British commanding general. It was decided that they should immediately ride out on their bicycles and inform Lord Roberts that the military authorities had left the town and that Mr Potgieter, as head of the civil administration, had been ordered to surrender Pretoria to him.

While still discussing the matter they were interrupted and told that a British officer had arrived at the artillery camp and was about to hoist the Union Jack over Pretoria. They went to see him and found that he was not acting under orders. He was told to desist until Lord Roberts' wishes became known.

After the British forces had been notified of the surrender, the troops moved into town. Ian Hamilton's column entered Pretoria from the western side. Churchill, with his cousin Sunny, Duke of Marlborough, wanted to be among the very first to arrive at the station. From there they would follow the route to the State Model School where he had been imprisoned. He wrote:

> We passed through a narrow cleft in the southern wall of mountains, and Pretoria lay before us — a picturesque little town with red or blue roofs peeping out among masses of trees, and here and there an occasional spire or factory chimney. Behind us, on the hills we had taken, the brown forts were crowded with British soldiers. Scarcely two hundred yards away stood the railway station.[4]

General Pole-Carew, whom they had passed earlier in their haste to be at the forefront of the victorious British Army, had to wait for his infantry to catch up with him. This delayed Churchill and the Duke, and while they sat watching the proceedings from their horses, they heard a locomotive whistle loudly, 'and, to our astonishment — for had not the town surrendered? — a train drawn by two engines steamed out of the station on the Delagoa Bay line'.[5]

A group of officers, aides-de-camp, and orderlies gave chase, but with wire fences and gardens in their way, their efforts in trying to stop the train or shoot the engine-driver were unsuccessful. Churchill counted ten trucks of horses, 'which might have been very useful', and a truck-load of what he called 'Hollanders'[6] who got away while he sat looking on helplessly. That was how he remembered the event in *Ian Hamilton's March*. However, in *My Early Life,* Churchill doesn't mention the ten trucks of horses. In that account the long train steaming slowly before their eyes was 'crammed with armed Boers whose rifles bristled from every window'.

The large group of officers that he and Sunny joined at the outskirts of the town were waiting at the closed gate of the railway level crossing. 'We gazed at each other dumbfounded at three yards distance. A single shot would have precipitated a horrible carnage on both sides. Although sorry that the train should escape, it was with unfeigned relief that we saw the last carriage glide slowly past our noses.'[7]

But all was not lost. Three more fully loaded trains with steam up, ready to follow the one that had escaped, were captured by the leading company of Grenadiers. The Boers in these trains 'attempted to resist the troops with pistols, but surrendered after two volleys had been fired, no one, fortunately, being hurt in the scrimmage'.[8]

From the station the Guards, with bayonets fixed, marched along Market Street towards Church Square in the centre of the town. Crowds lined the street and sentries and pickets were posted as they moved on. Churchill's former prison was only a few blocks away from the main street. Anxious to learn what had happened to his fellow prisoners, he made enquiries, only to be told by a mounted 'Dutchman' that they had been moved to the vicinity of Dr Gunning's zoological garden. Dutchmen were immigrants to the Transvaal — but not necessarily Hollanders — who were not naturalised citizens. This one offered to guide Churchill and his cousin to the 'Bird Cage', as the new prison was called. Without waiting for the troops to catch up, the three rode off.

They soon arrived at a long tin building with a corrugated iron roof with a high barbed wire fence enclosing the property. A wash drawing by the Austrian painter and illustrator Nepomuck Schönberg appeared in the *Sphere* of London in 1900. This illustration, the original of which is in the collection of Museum Africa in Johannesburg, shows that the guarded Bird Cage was floodlit at night, so few opportunities to escape were provided.

Churchill, in his dispatch to the *Morning Post* of 8 June wrote: 'We saw before us a long building surrounded by a dense wire entanglement. I raised my hat and cheered. The cry was instantly answered from within. What followed resembled the end of an Adelphi melodrama'.[9]

The Duke of Marlborough called on the prison commander to surrender forthwith.

The prisoners rushed from the building into the yard, some wearing uniforms, some with flannels, hatless or coatless, but all violently excited. The sentries threw down their rifles. Gates were flung open and while the rest of the guards, numbering 52 in all, stood around uncertain what to do, the long-penned-up officers seized their weapons. Grimshaw of the Dublin Fusiliers produced a Union Jack (made during his imprisonment out of a *Vierkleur*). The Transvaal emblems were torn down, and amid wild cheers, the first British flag was hoisted at 8:47am on 5 June.[10]

The 129 British officer freed were handed over to the Duke of Malborough. The prison commander, who had replaced Opperman when he was posted to the front, formally surrendered along with four corporals and 48 Dutchmen. The Dutchmen were locked up, but since there were no complaints about the way they had been treating their former prisoners, they were offered the chance to take the oath of neutrality and return to their homes.

Churchill had arrived in the nick of time to have the British prisoners freed. As Lieutenant Frankland of the Royal Dublin Fusiliers noted in his diary, the commandant had awakened them at 1:30am and told them to get ready to march to the railway station. From there they would be transported to a camp on the Delagoa railway line beyond Middelburg. The prisoners were shocked at first, but they remembered hearing the firing of field guns, the pom-poms and Maxims the day before. They had used field glasses and telescopes to watch the lyddite shells throwing up clouds of brown earth. Later in the afternoon they had seen the Boers pulling back from the western ridges and trek across the plain before disappearing along the northern road.

The prisoners knew it would only be a matter of days, perhaps even hours, before the British occupied the town and freed them. To be moved when their release was so close was beyond contemplation, so they refused to budge. But the commandant was not prepared to consider their views. When he insisted that he had to follow his orders, the officers took both him and his lieutenant as prisoners. After a further argument followed by a threat to have the guards intervene, the officers released them. Colonel Hunt suggested that they should simply go back to bed. 'You cannot shoot a man in his bed', he opined, and following this advice, the men laid down and anxiously awaited further developments.

Hours passed. The sun rose and they saw lines of men moving about on the racecourse. They couldn't discern their identity, but suddenly two mounted horsemen in khaki appeared in the near distance. They cantered across a small stream, then galloped towards the camp. A horseman raised his hat and cheered. 'There was a wild rush across the enclosure, hoarse discordant yells, and the prisoners tore like madmen to welcome the first of their deliverers.'[11]

The drama of the surrender of the capital was nearing its climax. Civil servants, railway employees and other burghers going to work that Tuesday found printed notices everywhere setting out the terms under which individuals could accept British rule. Later in the morning, negotiations between British officers and such representatives of the citizens as were willing to co-operate with the British — including the Republican officials JJ Smit, JF de Beer and Louis de Souza — were conducted in the *Raadsaal*. It was arranged that the formal entry of Lord Roberts would take place in Church Square at 2.00 pm that day, 5 June 1900.

Meanwhile, British guards had been mounted on all important buildings, including those belonging to the Netherlands Railway Company, the Presidency and General Botha's home where Mrs Kruger was also staying. A great deal of confusion followed because nobody knew precisely where Lord Roberts was. A wild goose chase to locate him ensued and he was eventually located in the Fountains valley at the southern entrance to the town. It was there that he accepted the surrender of Pretoria.

Churchill described his arrival in Pretoria as follows:

At two o'clock Lord Roberts, the staff, and the foreign attachés entered the town, and proceeded to the central square, wherein the Town Hall, the Parliament House, and other public buildings are situated. The British flag was hoisted over the Parliament House amidst some cheers. The victorious army had begun to parade past it, Pole-Carew's Division, with the Guards leading, coming from the south, and Ian Hamilton's force from the west. For three hours the broad river of steel and khaki flowed unceasingly, and the townsfolk gazed in awe and wonder at those majestic soldiers, whose discipline neither perils nor hardship had disturbed, whose relentless march no obstacles could prevent. With such pomp and the rolling of drums the new order of things was ushered in. The former Government had ended without dignity. One would have thought to have found the President — stolid old Dutchman — seated on his stoep, reading the Bible and smoking his pipe. But he had chosen a different course. On the Friday preceding the British occupation he had left the capital and had withdrawn along the Delagoa Bay Railway, taking with him a million pounds in gold and leaving behind him a crowd of officials clamouring for pay and far from satisfied with the worthless cheques they had received, and Mrs Kruger, concerning whose health the British people need not further concern themselves.[12]

Church Square was filled with 3 000 troops when the white-haired, 68-year-old Field Marshall stood to attention as the Union Jack was hoisted and 'God save the Queen' was played, followed by loud cheers. A photograph shows the time on the *Raadsaal* clock as 2.20pm. The biggest military march that Pretoria had ever seen followed. How different this was to that when, on 12 April 1877, Sir Theophilus Shepstone with eight civil servants and 25 mounted policemen formally annexed the Republic. The strength of the British army marching on Pretoria this time was 1 099 officers, 24 432 men, 6 971 horses, 12 heavy guns, 104 field guns and 176 machine guns.

Opposing them had been General Botha with 104 officers and 3 039 men.

Other witnesses recorded their impressions of that momentous day in the history of Pretoria. Almost every account describes the end of the long march and proceedings that led to a climax when the Union Jack was hoisted on the *Raadsaal* amidst the cheers of the victorious British troops basking in the glory of the moment.

While the quintessence of history is so elusive that it is only given to the really great historian to reveal an account not clouded by bias, patriotic sentiment or sheer misinterpretation of facts — as is so often the case — it is perhaps interesting to read extracts from an account by American journalist, HF Mackern, if only for the details.

Next morning, 5th June, the 11th Division awoke from their bivouac uncertain whether or not the enemy was still in position of the hills in front of them: we had as yet not heard of any surrender. No movement could be detected on the hills around Pretoria and gradually the news began to leak out that Pretoria had been evacuated during the night. General Pole-Carew and the Guard's Brigade moved in cautiously ... I rode on, following some of the troops who were evidently taking the main road and came to a halt just on the outskirts.[13]

Mackern could see the railway station in front of him. He did not mention any trains but he was aware of unusual activity. On one side of the station he noticed a motley crowd of excited Pretoria citizens. General Pole-Carew was all smiles as he gave orders to some of his staff who were engaged in looking after prisoners. 'After an hour or so, search parties began coming into the station with their arms full of rifles, carbines, shotguns, swords, and arms of every description. These, as they were piled up, presented a collection varied enough to have satisfied any curiosity hunter ...'[14]

It was close to 2.00pm when Mackern arrived at Church Square. The Guards Brigade was already drawn up close to the pavement, in single file all around and facing the Dutch Reformed Church or centre of the square. Beyond the soldiers, people, dressed in what seemed to be gala attire, had turned out en masse; some who were at last able to express their long pent-up feelings, came from motives of patriotism; others, doubtless the majority, came from mere curiosity. He continued:

At the head of Market Street, opening into the square, a large number of officers could be seen. There is something about their appearance that attracts my attention as differing from the rest. Their faces, instead of being sunburnt and having that fresh, healthy look derived from life on the veld, are pale, and appear as though they must have been in confinement for some time. Their uniforms, differing from those of their fortunate comrades, are neat, the light colour of khaki giving but too strong evidence of many types of washing. Some look thoughtful; some are unable to shake off that constrained look; some, by a nervous sort of laugh, show feelings of a strained temperament. Who are they? These are the greater part of the British officers who were released that morning.

The crowd is getting thicker and thicker; the balcony of the Grand Hotel to the left of the *Raadsaal*, and opposite the Dutch Reformed Church, is full of people; the column to the right of the church, on which the statue of Mr Kruger was to have been placed, is thronged with people endeavouring to get a good point of vantage. The ever-irrepressible small boy has long ago chosen his favourite gallery seat on the tops of lampposts, or on rickety building scaffolding. All of a sudden across the square, near where the ex-prisoners are standing, the people break away, and the line of Guardsmen make an opening, as Lord Roberts accompanied by his entire staff, the foreign attachés, and the bodyguard, amid a waving of handkerchiefs and huzzas from the people, rides into the square and takes up a position in front of the church, directly opposite the *Raadsaal*. An undercurrent of suppressed excitement seems to be visible during the next few moments. All faces are turned towards the flagstaff on the top of the *Raadsaal*. A little flutter of something red, white and blue rivets our attention, and slowly, but surely, symbolic of progress and civilisation, the Union Jack rises to the top.

It was rather a strange coincidence as I was standing on the back of my faithful old 'Blunderbuss' I should see standing beside me none other but Captain Arthur Haggard, whose brother, the noted author, with his own hands, in 1871, under the Shepstone régime, raised the Union Jack over the same capital. That flag was raised with a wavering hand, only to come down; but this one, never again!'[15]

Early that morning Churchill had booked a room at the Grand Hotel with a balcony overlooking Church Square. When the 60-bedroom hotel was built in 1890 it was named the President. It is not known whether Kruger was pleased with the name, but what he didn't like was that the three-storeyed building would overshadow the prestigious two storeyed *Raadsaal* designed by his Dutch architect, Sytze Wopke Wierda. The *Raadsaal*, he insisted, should also have three storeys and with its dome and clock tower, would be the dominant building on the square.

In spite of its enviable position, the owner of the 'finest building with three storeys in the Transvaal capital', a German by the name of HWF Bürger could not make a success of the hotel and consequently, in 1895, Solomon Schlomer took over the lease and changed its name to the Grand Hotel.

On the morning of 4 June Churchill's Aunt Sarah, accompanied by Mrs Godley, began travelling by cart to Pretoria from Mafeking. After that they intended to continue on to Johannesburg, then through the Orange Free State to Cape Town where they would board a liner that would take them back to England. They arrived in Pretoria on 7 June to find the town bustling with troops and the square blocked with carts and wagons. They were told the Transvaal Hotel close to the square and all other hotels in town were fully booked.

In desperation they made their way to the crowded Grand Hotel. The manager tried to be helpful. He knew that a guest was about to leave and took the two ladies to show them the suite. Great was Sarah's surprise to discover that the khaki-clad gentleman busy stowing away papers and packing clothes was her nephew Winston. Accounts of his imprisonment and escape had reached her in Mafeking, but she wanted to hear all the details of his adventures from him personally. Churchill thus postponed his departure by 24 hours and offered to share his suite with Sarah and Mrs Godley.

Churchill made no mention of the two ladies in his last dispatch from Pretoria on 8 June. With the Boer capital in British hands, he also intended to go home. 'Politics, Pamela, finances and books all need my attention', he wrote to his mother, but first he had to catch up with Sarah's adventures in Mafeking, and she with his.

The following morning the troops were given a special send-off by Lord Roberts. Churchill, Sarah and Mrs Godley watched the procession and were delighted when the commander-in-chief with Baden-Powell at his side halted his horse and exchanged a few words with them. The two ladies were the first Englishwomen to enter 'British Pretoria' and Roberts commended them for their daring.

Later in the day Churchill showed his aunt and Mrs Godley around town, including taking them to the prison camp and the State Model School. Later at the Grand Hotel, a group of army officers entertained Churchill to a farewell dinner.

25

Escape of Haldane and Co.

On 11 March 1900, Frankland recording his experiences as a prisoner at the State Model School in his journal, wrote:

'I drew another picture on my wall, a sequel to the first. It represents Kruger just escaping from Lord Roberts, also with drawn sword appears to be running after him at a good pace. My picture No 1 is entitled "President Kruger goes to the front to exhort his *burghers*"; picture No 2, "But returns on urgent business"'.[1]

The following day Frankland wrote: 'Opperman saw my portraits of Kruger this morning; I am afraid he did not appreciate them as he should have done. However, I told him that with a pail of whitewash and a brush he might obliterate them if he chose. (Such is the procrastinating nature of these Boer-Hollander people that Opperman never had the pictures removed, and this with other things had, I believe, a good deal to do with his own removal).'[2]

One person who did not appreciate the caricatures was the Superintendent of Education, Dutch-born Dr Nicholas Mansvelt. When the building reverted to its original use as a school, he took photographs of the map and the drawings and wrote to the State Secretary requesting that the map and the drawing of the skeleton be preserved for the purpose of historical memories and for future use in classes. Mansvelt also described the drawings in the second classroom before he ordered them removed. A translation of his description reads as follows: 'One painting shows HH going to the front to strengthen his burghers with a Bible under one arm and an umbrella in the other hand. The other shows HH returning on urgent business, dropping his Bible and losing his hat and chased by a British officer with a drawn sword, perhaps representing Lord Kitchener.'[3]

Churchill said nothing about his last visit to the State Model School, nor did he say anything about the caricatures. It was only in September 1951 that attention was drawn to them by Pretoria historian, Dr Jan Ploeger, who wrote about them in *Pretoriana*, the first issue of the journal of the now defunct Old Pretoria Society. It appears that no one could remember them, but five years later Dr Ploeger received a letter from a Mr JH Broekman of Bergen in the Netherlands. Mr Broekman enclosed copies of two old photographs of Frankland's Kruger caricatures,

Lieutenant Frankland's cartoons drawn on a wall at the State Model School. First depicts Paul Kruger going to the front to strengthen his burgers. The second depicts him being chased back to Pretoria by General Lord Roberts.

which fitted Dr Mansvelt's descriptions.

Frankland told Churchill about the dramatic escape of Captain Haldane, Lieutenant Le Mesurier and Sergeant Brockie from the State Model School at the end of February when he and Sunny arrived at the Bird Cage. On returning to England, Churchill included extracts from Frankland's journal in his book *From London to Ladysmith via Pretoria*.

In 1900 Haldane published his book titled *How we escaped from Pretoria*, which dealt with the trio's escape from the State Model School in 1900. There is no doubt that the sheer audacity and endurance of their bid for freedom had never been equalled in South Africa. Yet their story was overshadowed by Churchill's reports. Churchill was the first to write about his extraordinary experiences in a mass circulation newspaper and this, coupled with his reputation and a remarkable imagination, helped him gain worldwide fame.

After Haldane's first plan to escape with Brockie had turned out so disappointingly, he was more determined than ever to get away. 'Tales of escape from prison had always had a fascination for me, and I was familiar with the true account of Latude's escape from the Bastille and Jack Sheppard's from the castle-ward in old Newgate, as well as the fictitious escape of Edmund Dantés from the Château d'If', Haldane wrote in *How we escaped from Pretoria*. 'Our next plan, [after Churchill inserted himself into the plot and left without his co-conspirators] was to be on the lines of the last of these.'

When Haldane first arrived at the prison his first thought was to dig his way out. Two days after Churchill's escape, he checked to see if there was space beneath the floorboards and discovered a trapdoor under one of the beds. Haldane and his co-conspirators explored the possibility of escaping by escaping via the trapdoor and making their way out beneath the floorboards. They would then cut the light cable and in the darkness climb over the fence in the same way as Cahill, Bridge and Churchill had done. They discussed other options at length, but finally decided that their best means of escape lay under the floorboards.

Rumours that the prisoners were about to be transferred to a higher security prison became more persistent and they decided to make their move before it was too late. On 18 February, after provisioning themselves, the three men dropped through the trapdoor. This was immediately secured so that nothing betrayed their absence except their three empty beds. They crept towards the ventilation duct below the floor and settled down to wait.

On 27 February Lieutenant Frankland noted in his journal: 'This morning Opperman came into our room as usual to count the number of prisoners in bed, and on seeing three beds empty he fairly staggered with astonishment.'[4] He left the room in a hurry, returning shortly afterwards with Dr Gunning. Later, Chief of Police du Toit arrived and he and Gunning examined the room and discussed the mystery. Then a posse of armed police searched the whole building. They brought a lantern, but did not think of looking under the floorboards. Du Toit found a saw that Haldane had made from a table knife and he connected this to a hole in the roof of the gymnasium and some cut wires. Once more orders were given for the houses in the neighbourhood to be searched. 'The rest, such is their trust of one another in this country', Frankland wrote, 'were quite sure somebody had been bribed.'[5]

Later, Opperman and Du Toit returned with a hat and news that the fugitives had been seen going over the hills towards Mafeking, so as far as they were concerned, their search had ended.

For 18 long days and nights Captain Haldane and his two companions were forced to remain in cramped positions near the ventilation duct. Above them their brother officers kept them informed of developments. Plenty of food and drink was provided and they made themselves as comfortable as possible, considering the dark and wet conditions and the company of straying rats that they had to put up with.

On the 17th day, a note came down: 'We move tomorrow after breakfast. Patience has carried the day; you deserve your luck.' [6] At daybreak on 16 March the inmates were told to pack their belongings. At 10.00am the first cabs, provided by the government but later charged to the officer-prisoners, arrived. 'The long column of vehicles was escorted by a motley guard, consisting of very old men and tiny boys armed with Sniders and sporting guns of ancient pattern.'[7]

The column soon reached its destination which was halfway up a hillside close to where Dr Gunning's zoological garden had been established. 'It is probably a much healthier place than the State Model School',[8] Frankland recorded. The officers, however, were in for a surprise. The complex comprised a long white galvanised-iron shanty set in a fairly large compound enclosed by barbed-wire entanglements. Plenty of powerful electric lights were in place. The 85 by 30 yard sleeping hall could accommodate 120 officers. Four bathrooms, a service compartment, kitchen and dining rooms were integrated into the building. There was no flooring and the drains consisted of open ditches. The immediate protest levied by the officers was noted.

Very early on the morning after the officers had been moved from, the State Model School, Captain Haldane pushed up the trapdoor. The three men — pale, thin and unshaven but in high spirits — hauled themselves up into the deserted building. Reeling like drunken men, their legs weary from the lack of exercise, they simply walked out of their prison.

They had taken a map from a book in the prison library and they used this to make their way out of town and head towards the Delagoa Bay Railway line. Brockie advised them to slouch along with knees bent and backs rounded so as to appear like Boers. Haldane found this difficult, 'for the exquisite sense of exhilaration which I was experiencing made me feel much more inclined to run, jump, or indeed do anything but walk soberly along'.[9] Brockie's suggestion, however, must have paid off for they passed a few Zarps and none of whom showed any interest in them.

The initial adrenaline that had kept them going soon wore off. They saw a coal train pass by before they reached the rails. Le Mesurier twisted his ankle and an exhausted Brockie 'insisted that he saw Boers under every tree and bush'.[10] The party reached Eerste Fabrieken 13 miles east of Pretoria well after midnight. They decided to rest on dry grass at the bottom of a deep ditch, but it turned out to be a hotbed of mosquitoes.

At 6:30am that morning the steam horn of Sammy Marks' Heatherly Distillery blew, reminding them that dawn had broken on their first day of freedom after nearly three weeks without seeing the sun. The following night they lost Brockie as dogs started to chase them. Diving into reeds in a river seemed the only way of avoiding detection by Boers who came to investigate. When they eventually emerged their food ration was spoilt, their chocolate soggy and their matches useless. The cork on Haldane's whisky flask had come out and the elixir of life had disappeared. The next day

Haldane discovered that he had left his compass and money belt containing £18 at their last hiding place, but they couldn't go back. They went to a railway gradient and waited for a train to appear, only to realise after a long wait that the night service no longer ran. Haldane and Le Mesurier wondered what had happened to Brockie. They began walking along the railway line at night and slept in the veld during the day, but there was a lack of trees to shelter under and they became badly sunburnt. Calculating distances at various points along the line, they calculated that they had covered 36 miles in four days. There was another 21 miles to go before they reached Balmoral where they hoped to get help from Englishmen working at the collieries. Fortunately there was no shortage of drinkable water in pools and streams en route. An army emergency ration and a little biltong was eventually all they had left to eat.

In the next two or three days they finished the biltong and turned to eating wild mushrooms. Then they stumbled on an African hut. 'There were five thick-lipped, ebony coloured Negroes seated around a cauldron, which, turned on its side, displayed its half-eaten contents — thick dry mealie porridge'.[11] The Africans readily shared their food. Lack of comprehension of each other's language limited the exchange of essential information, but they were directed to a house where it was expected they would get a friendly reception.

The occupant turned out to be Danish and he willingly offered to help. He called a Mr Moore, the manager of the Douglas Colliery store, who gave the half-starved pair a feast of tinned salmon and cocoa. They were provided with accommodation in a forage shed. The next morning Dr Gillespie, the medical man in charge of the mines, arrived. He had heard of the escape and was told that the escapees were at Moore's house. To his surprise, Haldane learnt that Gillespie had helped Churchill three months earlier; which erased any doubts that the doctor would offer the same assistance to himself and Le Mesurier.

As with Churchill, a description of the three fugitives had been circulated by Pretoria to the police in Johannesburg as soon as their disappearance was discovered. A translation of the notice read as follows:

8.20am., 27th February 1900.

Yesterday evening three officers, prisoners of war, escaped from the State Model School, viz.: Captain Haldane. — About 6 feet 1 inch tall, walks with a slight stoop, thin, complexion and dark moustache, wearing a dark-coloured suit. Lieutenant Brockie. — about 5 feet 9 inches tall, erect, light complexion and a fair moustache. Has a habit of raising his eyebrows when talking. Has an elongated face, and was wearing a chocolate-brown suit. Lieutenant Le Mesurier. — About 5 feet 9 inches tall, strongly built, round face, complexion and moustache fair, small eyes. Wearing a grey suit. Muscles powerfully developed, blinks his eyes.

At Moore's place nothing was said about hiding the escapees in the mine. 'During the day a gramophone played numerous topical airs for our amusement', Haldane wrote, 'and when it grew dark Moore came and took us again to his house. Here we found, thanks to his thoughtful kindness, a complete change of garments, for our own were fit for nothing but the dust-heap. We also enjoyed the luxury of a bath, and were much amused at the reflection of ourselves in a looking glass'.[12]

After supper some of the Englishmen employed on the mine came to see them. Afterwards Dr Gillespie took them in a two-wheeled dogcart to see Howard of the Transvaal Delagoa Bay Colliery. They arrived at his office at 1:30am on Saturday 24 March. 'To make the arrangements safe, it would be necessary to take into our confidence two English servant-girls and a Kaffir boy.'[13] It was another hour and a half before they reached Howard's house, but before they were allowed to sleep, the mine manager insisted they have another meal.

By pure coincidence Brockie had shown up at Moore's mine store that very morning. They had helped him get on his way to Kaapmuiden, close to the Portuguese East African border, but he had already left by the time his erstwhile companions arrived.

Haldane and Le Mesurier stayed on for a few days in Howard's house, sleeping in a room with the blinds drawn. Dr Gillespie came to check their health and after dark Howard took them for a walk towards the Witbank lights.

On 26 March a firm in Lourenço Marques agreed to purchase a consignment of wool from Burnham on satisfactory terms. The risk of smuggling the men out of the country hidden in the wool was far greater than it had been for Churchill, for Burnham had already fallen under suspicion. A member of the firm to whom the wool was consigned had noticed some grease marks on the bales. He asked Burnham for an explanation and suggested that someone had occupied the truck. Burnham pleaded ignorance.

Gossip suggested that he had been seen walking in Lourenço Marques with a stranger after the wool was delivered. Shortly afterwards a Boer in Pretoria had asked him outright how much he had been paid to get Churchill out of the country. He knew he was on dangerous ground, but he nevertheless he took the calculated risk of offering to help the officers.

Two days later an empty coal truck had been loaded with 16 bags of wool at Witbank station. A space of 3ft by 7ft had been left in which the two escapees could hide. Before dawn on Thursday 29 March Haldane and Le Mesurier burrowed under the bales of wool and they were soon on their way. This time their benefactor didn't find it necessary to bribe officials with bottles of whisky for their safe passage to neutral territory.

Later, when Haldane and Le Mesurier boarded the *SS König* bound for Durban, they were astonished to meet up with Sergeant-Major Brockie, who had arrived in Lourenço Marques the previous evening.

In *Churchill Wanted Dead or Alive* Celia Sandys wrote: 'Churchill had been on the run for 30 hours. Haldane and Le Mesurier, who would escape with Brockie the following March, and who would follow the same route, took six days to cover the same distance, losing Brockie on the way and being reunited with him only when they reached Lourenço Marques. The comparison makes nonsense of Haldane's claim that had Churchill carried out the arrangements carefully thought out by Haldane and Brockie, he would have been able to foresee and surmount most of the difficulties he experienced'.[14]

Haldane's was no doubt disappointed that he and Brockie had been unable to get away when Churchill escaped, particularly as he had so carefully planned it. That Churchill had indeed followed the plan hatched by his friends he confirmed in *My Early Life*. He sought the railway line leading to Delagoa Bay and boarded a train that he knew was arriving at a certain time at Pretoria station. That he could not foresee the difficulties he would face is obvious.

In the same way Haldane and his partners also had to face the unexpected — such as being detected by Boer dogs, losing their provisions and papers and parting company with Brockie while taking refuge in the reeds. The main difference between the two escapes who used the same route, was that Haldane and his friends had spent 18 gruelling days confined below the floor of the prison before they could get away. They had to re-accustom themselves to standing up and walking while they slowly limped out of town. Le Mesurier's twisted ankle was an additional burden and because of the lack of trains they had to walk all the way to Witbank.

On the other hand Churchill scaled the fence with ease and 'walked on leisurely through the night, humming a tune and choosing the middle of the road' en route to boarding a train. He spent the major part of his 30 hours on the run, sleeping on the train that carried him towards Balmoral, resting in a shady grove of trees and hiding behind bushes while he waited for another train to carry him forward.

Churchill had four slabs of chocolate and some biscuits to sustain him and hunger was the furthest thing from his mind. Haldane and Le Mesurier, on the other hand , were near starving when they shared porridge with hospitable Africans after a tough six-day route march. All four men essentially followed the same route, but Haldane and Le Mesurier didn't encounter the guarded bridges and villages and the swamps that Churchill claimed he had fallen into. There is no record whatsoever of the privations that Brockie might have endured.

One would expect that the Boer authorities would have been more anxious to recapture three serving officers on the run than they would have been with one non-combatant correspondent, particularly as was about to be paroled by government order anyway.

Other anomalies are evident when the various records are examined. The two Dutch servant girls Howard had been careful to keep concealed from Churchill had become English lasses who were informed of the unexpected arrivals. Howard did not deem it necessary to hide Haldane and Le Mesurier in the mine or maintain any great secrecy. There was no field cornet snooping around. Spiriting the officers out of the country under a quickly arranged consignment of wool seemed to pose no great problem either.

Indeed, in the doing, the tribulations of Haldane, Le Mesurier and Brockie seem to surpass or at least equal Churchill's adventures, yet few got to hear of their stories. Churchill, of course, was not only the son of a flamboyant English lord he was also the acknowledged master of the written word when recording dramatic moments and evoking images in the minds of his readers. Besides that, he had the advantage of having already been publicly hailed for his heroism at Chieveley and being a widely read correspondent as well as an established author of note.

It seems odd that the escapes of Privates Bridge and Cahill escaped mention in his book, despite them having been the first to escape. Perhaps in the way of the world in those snobby Victorian times he didn't think they merited mention because of their lowly rank status.

26

A final act of courage

Although the main cities in the Transvaal and the Orange Free State were firmly in British hands, Churchill concluded that the South African War — the last gentleman's war — was far from over. Armed conflicts are always cruel undertakings — as Stuart Cloete put it: '... men who are killed, whether in a gentlemanly fashion or not, are dead, and their women — the colonel's lady or Judy O'Grady — are widows and their children fatherless.'[1] Churchill knew that the conflict wouldn't end with the occupation of Pretoria and that it would develop into a guerrilla war in which he would play no part.

Lord Roberts was poised to launch his army against Louis Botha and Koos de la Rey to drive the Boers farther away from Pretoria. The Boer generals had rallied a force of 6 000 burghers who were deployed along a chain of hills some 25 kilometres to the east of Pretoria. Their intention was to cut the main roads to Pietersburg and Middelburg and disrupt the Delagoa Bay railway line.

Churchill saw the forthcoming skirmish as his last chance to see action in South Africa, and perhaps to gain the official recognition he so desperately sought. Once this was over and he had come through it all right, he promised in a letter to his mother that he wrote to her on his last day in Pretoria, that he would finally turn his face towards home.

Lord Roberts approached the Boer forces with an army of almost 30 000 men and a hundred guns. His orders were to clear the enemy from the neighbourhood. The operation began on 11 June 1900 on the farm donkerhoek (Dark Corner), a name which is said to derive from the fact that the farm is situated so that it is almost always in the shade. On a map of 1898 the word 'diamonds' is printed at the site, hence British historians referred to Donkerhoek as 'Diamond Hill'[2]. General John French (later Field Marshall Earl French of Ypres) and the cavalry forming the flanks on either side of the infantry regiment came under heavy rifle fire from Botha's men occupying well-protected defensive positions. Although the British's big guns were well placed, they had made little impact by the time the day drew to a close.

The battle continued the next day with some 30 British soldiers killed and 150 missing. The number of casualties was not considered unduly large and was credited to the fact that the British were also enjoying good defence positions.

On 13 June Churchill, who had accompanied Ian Hamilton's column, saw his chance to get the attention he so badly wanted. He gives a full account of the three-day battle of Diamond Hill in the *Morning Post*, but surprisingly does not mention his own role in it. In *My Early Life* he wrote: 'I had one more adventure in South Africa', and dismisses the battle with the words: 'After taking part a fortnight later in the action of Diamond Hill, fought to drive the Boers farther away from Pretoria, I decided to return home'.

It was left to General Sir Ian Hamilton to outline Churchill's role in his memoirs, *Listening to the Drums*. By his account Churchill showed courage and 'conspicuous gallantry' at Diamond Hill. He had come to the realisation that the key to the battle lay on the summit of the hill. Without announcing his intentions, he undertook a scouting operation single-handedly. He climbed the hill and found a protected niche amongst the rocks. The British troops were astonished to see him waving a handkerchief on a stick high up on the hill indicating the way up. The Boers could easily have shot him if they had detected him during his climb, but once again Lady Luck was on his side.

According to General Ben Viljoen — the Assistant Commandant-General of the Transvaal Burgher Force and the member for Johannesburg in the Transvaal Volksraad — who described the battle in his book *My Reminscences of the Anglo-Boer War* — it was General Tobias Smuts who had 'made an unpardonable blunder by falling back with his commando'.[3] So although he wasn't aware of it, which does not detract from his bravery, Churchill was in no danger of being detected by the retreating enemy.

When General Jan Smuts applied for urgent reinforcement during the course of the afternoon, the British troops who had followed Churchill were already at the summit of the hill. Viljoen and his men, who were ordered to go to Smuts' aid, were met with a hail of bullets and with shells flying over their heads. They took cover in the rocky terrain and returned fire realising that Tobias Smuts and his burghers had retreated from the position. Viljoen wrote: 'At first I was rather in the dark as to what it all meant until we discovered that the British had won Smuts' position, and from it were firing upon us. We fell down flat behind the nearest cliffs and returned fire, but we were at a disadvantage, since the British were above us.'[4]

Celia Sandys had no doubt that Hamilton used the term 'conspicuous gallantry' which as the language in citations for the Victoria Cross. She writes in *Churchill Wanted Dead or Alive* of 'initiative and daring and of how he had grasped the whole layout of the battlefield'.[5] Although Churchill hadn't known that the Boers had vacated their position when he began his climb, he obviously realised it as he approached the summit, so his signal to the troops was done in the full knowledge that it was safe for them to follow him.

Hamilton blamed Roberts and Kitchener for ignoring his appeals to reward someone whom they disliked and who was after all only a press correspondent. Celia Sandys is of the opinion that 'the military establishment [was] unlikely to give a medal to a bumptious young subaltern who had so often outsmarted and outperformed them'.[6]

It was possibly Churchill's disappointment at his failure to achieve official recognition for the bravery he displayed during this, the last battle he played a role in, that prompted him to ignore the Diamond Hill episode in *My Early Life*. He probably realised that a large measure of the public admiration for him had been created by his pen. Perhaps he instinctively felt that too much self-glorification might tarnish the image he had so carefully created. It was time to move on. 'With the consent of the authorities I resumed my full civilian status and took the train for Cape Town'.[7]

But there was still another adventure in store for Churchill and it occurred on that train trip. Churchill was breakfasting in the dining car with the Duke of Westminster when the train jerked to a halt just beyond Kopjes Station, about 160 kilometres south of Johannesburg. As they climbed out on to the line, a shell from a small Boer gun exploded 'almost at our feet, throwing up clods from the embarkment'.[8] Just ahead a wooden bridge was in flames. The train was crowded with soldiers but no officer seemed to take command of the situation. 'In their absence, he once again took charge of a train, as he had done eight months previously'.[9] He ran along the line, climbed into the cab and persuaded the driver to reverse until they reached the safety of a fortified camp some three miles back.

When they arrived, Churchill saw 'a cluster of dark figures' in a dry watercourse nearby. 'These were the last Boers I was to see as enemies. I fitted the wooden stock to the Mauser pistol and fired six or seven times at them. They scattered without firing back'.[10]

Churchill once again emerged as the hero of the situation.

When Churchill walked down the gangplank of the *Dunnotar Castle* at Southampton on 20 July 1900, he was given a welcome that matched the farewell given to General Buller when both had embarked on the same vessel nine months earlier. His mother Lady Randolph was not there to witness the hero's reception accorded to her son, because she was busy preparing for her marriage to George Cornwallis-West.

The war that the world's mightiest empire had forced on to a small nation in the remote interior of Africa raged on for another two years. Lord Kitchener, who succeeded Lord Roberts as Commander-in-Chief, introduced his reprehensible scorched earth policy — the burning of farms and the destruction of farm animals. Women and children were herded into two dozen concentration camps where 26 000 of them perished. It was only on 31 May 1902 that peace was finally declared. In terms of the provisions of the Treaty of Vereeniging, the two Boer republics ceased to exist and became part of the British Empire.

27

Mystery of the eight watches

In a letter from Canada dated 9 January 1901, Churchill asked his mother to 'select some watches for the men and a broach for the women who had helped him escape from the Boers: I am sure you will choose much better than I shall'.[1] He had doubtless discussed the subject with Jennie before he left for his American lecture tour. The next reference to the gifts can be found in a letter he addressed to John Howard of the Witbank colliery on 25 February 1901.

> I am sending to South Africa by next week's mail a consignment of 8 gold watches, which are all of them engraved with suitable inscriptions. I thought it better in the present state of the country not to send these watches further than the Standard Bank of Cape Town, and I have instructed the Manager of the Standard Bank to hold them until you or Mr Addams (sic) are able to take them yourselves personally. I hope you will do me the honour to accept these small keepsakes of our remarkable adventure, and believe that they also represent my sincere gratitude for the help and assistance you all afforded me. I may add that I am bringing your names to the notice of the Secretary of State for War in the hope that you may be granted a medal, but it is not of course in my power to decide that point. I will instruct the bank to notify you when the watches arrive.[2]

Churchill indeed recommended to the Secretary for War 'that those who had helped him should receive a medal for their actions, but given the War Office's ineptness in arranging suitable awards to loyal civilians, it was not surprising they ignored Churchill's recommendation', Celia Sandys wrote.[3] Considering Churchill's position during the South African War, the circumstances of his escape and the immediate controversy it attracted, it is a matter for conjecture whether the War Office's attitude can really be interpreted as ineptness. As far as Churchill was concerned, however, he would show his personal appreciation to those who had helped make good his escape.

Churchill wrote the names of the men to be engraved on the inside of the 18-carat gold pocket watches in a note to his secretary, followed by the words: 'From Winston

S Churchill in recognition of timely help afforded him in his escape from Pretoria during the South African War. Dec 13 1899.'

The names included Dr James Gillespie, the man who supplied a roasted chicken, took him for a walk and examined him after he had refused to go back into the mine; JR Adams, the mine secretary; JD Dewsnap, the mining engineer who, according to Churchill, took him down the mine shaft; Joe McKenna and Joe McHenry, the miners who took the mattress, pillow and blankets to the stable; and Charles Burnham, the businessman who arranged for the bales of wool to be railed to Lourenço Marques. Ellen David and Ada Blunden — the two women who were sworn to secrecy when asked to provide Churchill with meals while he was hiding in Howard's storeroom — were also on the list. The instruction was that their inscription had to be the same as for the men, except that the words had to appear on the dome of the watches. These women were never mentioned in subsequent accounts relating to the watches and broaches.

When the precious parcel arrived at Standard Bank in Cape Town, the manager, J. Fitzwilliams, notified Howard and offered to send it on to Witbank. With the war still raging in the Transvaal, Howard felt it would be safer to have the consignment collected. It so happened that John Adams was due to travel to Cape Town on holiday and it was arranged that he would collect the package.

There was great excitement when the parcel was opened at Witbank, but this turned into disappointment for Howard when he discovered there was no watch bearing his name. If the ladies had received their broaches, there should have been nine items in the parcel., but it contained only five watches. Immediate enquiries to find out what had happened to Howard's watch were fruitless. His name was not even on the list that Churchill had given to his secretary. It seems that the key figure among those who had hidden Churchill and helped him to get out of the country had been overlooked when the gifts were ordered? Churchill was notified and asked to rectify the mistake. Howard, however, never received the precious souvenir that he had looked forward to receiving as a reminder of those eventful days during the war.

In July 1955, 83-year-old Charles Burnham presented his watch — as well as a silver cigarette case with Aylmer Haldane's name engraved in appreciation for having helped Churchill escape — to Miss Killie Campbell of the Durban Africana Museum for public display. A report appeared in the *Natal Mercury*, under the headline 'Churchill rescuer gives watch to museum', together with the caption: 'Churchill sent eight such watches to South African helpers', and 'Only two remain.'[4]

Burnham was described as 'the grandson of Jeremiah Cullingworth, the printer who brought Durban's first printing press to Natal'. This was followed by a brief outline of how he had smuggled Churchill, Haldane and Le Mesurier out of the Transvaal and helped them escape to Lourenço Marques. In whose possession the two remaining watches were the paper did not reveal. If it were not for Pretoria hotelier Jimmy McLachlan, it is likely the story would have ended there.

Jimmy McLachlan and his brother Archie opened the Boulevard Hotel in Pretoria in 1954. He named a popular bar in this hostelry *Dromedaris* after the ship that brought Jan van Riebeeck to the Cape of Good Hope in 1652 to establish a victualling station for Dutch sailing vessels bound for the East Indies.

When the McLachlans were ready to open a second Boulevard Hotel in Witbank in 1968, Jimmy offered £50 to anyone who came up with an appropriate name that linked its bar to the history of the mining town. It would not only remind patrons of a memorable moment in Witbank's history, before the town itself was established in 1903; but Jimmy felt it would also be a novel way of paying tribute to the place that afforded him the opportunity to expand his business.

Suggestions such as 'Utopia' and 'Leisure Island' indicated that the people of Witbank did not recall any historical event that was worthy of immortalizing as the name of a bar in their newest hostelry.

Jimmy came across an article about the State Model School, which had been declared a national historical monument, and he decided to visit Churchill's former prison. There he was shown the letter Churchill had written to John Howard, notifying him of the consignment of watches he was sending to Cape Town. John Howard's son Lewis had presented the letter to Dr PJ du Toit, chairman of the Historical Monuments' Commission, on the occasion of the unveiling of the Commission's plaque on 20 May 1963. This letter provided Jimmy with an answer for the name of the bar: 'Churchill's' seemed to be appropriate.

But then a puzzling question raised its head. What had happened to the watches? The prospect of discovering the details enthralled him. Little did Jimmy realise that his search would captivate his mind for the next 30 years and take him as far away as Scotland.

By the close of 1969 Jimmy had learnt that Burnham's watch was exhibited in the Killie Campbell Africana Museum in Durban and that Errol Dewsnap, grandson of John Dewsnap, the mining engineer of the Transvaal and Delagoa Colliery, then living in Edenvale near Johannesburg, possessed his grandfather's watch. Jimmy hoped to trace the whereabouts of the remaining watches with the help of the press.

A press conference was arranged at the Boulevard Hotel in Struben Street, Pretoria on 27 January 1970. Errol Dewsnap arrived to show off the gold watch that had been passed on to him. (Today this family heirloom is believed to be in Vereeniging, the town where the treaty was signed that brought an end to the South African War.) The proud owner also displayed a walking stick and a knife given to Howard as mementoes by Aylmer Haldane. These items had also been passed on to Errol. Holding Dewsnap's watch in the palm of his hand for a fleeting moment was one of the greatest thrills in Jimmy's life. The sensation was probably akin to an archaeologist finding a rare relic of the distant past.

The following day the *Pretoria News* reported under the headline: 'Churchill's Watches sought ... bid to find eight Churchill Watches', that it was Jimmy McLachlan's plan to open a historical nook at his Witbank hotel on Churchill's birthday in November 1970. 'The pub was to have been called Churchill's — with the written permission of Lady Churchill, but plans now are to call it "The Eight Watches".[5] Pretoria's Afrikaans daily, *Hoofstad*, also featured an article on Jimmy's search, and within days John Howard's son Lewis, then living in Germiston, contacted him and presented him with the a statement:

> Mr Adams who had by now collected the parcel of watches returned to his duties on the mine in Witbank, handing over the parcel to my dad, on his arrival back. As far as my dad could judge the parcel was intact, and appeared to be in good order in every respect, yet when my dad opened the parcel there were only seven watches, and none of them bore the inscription which should have gone with my dad's watch; all the others who had taken part in this great episode of helping Churchill to escape, received their watches in good order; but my father's watch was missing and incidentally he never in his lifetime, saw or received his watch.
>
> Whether Churchill had sent my Dad's watch out under separate cover or not remains a mystery. Churchill, I believe, when asked whether he had done so replied, 'he could not remember'.[6]

Jimmy discovered the whereabouts of the third gold watch after he read Dr Alexander JP Graham's 1965 publication entitled *The Capture and Escape of Winston Churchill during the South African War*. In a letter to Jimmy dated 11 February 1970, Dr Graham advised that Joe McKenna's watch was in the possession of his great-grandson, Joseph James Hagger of Salisbury, Rhodesia (now Zimbabwe). Joseph's mother confirmed this, writing that her grandfather, Joe McKenna, had bequeathed the watch to his eldest son, also Joe McKenna, who was her father. The latter, in turn, left the watch to Joseph. According to Jimmy McLachlan, the watch became a valued treasure of a McKenna family member in Guernsey. It is now on display in the Imperial War Museum in London.

Jimmy learnt that the fourth watch, that of Dr Gillespie, had been in the possession of Dr Elizabeth McMullen of Pretoria. She had passed it on to her nephew in Stirlingshire, Scotland. When the bar at the Witbank Boulevard Hotel was about to be opened, Jimmy decided to travel to Scotland to solve the mystery of the Gillespie watch.

Coincidentally, Jimmy had met the ageing Dr Gillespie in Witbank in 1947. The McLachlan brothers were building contractors engaged in the erection of a nurses' home adjacent to the hospital of which Dr Gillespie was in charge. At that time Jimmy was unaware of Churchill's gift to Dr Gillespie, and even if he had known, it would have been of no particular interest to him. It was only much later that the McLachlans, branched into the hotel business.

As far as McHenry's watch is concerned, Jimmy was told that he always wore it as a good luck charm. He served as a pilot in 17-Squadron Royal Air Force during World War-I and was shot down and killed. It seems McHenry was not wearing it on that fateful day for it is now on display at Churchill's country house, Chartwell in Kent.[7]

Of Adam's watch it was rumoured that it was destroyed in a fire. Celia Sandys also mentions this, but no confirmation is available.

According to Sandys, Howard, Burnham, McKenna and Adams continued corresponding with Churchill until long after the war. Adams, however, became a problem. 'In 1921, having fallen out with Howard, Adams wrote to a South African journalist, Dadge Stansfield, and tried to diminish Howard's role in Churchill's escape. He also contradicted parts of Churchill's own account'.[8] Churchill's version of the escape, as he recorded it 30 years after the event in *My Early Life*, does contain a remarkable number of conflicting statements. Sandys does not elaborate on Adams' allegations. But even if Howard and his colleagues were still alive today, it is unlikely that they would publicly contest their roles in the brilliantly told story of an episode in the life of the man to whose fame they were linked for posterity.

28

England's noblest hero

When Churchill came home to contest the 'Khaki Election' of 1900, the Conservatives in 11 different constituencies approached him. He chose, however, to go back to Oldham, the scene of his earlier defeat for a seat in parliament This time, however, things would be different. 'Oldham almost without distinction of party accorded me a triumph. I entered the town in state in a procession of ten landaus', Churchill wrote in *My Early Life*.[1] Bands played and banners declared: 'See the Conquering Hero.'

That night a meeting was held for the candidate in the Theatre Royal, and the crowds flocked to hear him speak about his adventures in South Africa. A woman in the front row wore a sash with the words embroidered on it: 'God Bless Churchill, England's Noblest Hero.'

The hero was in his element. He told the people his version of his escape, and when he mentioned the name Dewsnap — remembering that Dan Dewsnap, the mining engineer at the Witbank Colliery came from Oldham — the audience shouted: 'His wife's in the gallery.' A tumultuous cheer broke out. He went on to say that those who had aided him were now safe under British protection, and that he was free for the first time to tell the whole story.

The election was fought largely on the issue of the Boer War, with the Liberals being bitterly opposed to what they termed 'a wicked and unnecessary conflict', so it is hardly surprising that they attacked the Conservatives and tried to smear Churchill.

Chamberlain was accused of having deliberately engineered the war as a commercial venture and Churchill, it was suggested, had left the Army in disgrace. He had travelled to South Africa as a correspondent rather than as a soldier because he was a coward. The *Daily Mail* noted: 'In nothing does Winston Churchill show his youth more than in the way he allows slander to affect him ... they deeply wound him and he allows men to see it. When some indiscreet supporter brings these stories to him, his eyes flash fire, he clutches his hands angrily, and he hurries out to find opportunity of somewhere and somehow bringing his traducers to book'.[2]

The electioneering was drawn out over almost six weeks. In the final stages the Conservatives had a large permanent majority of the electorate. Chamberlain came to Oldham to speak for Churchill. The hall was jammed with supporters and the streets were crowded with booing opponents.

The press was ecstatic. London papers sent reporters to write the most beautiful eulogies on their national hero. Julian Ralph of the *Daily Mail* termed Churchill a genius. He wrote: 'The species is not so broad or so over familiar that one can carelessly classify a man as such. In this case there is no doubt'. On his personality he had this to say: 'He finds it easier to vault out of a landau than to open the door when he is getting out to address his electors and win their unqualified admiration if he can. He will take a bath 13 minutes before dinnertime, will not hesitate to advise or admonish the Government or newspaper in a letter, and will calmly differ from a bishop on a point of ecclesiastical law. But, mark you, he is usually diplomatic and considerate in speech and tone; he is boyishly handsome, has a winning smile, and is electric in brilliance and dash. That is why people rushed after him in crowds in Oldham, to see and hear him and to wring his hand. They called him, "Young Randy" and shouted God's blessing after him'.[3]

As was to be expected, the election was a success for the Conservatives who had a large permanent majority in Oldham. Churchill won by 222 votes. Prime Minister Lord Salisbury sent him a telegram of congratulations and within a few hours invitations arrived from all over the country for him to address meetings.

He was now an MP but there were still some months to go before he could take up his seat in the last of Queen Victoria's parliaments.

The question of money that had plagued Churchill for as long as he could remember was more acute than ever. To be a Member of Parliament in those days required a substantial private income, and this Churchill didn't have. He had earned about £4 500 from his books and for his columns in the *Morning Post*. Now he saw the opportunity of lecturing on his experiences during the South African War as a Godsend to improve his financial status. He received an invitation to address a meeting in London on the day after winning the election. Manchester followed, and then a succession of engagements around the country. Speaking every night at a different venue during the month of November at a fee of £100 to £300 a lecture, earned him a further £4 500.

Parliament was to sit at the beginning of December, but Churchill decided to undertake a lecture tour in the United States and Canada first. This allowed him to bank another £10 000. By the middle of January he was back in England and he continued to speak in various centres until the middle of February. He had spoken 'for more than five months for an hour or more almost every night, except Sundays, and often twice a day, rarely sleeping twice in the same bed'.[4] He was now independent and could start his life as a politician without financial worries.

While in Ottawa, Canada, Churchill unexpectedly met Pamela Plowden at a Christmas dinner given by another of his mother's admirers, the Governor-General of Canada, Lord Minto. Winston had shown little interest in women before he was introduced to her at a polo match at Secunderbad four years earlier. 'She is the most beautiful girl I have ever seen — bar one', he wrote to his mother, but although he met her occasionally and corresponded with her for two years, there was little else that he offered her.

It has been said that Churchill was something of a misogynist, but there is no doubt that he liked Pamela in his own way. She, on the other hand, accused him of lacking warmth and affection. Winston did not understand that the pretty girl yearned for more than letters in which he was the only one who seemed to matter. 'Why do you say that I am unable to offer affection?' he asked. 'Perish the thought. I love one above all others. And I shall be constant. I am no fickle gallant capriciously following the fancy of the hour. My love is deep and strong. Nothing will ever change it.'[5] Who was it that Winston loved with such singled-minded devotion? Ted Morgan asks. The answer, he said, was over the page — it was ... *himself*, Winston Spencer Churchill.[6]

Jennie had hoped that the two would marry. In a letter dated 26 May 1900, she told Winston: 'Pamela is devoted to you, and if your love has grown as hers — I have no doubt that it's only a question of time for you to marry.' She tried to paint a picture of him settling down in comfort, making a decent living out of writing and his political career leading to big things. His mother meant well and although Winston told her that Pamela was the only women he could ever live with, he was not, in fact, convinced that this was so. Pamela, too, considered her future and had ended the 'romance' a few months before the two had met by chance in Ottawa.

When it became known that Winston would not marry Pamela, Colonel Brabazon told Jennie that he was pleased, believing she should be a rich man's wife. Churchill may not have been rich, but his income from his books and his public lectures was now substantial. He proudly mentioned to his mother that there was not one person in a million who had earned £10 000 at the age of 25 without any capital in less than two years.

When Parliament reassembled in February, Churchill took his father's old seat on the back benches. Every one of the goals he had set himself had been achieved. He was famous, an established writer and comfortably off. Crowning it all, he was in the House of Commons to make his mark on world politics.

In May 1901 he felt the time had come to pursue the matter of being awarded a medal for his actions at Chieveley. When one looks at his blunt request for official recognition, it becomes clear that there was more to receiving a medal than simply commemorating a battle in which he took part. He included Haldane's report of his heroism at Chieveley in a letter to his friend, the Colonial Secretary Joseph Chamberlain: 'It had occurred to me that if papers sent by the Natal people to the Colonial Office were forwarded to the War Office, they would look very imposing taken in conjunction with his dispatch, and I might get some military mention or decoration.' In trying to mellow the wording of his appeal, he added: 'Of course in common with all the other members of Parliament I care nothing for glittering baubles of honour for my own sake: but I have like others — to think of my constituents — and perhaps I ought to consider the feelings of my possible wife. This being so if you can trace these papers and feel inclined to send them to the War Office, I shall be much obliged. The case would then be considered with other cases.'

However, Churchill was not the most popular man among the higher echelons of the army, and to his dismay, no one at the War Office took the matter further. As far as the medal he had promised the driver of the armoured train was concerned, nothing came of that either. Churchill had written a letter to the Prince of Wales, on 30 November 1899 — his 25th birthday — while in prison in Pretoria, requesting some recognition for the gallantry of the driver. In later years, Churchill was frequently reminded of Charles Wagner for his part in bringing the wounded to safety. Querulous letters from the driver's colleagues expressed the thought that he had been gracelessly treated, and Churchill agreed. In response to an article about the armoured train in the *Spectator*, Churchill wrote that 'the driver had received no recognition of any kind from the War Office ... although one would have thought his services not less valuable and deserving than those of several young gentlemen who adorned the headquarters staff'.

One could, of course, speculate that political intrigues were at play. With Churchill having been denied official recognition for his part in the rescue of the engine and the wounded men, it would have been out of the question to treat Wagner differently. However, an appropriate honour would come Wagner's way, although it would take all of ten years. In 1910 Churchill was Home Secretary and in a position to advise King George V. He recommended that the footplate heroes be awarded the Albert Medal for their devotion to duty at Chieveley in 1899. The King consulted the records of the war and the Governor of Natal, Sir Walter Hely-Hutchinson, and the railway company was contacted.

Although Churchill did not mention Wagner by name, either in the dispatches he had published in the *Morning Post* or in his biography, the engine driver was finally honoured with the Albert Medal First Class, the highest awards for gallantry open to civilians. The train's second engineer, Alexander Stewart, received the Albert Medal Second Class.

The citation, no doubt, written by Churchill himself, was full of praise for the courage Wagner and Stewart had displayed, while rescuing the wounded. He pointed out that the injured crowded the engine and its tender and that the danger that the shells could have exploded the boiler was exceptional. It was suggested that the railway men were the real heroes of the incident, but be that as it may, Churchill had finally been able to fulfil the 11-year-old promise.

On 14 December 1901, on Churchill's first evening as a member of the Government, Eddie Marsh, who was an obscure clerk in the West African Department of the Colonial Office, came into Churchill's life. They were introduced at a dinner party arranged by Lady Grandy. Marsh noticed that Churchill was staring in his direction as the evening progressed. The following day Churchill asked for him. Marsh was petrified. As it happens, Churchill was in need of a private secretary.

They met at Churchill's flat in Mount Street where, at a *dinner à deux,* he charmed the man, who was two years his senior. Although Eddie had doubted that he could have anything in common with Winston, within three weeks of their meeting the two had taken up rooms at the Midland Hotel in Manchester. Churchill had chosen the city to serve as his base for his first campaign as a Liberal candidate.

Lady Randolph was at first not keen on Marsh being her son's secretary. She remembered the homosexual affair Winston had been accused of at Sandhurst, and with Marsh being overtly homosexual (as the years passed he became recognised as the centre of a large homosexual artistic colony in England) she feared that the association would adversely affect her son's political career. But Jenny need not have worried. Marsh not only loyally served Churchill as his secretary for 20 years, but also remained an inseparable companion to him, following him with devotion from office to office throughout the many downturns in his career. The friendship between the two men which commenced on 15 December 1901 lasted until 1953 when Marsh died.

Marsh, who became Sir Edward, was imbued with impeccable taste. He was a fine classical scholar and had inherited money which he used in patronage of the arts. He collected paintings and beautiful young men like the poet Rupert Brooke and the actor Ivor Novello, who also became well acquainted with Churchill in later years.

Violet Bonham Carter — the daughter of HH Asquith, Chancellor of the Exchequer and later Prime Minister of England — described Marsh as having 'a head cocked to attention like a bird's, bristling eyebrows always agog with eagerness, ecstatically expressing every mood, in one eye a monocle which he occasionally removed to wipe away from it a tear, evoked by laughter or a line of poetry or a play — and a falsetto voice which was like a high-pitched chirrup'. He would get quite upset by the 'vexatiously frequent responses of "Yes, madam" to his "Hallo" on the telephone, and often assured his friends that he had what he called "deep organ tones" at his command, but could never manage to use them in conversation in what seemed to him to be a natural manner'.[7]

Jennie became quite fond of Eddie Marsh and by the time her son took him along on a four-month trip to Europe and British East Africa, the Sudan and Egypt in late 1907, this was evident from a letter to him in which she asked him to look after her precious Winston.

After Pamela's break with Churchill, he might well have believed that there would never be another suitable woman in the world for him. But it was not too long before he became enamoured with the American actress Ethel Barrymore. He sent her flowers every day and almost every night went to Claridge's Hotel for supper, knowing she always went there after her performance at the theatre. Enchanted by her beauty and dignity, he took her to Blenheim Palace where he proposed to her in July 1902. But Miss Barrymore turned him down. Winston was just one of her many hopeful admirers and the actress had no desire to exchange the theatre world for a life of politics.

Whether Jennie would have approved of her son marrying the American actress is questionable, but there seemed to be no urgency for him to seek nuptial bliss. It became increasingly worrisome for his mother, though, that Winston was still a bachelor at the time of his African tour, and moreover, was speaking of women as 'lesser beings who did not do justice to the complexity of life'.[8] Jack had tied the matrimonial knot on 7 August 1908, and Winston would be 'the next to pop off',[9] Jennie announced at the wedding. She was right.

Winston had his eye on Clementine Hozier, one of four daughters of Lady Blanche Hozier whose marriage to an ex-cavalry officer, Colonel Sir Henry Montague Hozier, broke up in 1891. According to Winston's daughter Mary Soames, 'in her later life Clementine became convinced that she was not the child of Henry Hozier ... '[10] Lady Soames, in her introduction to her edited volume of the letters her parents wrote to each other, made it clear that there was no doubt that Blanche Hozier was promiscuous. 'At the time when her husband was threatening her with divorce, gossip had it that she had at least nine lovers.'[11]

To determine whom Clementine's father was difficult. Bertram Mitford, who became the first Lord Redesdale in 1902 was named as a possible candidate, and also William Middleton, a member of the diplomatic service who would marry Lady Hozier's young sister.

Churchill first saw Clementine when she was 19, at a dance given by Lady Crewe in 1904. Clementine later said: 'He never asked me for a dance, he never asked me to have supper with him. I had of course heard a great deal about him — nothing but ill. I had been told he was stuck-up, objectionable, etc. And on this occasion he just stood and stared.'[12]

It took a long time for them to get acquainted. Winston eventually asked his mother about the girl. Jennie arranged for them to meet at a party given by her great-aunt, Lady St Helier, in London in March 1908. He arrived late 'as usual ... eyes turned to watch his entrance, not that he was a handsome figure of a man — he wasn't. But the atmosphere of his personality, his very presence was electric. His blazing red hair, and his equally blazing blue eyes, compelled attention'.[13]

Winston told Clementine about the biography he had written on his father and asked her whether she had read it. She had not. He promised that he would send her the book the following day, but he never did.

Two years earlier Winston had demonstrated his gaucherie with Violet Asquith. 'After a long silence he suddenly asked her how old she was. She replied that she was 19'. Winston said that he was already 32, but assured her that he was 'younger than anyone else who counts'.[14] Whether this awkward approach from a considerably older man was likely to entice a girl — even in Edwardian times when prospects were more important than love — is debatable. How Violet reacted to Winston's added comment: 'We are all worms, but I do believe I am a glow-worm', is not recorded.

On the day his brother Jack married, Winston wrote to Clementine telling her about the wedding. The next day he wrote again, inviting her to Blenheim Palace. His cousin Sunny, the Duke of Marlborough, expected them and Jennie came along as chaperone. The arrangement worked. Winston took Clementine for a walk in the late afternoon, and when it started to rain, they took cover in an ornamental temple overlooking the lake. It was here, in Diana's temple, that he proposed to her.

Clementine had been engaged twice, once to Sidney Peel, grandson of Sir Robert — Prime Minister and founder of the Metropolitan Police — and once to a civil servant named Lionel Earle. This time she had no doubt that she had found the right man to share her life with.

Winston held a stag party at his house in Bolton Street, London, and Clementine entertained close friends to tea at Portland Place. Many of the guests expressed serious doubts whether the union would last, with Lord Roseberry giving the couple six months. He justified his prediction by insisting that Winston was not the marrying kind.

On 12 September 1908 Winston married 23-year-old Clementine. Lord Roseberry and the other sceptics couldn't have been more wrong. Winston summed it up neatly in 1930: 'I married and lived happily ever afterwards.'[15] And indeed that state prevailed until Winston's death in 1965.

The couple commenced their honeymoon at Blenheim Palace, where he revised the final text of his book on Africa. Then they travelled to Venice, where Winston busied himself with official documents and memoranda while Clemmie, as he called her, was to discover that her husband wore very finely woven silk underwear of a pale pink colour. On their return to London Clementine confided this intimate detail to her friend Violet Asquith. She herself wore cheap chemises, but his underclothes, she told Violet, came from the Army and Navy Stores and cost about £8 a year. Winston disclosed the reason for this extravagance to Clementine by telling her that it was essential to his well-being and pointed out that he had a very delicate and sensitive cuticle which demanded the finest covering.

While much has been written about Churchill's depressive moods, authors of books on him have not looked beyond this mental disorder that affected him all his life. Neither he nor those close to him realised that he was afflicted with symptoms of the neurobiological condition now known as Asperger Syndrome. It was only in 1944 that it was identified in a paper published by the Viennese psychiatrist and paediatrician Hans Asperger; he outlined a pattern of behaviour in a number of young boys with normal intelligence and language development, but who also exhibited autistic-like behaviours and lacked social and communication skills. Another 50 years would pass before Asperger Syndrome was recognised by professionals and parents of afflicted dependents.

Children diagnosed with the disorder find it difficult to make friends and learn social skills. They tend to be bullied at school due to their 'differentness', their use of language and their idiosyncratic behaviour. Their marred capacity to respond in socially expected ways to signs and body language makes them particularly vulnerable to abuse.

They have difficulty in demonstrating empathy and affection. Their deficiency in social skills is sometimes expressed in bumptiousness that is often seen as rudeness. They are usually intelligent but are looked on as self-centred, egotistical and uncaring individuals. Some people with the syndrome use words in odd combinations; they coin new phrases and seem to have a remarkable memory for lengthy texts. This, together with their preference for monologues over conversation often leads to difficulty in finding a life partner.

Churchill displayed most of the symptoms associated with Asperger Syndrome. His lack of learning ability at school led him to be seen by his teachers as a problem child. He acquired a rich vocabulary but developed idiosyncrasies in speech and language. His quick wit and the ability to coin expressions and create clever puns never ceased to amuse his audiences. He did prefer monologues over conversation and displayed a social aloofness and a lack of interest in other people. He found it difficult to foster friendships and, as we have seen, was inept at entering into relationships with members of the opposite sex.

The story of Winston Churchill as a politician has been exhaustively documented and a summary of his long life after his triumphant return from South Africa would not do justice to the man.

As far as his association with South Africa was concerned, he never returned to the country that afforded him fame and was instrumental in launching his illustrious political career.

When Pretoria celebrated its centenary on 16 November 1955, Churchill was invited as a guest of honour by the city fathers. He had never liked to travel by air and, at the age of 80, declined the invitation, writing:

'It is my privilege, as one not unacquainted with Pretoria's hospitality, to offer the city my heartiest congratulations.'

Bibliography

Books

Atkins, JB. *Incidents and Reflections*, (Christophers, 1947); **Batts, HJ**, *Pretoria From Within During The War 1899–1900*, (John F. Shaw and Co London, undated); **Bonham Carter, Violet**. *Winston Churchill As I knew Him*, (Eyre & Spottiswode and Collins, London, 1965); **Bolsmann, Eric**. *Pretoria—Artists' Impressions 1857-2001*, (Protea Book House, Pretoria, 2001), *The Mount Nelson*, (Haum Publishers, Pretoria, 1978); **Botes, Prof. Paul**. *History of Witbank*, (City Council of Witbank, 1994); **Boyden, PB. et al** (Ed). *Ashes and Blood: The British Army in South Africa 1795-1914*, (National Army Museum, London, 1999); **Brennand, Frank**. *The Young Churchill*, (New English Library, London, 1965); **Breytenbach, JH**. *Die Geskiedenis van die Tweede Vryheidsoorlog in Suid-Afrika*, 1900-1902 4 Vols, (Pretoria, 1969-1877); **Butterfield, Paul H**. *Centenary, The first 100 years of English Freemasonry in the Transvaal*, 1878-1918, (Private publication); **Chisholm, Ruari**, *Ladysmith*, (Jonathan Ball Publishers, Johannesburg, 1979); **Churchill, (Lord) Randolph**, *Men, Mines and Animals in South Africa*, (Sampson Low, London, 1892); **Churchill, Randolph S**. Winston S. Churchill, Young Statesman, 1901-14; **Churchill, Winston S**. *From London to Ladysmith via Pretoria*, (Longmans, Green, London, 1900), Ian Hamilton's March, (Longmans, Green, London, 1900), *My Early Life 1874-1908*, (Fontana/Collins, London, 1959); **Cloete, Steward**, *African Portraits*, (Constantia Publishers, Cape Town, 1969); **Cowles, Virginia**, *Winston Churchill, The Era and The Man*, (Hamish Hamilton, London, 1953); **Davitt, Michael**, *The Boer War Fight for Freedom*, (Funk & Waggnalls, New York and London, 1902); **Oakes, Dougie (Ed)**, *Illustrated History of South Africa*, (Reader's Digest Association South Africa, 1988); **Fishman, Jack**, *My Darling Clementine*, (WH Allen, London, 1963); **Gilbert, Martin**, *Churchill: A Photographic Portrait*, (Heineman, London, 1974); **Guedalai, Philip**, *Mr Churchill, A Portrait*, (Hodder and Stoughton Ltd., London, 1941); **Haldane, Captain Aylmer**, *How We Escaped from Pretoria*, (Africana Book Society, Johannesburg, 1977); **Holmes, Richard**, *In the Footsteps of Churchill*, (BBC Books, London, 2005); **Hofmeyr, Adrian**, *The Story of My Captivity During the Transvaal War*, (Edward Arnold, London, 1900); **Jenkins, Roy**, *Churchill*, (Macmillan, London, 2001); **Geen, MS**, *The Making of South Africa*, (Maskew Miller Ltd., Cape Town, 1958); **Kruger, Rayne**, *Goodbye Dolly Gray*, (Pimlico, London, 1996); **Martin, Ralph G**, *Lady Randolph Churchill, Vol. I*, (Sphere Books, London, 1974); *Lady Randolph Churchill, Vol. II*, (Cassel, London 1971); **Meintjes, Johannes**, *General Botha*, (Cassel & Company, London, 1970); *The Commandant-General : The life and times of Petrus Jacobus Joubert of the South African Republic, 1831-1900*, (Tafelberg Uitgewers, Cape Town, 1971); **Milner, Charles**, *The Lunatic Express*, (Macmillan,

London, 1972); **Morehead, Alan**, *Churchill and his world*, (Thames and Hudson, London, 1965); **Morgan, Ted**, *Churchill The Rise To Failure: 1874-1915*, (Triad Panther Books, London, 1984); **Packenham, Thomas**, *The Boer War*, (Futura, London, 1982); **Peacock, Robert**, *Die Geskiedenis van Pretoria 1855-1902*, (Unpublished PhD Thesis, University of Pretoria); **Reitz, Deneys**, *Commando*, (Faber & Faber, London, 1929); **Roberts, Brian**, *Churchills in Africa*, (Hamish Hamilton, London, 1970); **Rose, Norman**, *Churchill, An Unruly Life*, (Touchstone Books, London, 1998); **Sandys, Celia**, *Churchill Wanted Dead or Alive*, (Jonathan Ball Publishers, Johannesburg, 1999); **Theron, Bridget**, *Pretoria at War 1899-1900*, (Protea Book House, Pretoria, 2000); **Thomson, Malcolm**, *Churchill His Life and Times 1874–1965*, (Oldhams Books, Limited, London, Special Memorial Edition,1963); **Trew, Peter**, *The Boer War*, (Jonathan Ball Publishers, Johannesburg, 1999); **Viljoen, Ben**, *My Reminiscences of the Anglo-Boer War*, (Hood, Douglas, & Howard, London, 1903); **Warner, Philip**, *Kitchener, The Man behind the Legend*, (Cassel, London, 2006); **Warwick, Peter**, General Editor, *The South African War*, (Longman Group Ltd, Harlow, 1980); **Wilson, HW**, *With the Flag to Pretoria*, (Harmsworth Brothers Limited, London, 1901); **Woods, Frederick**, (Ed), *Young Winston's Wars 1897-1900*, (Sphere Reference, London, 1972).

Newspapers, journals etc
Africana Notes and News, Vol. 23 No 5, March 1970; *Daily Nation*, 16 Dec 1899; *Daily Telegraph*, London, 15 Dec 1899; Journal, Old Pretoria Society, Pretoria, No 20, 32, 1956; *Mail & Guardian*, Johannesburg, 6 Aug 2006; *The Standard Diggers' News*, Johannesburg, 14, 24, 25 Dec 1899; *The Star*, Johannesburg 11, 22 Dec 1923; *The Strand Magazine*, London, Dec 1923; Feb 1946; *Natal Mercury*, Durban, 16 Nov, 22, 23 Dec 1899, 6 July 1955; *Pretoria News*, 28 Jan 1970; *Staats-Courant, Zuid-Afrikaansche Republiek*, 18 Nov 1899

NOTES

Chapter 1

1. Brennan, Frank, *The Young Churchill*, p9.
2. Morgan, Ted, Churchill: *The Rise to Failure*: 1874-1915, p23.
3. Manchester, William, *The Last Lion*, p137.
4. Morgan, Ted, quoted in Churchill, *The Rise to Failure*: 1974-1915, p27.
5. Churchill, Winston S, *My Early Life*, p9.
6. Ibid, p10.
7. Ibid, p14.
8. Ibid.
9. Manchester, William, *The Last Lion*, p119.
10. Ibid, p23.
11. Churchill, Winston S, *My Early Life*, p17.
12. Ibid, p20.
13. Ibid.
14. Manchester, William, *The Last Lion*, p24.
15. Churchill, Winston S, *My Early Life*, p21.
16. Ibid p12.
17. Ibid
18. Manchester, William, *The Last Lion*, p137.
19. Ibid, p138.
20. Churchill, Winston S, *My Early Life*, p13.

Chapter 2

1. Churchill, Winston S, *My Early Life*, p24, 101.
2. Morgan, Ted. Quoted by in *Churchill, The Rise to Failure*: 1874-1915, p47-48.
3. Churchill, Winston S, *My Early Life*, p101.
4. Ibid, p46.
5. Ibid, p27.
6. Brian, Roberts, *Churchills in Africa*, p35.
7. Ibid, p35-36.
8. Volksstem, 14 July 1891.
9. Roberts, Brian, Churchills in Africa, p82.
10. Churchill, Winston S, My Early Life, p38.
11. Churchill, Randolph S, *Winston S. Churchill*, Youth, Vol. I, p189.
12. Ibid, p194
13. Churchill, Winston S, *My Early Life*, p70.
14. Manchester, William, *The Last Lion*, p27.

Chapter 3

1. Milner, Charles, *The Lunatic Express*, p267.
2. Morgan, Ted, *Churchill: The Rise to Failure*: 1864-1919, p81.
3. Ibid, p83.
4. Ibid, p85.
5. Martin, Ralph G, *Lady Randolph Churchill*, p42.
6. Milner, Charles, *The Lunatic Express*, p267.
7. Churchill, Randolph S, quoted in *Winston S Churchill*, Youth, Vol. I, p252.
8. Ibid, p251.
9. Ibid,
10. Ibid, p252.
11. Churchill, Randolf S, *Winston S. Churchill*, Youth, Vol. I, p252.
12. Milner, Charles, *The Lunatic Express*, p267-269.
13. *Truth*, October 1896.
14. Manchester, William, *The Last Lion*, p212.
15. Morgan Ted, Churchill, *The Rise to Failure*: 1895-1915, p47.

16. Martin, Ralph, *Lady Randolph Churchill*, p44.
17. Manchester, William, *The Last Lion*, p153.
18. Martin, Ralph, *Lady Randolph Churchill*, p79.
19. Manchester, William, *The Last Lion*, p285.

Chapter 4

1. Churchill, Winston S, *My Early Life*, p91.
2. Ibid, p88.
3. Morgan Ted, Churchill, *The Rise to Failure*: 1874-1915, p89.
4. Ibid, p89.
5. Morgan, Ted, quoted from the *Newcastle Leader* of 7 December1895 in *The Rise to Failure*: 1874-1915, p89.
6. Churchill, Winston S, *My Early Life*, p84.
7. Ibid,
8. Manchester, William, *The Last Lion* p230.

Chapter 5

1. Maylam, Paul, *Mail & Guardian*, 4 Aug 2006.
2. Ibid,
3. Roberts, Brian, *Churchills in Africa*, p112.
4. Ibid, p114.
5. Churchill, Randolf S, *Winston S. Churchill*, Youth, Vol. I, p449.
6. Ibid, p449-450.

Chapter 6

1. Churchill, Winston S, *My Early Life*, p96.
2. Ibid,
3. Ibid, p112.

4   Ibid, p113.
5   Ibid, p114.
6   Morgan Ted, Churchill, *The Rise To Failure*: 1874-1918, p95.
7   Ibid, p96
8   Companion Volume 2, p784.
9   Morgan Ted, *Churchill, The Rise to Failure*: 1874-1915, p98.
10   Churchill, Randolf S, *Winston S. Churchill*, Youth, Vol. I, p352.
11   Ibid, p353.
12   Ibid, p354.
13   Holmes, Richard, quoted *In the Footsteps of Churchill*, p59.
14   Manchester, William, *The Last Lion*, p254.
15   Churchill, Winston S, *My Early Life*, p165.
16   Ibid, p165.
17   Ibid, p167.

Chapter 7
1   Woods, Frederick, *Young Winston's Wars*, pp122-123.
2   Churchill, Winston S, *My Early Life*, p168.
3   Ibid, p169.
4   Warner, Phillip, *Kitchener, The Man Behind The Legend*, p90.
5   Manchester, William, *The Last Lion*, pp264-265.
6   Churchill, Winston S, *My Early Life*, p170.
7   Manchester, William as quoted in *The Last Lion*, p265.
8   Churchill, Winston S, *My Early Life*, pp170-171.
9   Ibid, p171.
10   Ibid, p174.
11   Ibid, p175.
12   Ibid, p183.
13   Ibid, p183-184
14   Warner, Phillip, *Kitchener:*

The Man Behind The Legend, p91.
15   Ibid, pp99-100
16   Churchill, Winston S, *My Early Life*, p200.
17   Warner, Phillip, *Kitchener: The Man Behind the Legend*, p99-100.
18   Ibid,
19   Morgan Ted, *Churchill, The Rise to Failure*: 1974-1915, p146.
20   Ibid, p118
21   Churchill, Winston S, *My Early Life*, p205.
22   Churchill, Randolf S, *Winston S. Churchill*, Youth, Vol. I, p431

Chapter 8
1   Fishman, Jack, *My Darling Clementine*, p23
2   Ibid, p22.
3   Churchill, Winston S, *My Early Life*, p232.

Chapter 9
1   Chisholm, Ruari, *Ladysmith*, p119.
2   Churchill, Winston S, *My Early Life*, p238.
3   Ibid, p336.
4   Churchill, Randolf S, quoted in *Winston S. Churchill*, Youth, Vol. I, p453.
5   Atkins, J B, *Incidents and Reflections*, London 1947.
6   Churchill, Winston S, *My Early Life*, p241.
7   Ibid, p243.
8   Ibid, p243.
9   Churchill, Winston S, *From London to Ladysmith via Pretoria*, p13.
10   Atkins, JB, *Incidents and Reflections*, London 1947.

Chapter 10
1   Kinsey HW, *.Military History Journal*, p122.
2   Ibid,
3   Atkins, JB, *Incidents and Reflections* p122.
4   Roberts, Brain, *Churchills in Africa*, p166.
5   Churchill, Winston S, *My Early Life*, p252.
6   Ibid, p252.
7   Ibid, p254.
8   Ibid,

Chapter 11
1   Churchill, Winston S, *My Early Life*, p257.
2   Ibid, p257.
3   Ibid, p258.
4   The Star, 30 April 1960.
5   Churchill, Winston S, *From London to Ladysmith via Pretoria*, p48.
6   Churchill, Winston S, *My Early Life*, p258.
7   Ibid, p259.
8   Manchester, William, *The Last Lion*, p301, Haldane, Aylmer Haldane, *How we Escaped from Pretoria*, p3.
11   As quoted by Churchill, Randolf S, in Winston S. Churchill, Youth Vol. I, p464.
12   Churchill, Randolf S, *Winston S. Churchill*, Youth, Vol. I, p471.
13   Jenkins, Roy, *Churchill*, p53.
14   Churchill, Winston S, *My Early Life*, p259.
15   Ibid, p259-260.
16   Ibid, p260.
17   Morgan., Ted, *Churchill: The Rise to Failure*: 1874-1915, p132.
18   Sandys, Celia, *Churchill Wanted Dead or Alive*, p60.
19   Roberts, Brian, *Churchills*

in Africa, p170.

20   Churchill, Randolf S,
      Winston S. Churchill,
      Youth, Vol. I, p473.
21   Leyds, 719, p541, *Genl
      Louis Botha aan Mev.
      Botha,* dd. 16 Nov 1899
22   Sandys, Celia, *Churchill
      Wanted Dead or Alive,*
      p60.
23   Ibid, p58.
24   Jan Smuts, *Memoirs of the
      Boer War,* p74
25   Telegram 434, State
      Archives of South Africa,
      28 November 1899.
26   Sandys, Celia, *Churchill
      Wanted Dead or Alive,*
      p58.
27   Ibid, p60.
28   Churchill, Winston S,
      *From London to Ladysmith
      via Pretoria,* p45.
29   Ibid, p260.
30   Ibid,
31   Ibid, p263.

Chapter 12
1   Haldane, Aylmer Haldane,
      *How We Escaped from
      Pretoria,* p6.
2   Ibid,
3   Ibid,
4   Churchill, Winston S,
      *From London to Ladysmith
      via Pretoria,* p47.
5   Churchill, Winston S, *My
      Early Life,* p264.
6   Sandys, Celia, *Churchill
      Wanted Dead or Alive,*
      p57.
7   Churchill, Winston S,
      *From London to Ladysmith
      via Pretoria,* p49.
8   Churchill, Winston S, *My
      Early Life,* p264.
9   Jenkins, Roy, *Churchill,*
      p54.
10   Churchill, Winston S, *My
      Early Life.* p264.
11   Churchill, Winston S,

*From London to Ladysmith
via Pretoria,* p49.
12   Haldane, Aylmer, *How We
      Escaped from Pretoria,*
      p12.
13   Ibid, p12-13.
14   Churchill, Winston S,
      *From London to Ladysmith
      via Pretoria,* p50.
15   Ibid, p50.
16   Haldane, Aylmer, *How We
      Escaped from Pretoria,*
      p15.
17   Ibid,
18   Haldane, Aylmer, *How We
      Escaped from Pretoria,*
      p27.
19   Ibid,
20   Izedinova, Sophia, *A Few
      Months With The Boers,*
      p64.
21   Ibid,

Chapter 13
1   Churchill, Winston S,
      *From London to Ladysmith
      via Pretoria,* p35
2   Ibid, p65.
3   Ibid,
4   Haldane, Aylmer, *How we
      escaped from Pretoria,*
      p35.
5   Ibid, p35.
6   Churchill, Winston S,
      *From to Ladysmith via
      Pretoria,* p35.
7   Churchill, Randolf S,
      quoted in *Winston S.
      Churchill,* Youth, Vol. I,
      p478.
8   Sandys, Celia, *Churchill
      Wanted: Dead or Alive,*
      p84.
9   Ibid, p84.
10   *Natal Witness,* 10
      November 1899.
11   Ibid,
12   Churchill, Randolf S,
      quoted in *Winston S.
      Churchill,* Youth, Vol. I,
      p467.

13   Ibid, p467.
14   Churchill, Winston S,
      *From to Ladysmith via
      Pretoria,* p67.
15   Ibid,
16   Ibid,
17   Ibid,
18   Ibid,
19   Ibid, p72.
20   Ibid, p70.
21   Ibid, Lord Methuen fought
      the Boers at Belmont, a
      small town in the Cape
      on 21 November, 1899.
      The Boers fled, leaving
      behind fewer than 100
      casualties.
22   Haldane, Aylmer, *How We
      Escaped from Pretoria,*
      p72.
23   Ibid, p71-71.
24   Roberts, Brian, *Churchills
      in Africa,* p201.
25   Sandys, Celia, *Churchill
      Wanted: Dead or Alive,*
      p82.
26   Haldane, Aylmer, *How We
      Escaped from Pretoria,*
      p43.
27   Churchill, Winston S,
      *From London to Ladysmith
      via Pretoria,* p69.
28   Ibid,
29   Churchill, Winston S, *My
      Early Life,* p265.
30   Ibid, p269.
31   Ibid, p272.
32   Ibid, pp272-273.
33   Churchill, Randolf S,
      quoted in *Winston S.
      Churchill,* Youth, Vol. I,
      p479-480.
34   Ibid, p482-483.
35   Reitz, Deneys, *Commando,*
      p49.
36   Churchill, Randolf S,
      quoted in *Winston S.
      Churchill,* Youth, Vol. I,
      p483.
37   Ibid, p484.

38   Churchill, Winston S, *From London to Ladysmith via Pretoria*, p78.

Chapter 14

1   Churchill, Winston S, *From to Ladysmith via Pretoria*, p80.
2   Churchill, Winston S, *My Early Life*, p274.
3   Haldane, Aylmer, *How We Escaped from Pretoria*, pp52-53.
4   Cowles, Virginia, *Winston Churchill, The Era And The Man*, p62.
5   Haldane, Aylmer, *How We Escaped from Pretoria*, p53.
6   Morgan Ted, *Churchill, The Rise to Failure: 1874-1915*, p135.
7   Churchill, Winston S, *My Early Life*, p276.
8   Churchill, Randolf S, *Winston S. Churchill*, Youth, Vol. I p500.
9   Ibid,
10   Churchill, Winston S, *My Early Life*, p276.
11   Churchill, Randolf S, *Winston S. Churchill*, Youth, Vol. I, quoting from a memo written by Winston Churchill in 1912.
12   Churchill, Winston S, *My Early Life*, p276.
13   Ibid,
14   Ibid, p278.
15   Ibid, p277.
16   Haldane, Aylmer, *How We Escaped from Pretoria*, p53.
17   Ibid,
18   *Africana Notes and News*, March 1917, p198.
19   Churchill, Winston S, *My Early Life*, p267.
20   *Africana Notes and News*, March 1917, p199.

21   Churchill, Winston S, *My Early Life*, p277.
22   Theron, Bridget, quoted in *Pretoria at War*, p20.
23   Butterfield, Paul H., Centenary, *The first 100 years of English Freemasonry in the Transvaal 1878-1918.*
24   Churchill, Winston S, *My Early Life*, p278.
25   Ibid, p278.
26   Ibid, p279.
27   Ibid, p282.
28   Haldane, Aylmer, A Soldiers Saga, p195
29   Ibid, p283.
30   Ibid,
31   Churchill, Winston S, quoted in *From London to Ladysmith via Pretoria*, p88.

Chapter 15

1   Hofmeyr, Adrian, *The Story of My Captivity During the Transvaal War*, p134- 135.
2   Churchill, Randolf S, quoted in *Churchill, Winston S*, Youth, Vol. I p495.
3   Adrian Hofmeyr, *The Story of My Captivity During the Transvaal War*, p137.
4   Ibid,
5   Ibid, p136.
3   Ibid,
6   Sandys, Celia, *Churchill Wanted Dead or Alive*, p101.
7   Churchill, Winston S, quoted in *Ian Hamilton's March*, p361.
8   Rodda, TJ, Journal of the Old Pretoria Society, No 20, 1956
9   Ibid,
10   Ibid,

Chapter 16

1   Churchill, Winston S, *My Early Life*, p285.
2   Ibid,
3   Ibid,
4   Ibid, p286.
5   Ibid, p282.
6   Sandys, Celia, *Churchill wanted Dead or Alive*, p21.
7   Bonham Carter, Violet, *Winston Churchill As I Knew Him*, p55.
8   Churchill, Winston S, *My Early Life*, p288.
9   Ibid, pp288-289.
10   Ibid, p290.
11   Ibid, p291.

12   Hofmeyr, Adrian, *The Story of My Captivity During the Transvaal War*, p138.
13   *The Star*, Johannesburg, 11 Dec 1923.
14   Ibid,
15   Ibid,
16   Ibid,
17   Ibid,
18   Churchill, Winston S, *My Early Life*, p291
19   Ibid,
22   *The Star*, Johannesburg, 11 Dec 1923.
23   Churchill, Winston S, *My Early Life*, p292.
24   Graham, Alexander JP, *The Capture and Escape of Winston Churchill During the South African War*, p2.
25   *The Star*, Johannesburg, 11 Dec 1923.
26   *Daily Telegraph*, London, 15 Dec 1899.
27   *Daily Nation*, Dublin, 16 Dec 1899.
28   Churchill, Winston S, *My Early Life*, p292.
29   Sandys, Celia, *Churchill Wanted Dead or Alive*, p126.
30   Churchill, Winston S, *My Early Life*, p293.

31 Ibid,
32 Ibid
33 Ibid, p294.
34 Ibid
35 Ibid,
36 Ibid, p295.
37 Ibid,
38 Ibid,
39 *The Star*, Johannesburg, 22 Dec 1923.
40 Churchill, Winston S, *My Early Life*, p295
41 *The Star*, Johannesburg, 22 Dec 1923.
42 Ibid,
43 Ibid,
44 *The Star*, Johannesburg, 11 Dec 1923.
45 Churchill, Winston S, *My Early Life*, p296.
46 *The Star*, Johannesburg, 22 Dec 1923.
47 Churchill, Winston S, *My Early Life*, p297.
48 Ibid, p299.

Chapter 17
1 Churchill, Winston S, *From London to Ladysmith via Pretoria*, p89.
2 Ibid, p297.
3 Churchill, Winston S, *My Early Life*, p296.
4 Thomson, Malcolm, *Churchill, His Life and Times*, p61
5 Sandys, Celia, *Churchill Wanted Dead or Alive*, p103.
6 De Haas, L, *Churchill Dead or Alive, Strand Magazine*, February 1946, p40.
7 Ibid, p41.
8 Churchill, Winston S, *My Early Life*, p297.
9 Sandys, Celia, *Churchill Wanted Dead or Alive*, p103.
10 Ibid, p104.
11 Haldane, Aylmer, *How We Escaped from Pretoria*, p15.

Chapter 18
1 Churchill, Winston S, *My Early Life*, p299.
2 Ibid, p300.
3 Ibid, p301.
4 Roberts, Brian, *Churchills in Africa*, p245.
5 Ibid, p 246.
6 Churchill, Winston S, *My Early Life*, p302.
7 Ibid, p303.
8 Ibid, p303.
9 Ibid, 304.
10 Ibid,
11 Ibid, p304-305.
12 *Natal Mercury*, 22 Dec 1899.
13 Ibid, 23 Dec 1899.
14 Ibid,
15 Ibid,
16 Ibid,
17 Churchill, Winston S, My Early Life, p304.
18 Ibid,
19 Ibid, p304.
20 *Natal Mercury*, 24 Dec 1899.
21 Brian Roberts, *Churchills in Africa*, p252.
22 *Natal Mercury*, 24 Dec 1899.

Chapter 19
1 Churchill, Winston S, *From London to Ladysmith via Pretoria*, p95.
2 Ibid,
3 Ibid, p292.
4 Labuchere, Henry, *Truth*, 23 Nov 1899.
5 *Phoenix*, 23 Nov 1899.
6 Churchill, Winston S, *My Early Life*, p305.
7 Churchill, Winston S, *From London to Ladysmith via Pretoria*, p95.
8 Ibid,
9 *Westminster Gazette*, 26 Dec 1899.
10 Churchill, Winston S, *My Early Life*, p308.
11 Ibid,
12 Churchill, Randolf S, *Winston S. Churchill, Youth, Vol. I*, p498.
13 Sandys, Celia, *Churchill Wanted Dead or Alive*, p105.
14 Churchill, Randolf S, *Winston S. Churchill, Youth, Vol. I*, p498.
15 Ibid, p498.
16 Sandys, Celia, *Churchill Wanted Dead or Alive*, p106.
17 Ibid, p108.
18 Ibid,
19 Morgan, Ted, *Churchill, The Rise to Failure: 1874-1915*, p137-138.
20 Ibid, p138.
21 Ibid,

Chapter 20
1 Churchill, Winston S, *My Early Life*, p309.
2 Ibid, p308.
3 Ibid, p309.
4 Churchill, Winston S, quoted in *My Early Life*, p309.
5 Sandys, Celia, quoted in *Churchill Wanted Dead or Alive*, p143.
6 Churchill, Winston S, *My Early Life*, p312.
7 Ibid, p313.
8 Ibid,
9 Churchill, Randolf S, *Winston S. Churchill, Youth Vol. I*, p508.
10 Manchester, William, *The Last Lion*, p317.
11 Ibid,
12 Churchill, Winston S, *My Early Life*, p319.
13 Ibid,
14 Roberts, Brian, *Churchills*

in Africa, p279.

15 Manchester, William, *The Last Lion*, p319.

Chapter 21

1   Roberts, Brian, *Churchills in Africa*, p276.
2   Churchill, Winston S, *My Early Life*, p328.
3   Churchill, Randolf. S, quoted in *Winston S. Churchill*, Youth, Vol. I, p510.
4   Manchester, William, *The Last Lion*, p320.
5   Roberts, Brian, *Churchills in Africa*, p276.
6   Churchill, Winston S, *My Early Life*, p326.
7   Ibid,
8   Ibid, p326.
9   Ibid,
10 Ibid, p328.
11 Churchill, Randolf S, quoted in *Winston S. Churchill*, Youth, Vol. I, p511.
12 Roberts, Brian, quoted in *Churchills in Africa*, p285.
13 Churchill, Winston S, *My Early Life*, p333.
14 Churchill, Winston S, *From London to Ladysmith via Pretoria*, p209.
15 Churchill, Winston S, *My Early Life*, p333.
16 Morgan, Ted, *Churchill, Rise to Failure*: 1874-1915, p143.
17 Packenham, Thomas, *The Boer War*, p366.
18 Ibid,
19 Ibid,
20 Churchill, Winston S, *From London to Ladysmith via Pretoria*, p210.
21 Ibid,
22 Churchill, Winston S, *My Early Life*, p334.
23 Sandys, Celia, *Churchill Wanted Dead or Alive*, p178.
24 Churchill, Winston S, *From London to Ladysmith via Pretoria*, p213.
25 Ibid, p179.
26 Churchill, Winston S, *My Early Life*, p328.
27 Roberts, Brian, *Churchills in Africa*, p289.
28 Ibid, p289.
29 Ibid, p288.
30 Ibid, p289.
31 Morgan, Ted, *Churchill, Rise to Failure*: 1874-1915, p144.
32 Magee, Bryan, *Encounter*, Oct 1965.
33 Morgan Ted, *Churchill, Rise to Failure*: 1874-1915, p145.
34 Manchester, William, *The Last Lion*, p138.
35 Magee, Bryan, *Encounter*, Oct 1965; Morgan Ted, *Churchill, Rise to Failure: 1874-1915*, p145; Manchester, William, *The Last Lion*, p332.

Chapter 22

1   Churchill, Winston S, *My Early Life*, p341.
2   Churchill, Winston S, *From London to Ladysmith via Pretoria*, p115.
3   Churchill, Winston S, *Ian Hamilton's March*, p232.
4   *Cape Times*, 2 March 1899.
5   Churchill, Winston S, *Ian Hamilton's March*, p233.
6   Churchill, Winston S, *Ian Hamilton's March*, p233.
7   Churchill, Winston S, *My Early Life*, p342-343.
8   Ibid, p348.
9   Ibid, p349.
10 Ibid,
11 Ibid,
12 Ibid,
13 Ibid,
14 Manchester, William, *The Last Lion*, p325.
15 Churchill, Winston S, *Ian Hamilton's March*, p253.
16 Ibid,
17 Ibid, p254.
18 Ibid,

Chapter 23

1   Brian Roberts, *Churchills in Africa*, p316.
2   Churchill, Winston S, *My Early Life*, p353.
3   As quoted by Brian Roberts in *Churchills in Africa*, p226.
4   Churchill, Winston S, *My Early Life*, p354.
5   Ibid,
6   Ibid,
7   Churchill, Winston S, *Ian Hamilton's March*, p343.
8   Churchill, Winston S, *My Early Life*, p355.
9   Ibid,
10 Churchill, Winston S, *Ian Hamilton's March*, p345.
11 Ibid,
12 Ibid,
13 Churchill, Winston S, *Ian Hamilton's March*, p345.
14 Ibid, p347
15 Churchill, Winston S, *My Early Life*, p357.
16 Churchill, Winston S, *Ian Hamilton's March*, p349.

Chapter 24

1   Jan Smuts, *Memories of the Boer War*, p41
2   Sandberg, CGS, unpublished manuscript in Pretoria City Library
3   Ibid,
4   Churchill, Winston S, *Ian Hamilton's March*, p354.
5   Ibid,
6   Ibid,
7   Churchill, Winston S, *My Early Life*, p358.

8 Churchill, Winston S, *Ian Hamilton's March*, p354.
9 Ibid, p354-355.
10 Ibid, p355.
11 Ibid, p387.
12 Ibid, p355-356.
13 Mackern, HF, *Side Lights on the March*, p215-230.
14 Ibid,
15 Ibid,

Chapter 25.
1 Churchill, Winston S, quoted in *Ian Hamilton's March*, p371-372.
2 Ibid, p372.
3 Haldane, Aylmer, *How We Escaped from Pretoria*, p63.
4 Churchill, Winston S, *Ian Hamilton's March*, p369.
5 Ibid, p370.
6 Ibid, p373.
7 Haldane, Aylmer, *How We Escaped from Pretoria*, p120.
8 Churchill, Winston S, *Ian Hamilton's March*, p374.
9 Ibid,
10 Haldane, Aylmer, *How We Escaped from Pretoria*, p132.
11 Ibid, p138.
12 Ibid, p176.
13 Ibid, p187-188.
14 Ibid, p194.
15 Sandys, Celia, *Churchill Wanted Dead or Alive*, p122.

Chapter 26
1 Cloete, Stuart, *African Portraits*, p279.
2 The largest diamond known was found in Cullinan in 1905. It was a 3024,75 carat stone from which the 530-carat Star of Africa, the smaller Cullinan ii, iii and iv stones, and several brilliants were cut. All are set in the British Crown Jewels.
3 Viljoen, Ben, *My Reminiscences of the Anglo Boer War*, p101.
4 Ibid,
5 Sandys, Celia, *Churchill Wanted Dead or Alive*, p206.
6 Ibid,
7 Churchill, Winston S, *My Early Life*, p359.
8 Ibid,
9 Sandys, Celia, *Churchill Wanted Dead or Alive*, p208.
10 Churchill, Winston S, *My Early Life*, p360.

Chapter 27
1 Martin, Randolph G, *Lady Randolph Churchill*, Vol. II, 1895-1921, p209.
2 *Pretoriana*, April-August 1968.
3 Sandys, Celia, *Churchill Wanted, Dead or Alive*, p140.
4 *Natal Mercury*, 6 July 1955.
5 *Pretoria News*, 28 Jan 1970.
6 Ploeger, Dr Jan, unpublished manuscript re Churchill's escape compiled in March 1970.
7 Sandys, Celia, *Churchill Wanted Dead or Alive*, p141.
8 Ibid, p42.

Chapter 28
1 Churchill, Winston S, *My Early Life*, p362.
2 *Daily Mail*, 27 Sept 1900.
3 *Daily Mail*, 2 Oct 1900;
4 Churchill, Winston S, *My Early Life*, p369.
5 Morgan, Ted, quoted in *Churchill The Rise to Failure*: 1874-1914, p118-119.
6 Ibid, p119.
7 Bonham Carter, Violet, *Winston Churchill As I Knew Him*, p150-151.
8 Morgan Ted, *Churchill The Rise to Failure: 1874-1915,* p236.
9 Martin, Ralph, *Lady Randolph Churchill*, Vol. II, 1895-1921, p246.
10 Roy Jenkins, *Churchill*, p133.
11 Martin, Ralph, *Lady Randolph Churchill*, Vol. II, 1895-1921, p245.
12 Fishman, Jack, *My Darling Clementine*, p9.
13 Martin, Ralph, *Lady Randolph Churchill*, Vol. II, 1895-1921, p245.
14 Ibid,
15 Churchill, Winston S, *My Early Life*, p378.

Index